Traditional Enemies

Traditional Enemies
Britain's War with Vichy France
1940–1942

John D. Grainger

Pen & Sword
MILITARY

First published in Great Britain in 2013 by
PEN & SWORD MILITARY
An imprint of
Pen & Sword Books Ltd
47 Church Street
Barnsley
South Yorkshire
S70 2AS

ISBN 978-1-78159-154-3

Typeset by Concept, Huddersfield, West Yorkshire.

Printed and bound in England by
CPI Group (UK) Ltd, Croydon, CRO 4YY.

Pen & Sword Books Ltd incorporates the Imprints of Pen & Sword Aviation, Pen &
Sword Family History, Pen & Sword Maritime, Pen & Sword Military, Pen & Sword
Discovery, Wharncliffe Local History, Wharncliffe True Crime, Wharncliffe
Transport, Pen & Sword Select, Pen & Sword Military Classics, Leo Cooper, The
Praetorian Press, Remember When, Seaforth Publishing and Frontline Publishing.

For a complete list of Pen & Sword titles please contact
PEN & SWORD BOOKS LIMITED
47 Church Street, Barnsley, South Yorkshire, S70 2AS, England
E-mail: enquiries@pen-and-sword.co.uk
Website: www.pen-and-sword.co.uk

Contents

Maps

List of Maps

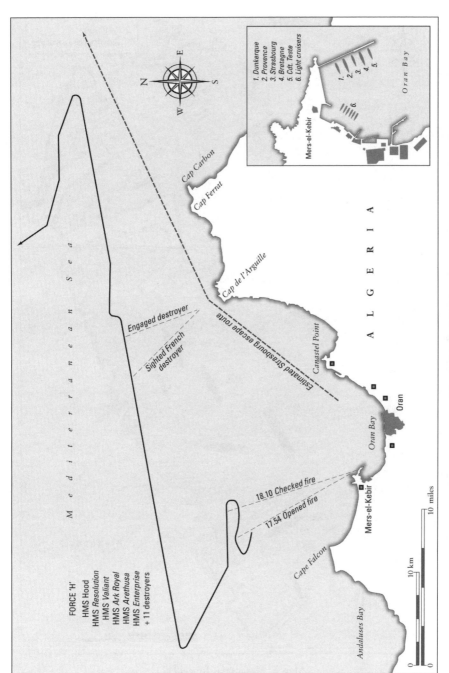

FORCE 'H'
HMS Hood
HMS *Resolution*
HMS *Valiant*
HMS *Ark Royal*
HMS *Arethusa*
HMS *Enterprise*
+ 11 destroyers

Mediterranean Sea

Engaged destroyer

Sighted French destroyer

Estimated Strasbourg escape route

Cap Carbon
Cap Ferrat
Cap de l'Arguille

Canastel Point

ALGERIA

Oran

Oran Bay

18.10 Checked fire

17.54 Opened fire

Mers-el-Kebir

Cape Falcon

Andaluses Bay

10 km

10 miles

0

0

Mers-el-Kebir

1. *Dunkerque*
2. *Provence*
3. *Bretagne*
4. *Cdt. Teste*
5. *Light cruisers*
6.

Oran Bay

Map 1. Mers el-Kebir

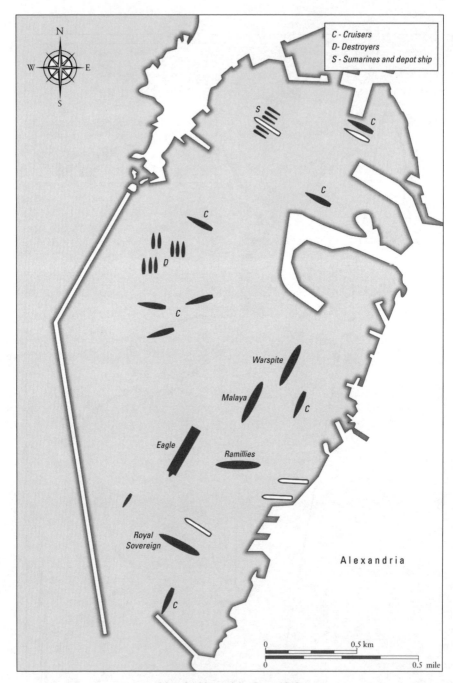

Map 2. Alexandria, June 1940

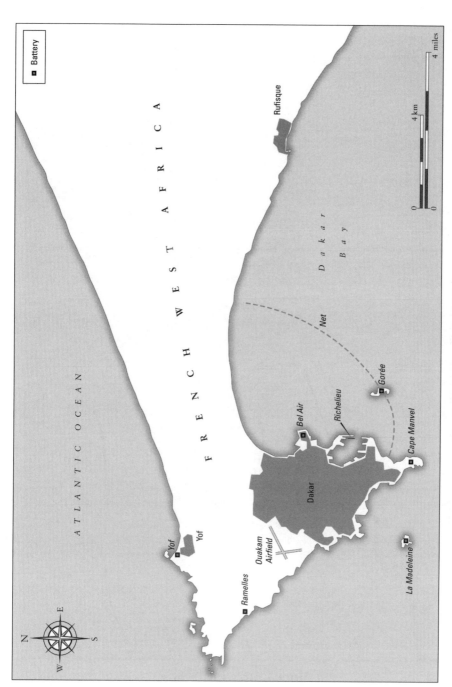

Map 3. Peninsula and Bay of Dakar

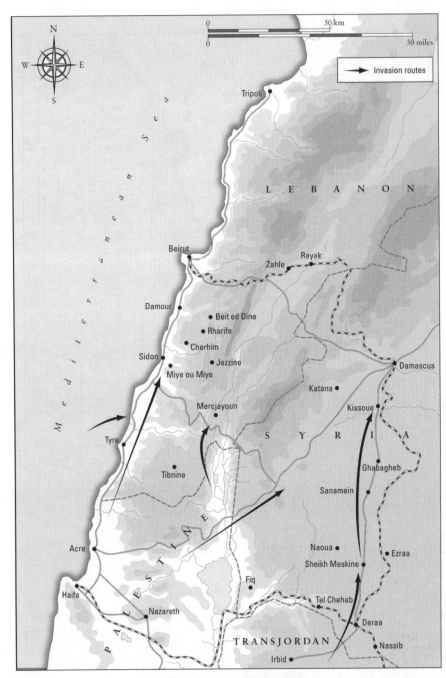

Map 4. Lebanon and SW Syria

Map 5. France: occupation and raids

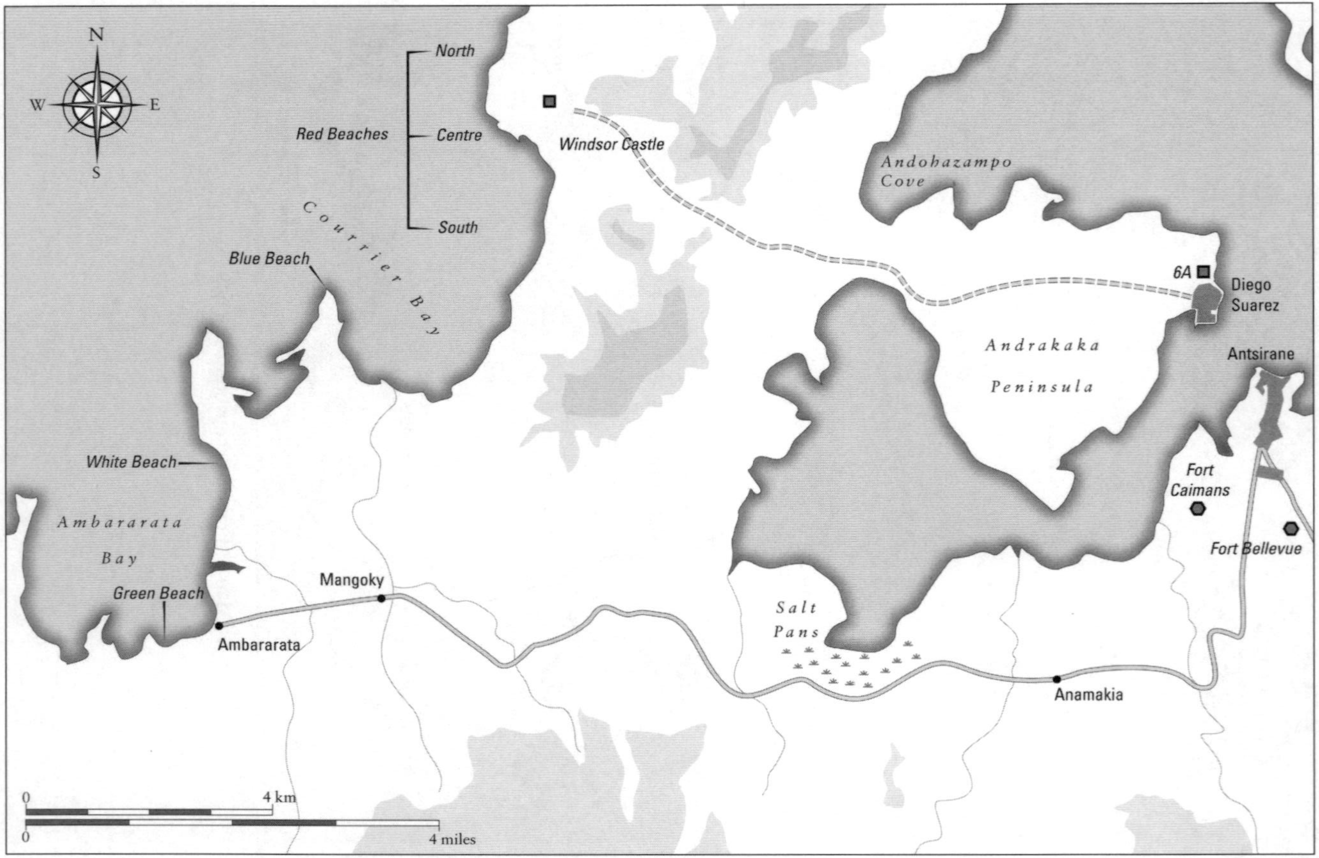

Map 6. Diego Suarez

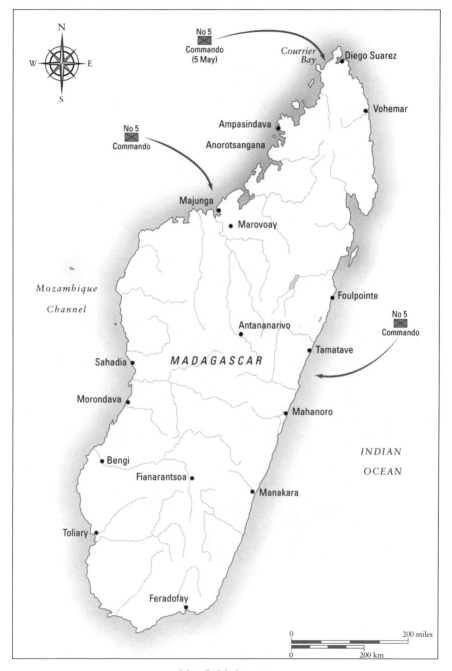

Map 7. Madagascar

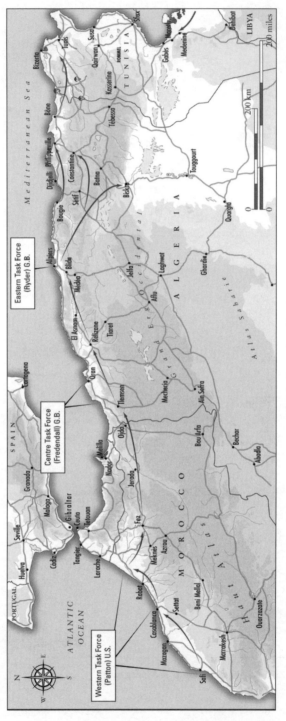

Map 8. Operation Torch

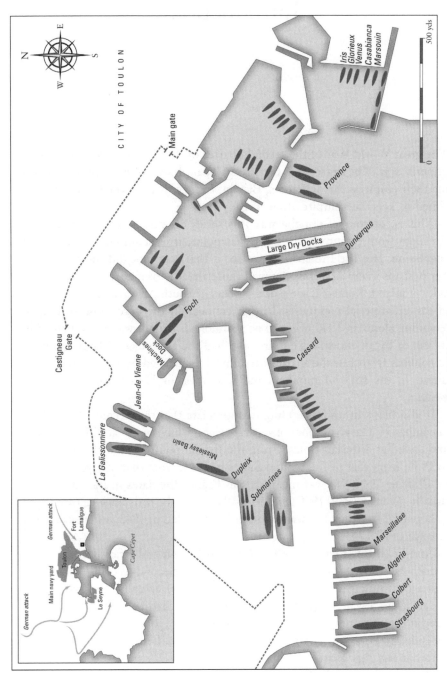

Map 9. Toulon: Scuttle

Introduction

The great World War of the second quarter of the twentieth century was an imperial war. The aggressors, Germany, Japan, Italy, were intent on expanding their empires; the defenders, Britain, France, Russia, the United States, aimed to keep the empires they already had.

This is, of course, not the way this series of wars is usually perceived. Freedom from tyranny is the usual viewpoint, at least among the victims of aggression. But the Indians did not see it that way, nor did the Egyptians, nor perhaps many Africans. Some of those already 'free' took the aggressors' side – Finland, Romania, some of the Boers of South Africa, and other victims of earlier imperial conquests. In that connection the perception of Britain 'standing alone' in 1940 needs to be abandoned. Britain was accompanied in its stance by an enormous empire, and had the assistance of large numbers of soldiers from European countries already squashed by the German conquest. In the scale of numbers and resources, in 1940 Germany was the weaker.

It also helps in understanding to appreciate that the Second World War encompasses a large number of separate wars, which began at different times and ended at different times. From the British point of view the war began in 1939; from that of the United States in 1941; from that of Japan in 1931, or 1937, or 1941. On war memorials in France the dates of the conflict are usually given as 1939–1940 and 1944–1945, with the resistance victims listed in between. For Italy the war began in 1940, ended in 1943, and began again at once until 1945.

And in all this there is the war between Britain and France. It is almost hidden beneath the tremendous events of the Second World War, but it was a continuing, if intermittent, conflict. Never actually declared, it was nevertheless a war between two countries which had been allies for a short time at the beginning of the overall war, and were to be on the same side at its end. In between they fought each other – or rather, perhaps it would be better to say that Britain fought France.

Between 1940 and 1942 Great Britain and France fought a series of conflicts in several parts of the world; Europe, Africa, the Mediterranean, even America, which in total added up, by 1942, to the destruction of the French overseas empire – an outcome in which the British were, ironically, assisted by the Germans, the Japanese, and the United States. Usually, amid the din of even greater events at sea, in Russia, in the Pacific, this conflict is too often more or less hidden away, though at times it surfaced to have an effect on the wider war; it is a series of events rather like rocks in the path of a steamship, appearing suddenly and sometimes unexpectedly in its path.

It has a wider significance, however. The restraint of the Vichy French government was quite remarkable under the stress of British attacks, and failure of the German government to appreciate their opportunity was no less surprising. Had the Vichy government declared war in 1940, after the events at Mers el-Kebir, the British position, in the Mediterranean and in the English Channel, would have been grave indeed. The prospect of dozens of French super-destroyers and destroyers assisting the Germans in the invasion of Britain is one which chills the blood. Beyond that, and back in the area of reality rather than supposition, the speed of the collapse of the French Empire should have been a clear sign to the British of the fragility of their own empire, which in fact lasted only a couple of years beyond the end of the wider war. There is no sign, however, that the lesson was taken on board, perhaps because the mindset of the British simply assumed the solidity and permanence of their empire.

Because France had been defeated in 1940 while Britain, also defeated, had survived in embattled freedom, the conflict was essentially one which was generated in and by Britain; that is, the aggression was almost always from the British side. It was conducted with very mixed emotions, ranging from the agony of the British naval officers who had to order the fleet to fire on French ships at Mers el-Kebir to the cheers which greeted the Prime Minister's announcement of that action from the MPs in the House of Commons. Later these emotions were more hidden, partly because later British attacks had a more obvious justification than Mers el-Kebir, but there was always a manifest British reluctance to be really ruthless and a constant wish to persuade the French to come to their senses, abandon their hostility to the British, and join in the war with Germany and Japan.

Mixed in with the overt conflict was the presence in Britain of Brigadier General Charles de Gaulle, claiming to be the legitimate representative of the soul and government of France, but doing so in a way which seriously angered his likely and actual allies. By taking Britain's part in the wider anti-Nazi war, de Gaulle was opening himself to vicious criticism from the actual legitimate government of France, which became established at Vichy. So the wider war hid the lesser conflict between Britain and France, and this conflict had a further layer of antagonism between two groups of Frenchmen, both claiming legitimacy. And there were also Frenchmen, principally Socialists and Communists, who did not like either the pretensions of de Gaulle or the defeatism and corporatism of Vichy.

This book, therefore, is an attempt to detail this complex conflict between empires, but since the events of the conflict were directed and instigated from Britain, it will be recited largely from the British point of view, with the internal French conflict less visible – as it was in fact. That internal feud, at least, has been properly delineated in French history, though de Gaulle's problems in Britain were clearly relevant to the international conflict, and at times it will be necessary to consider Vichy's policies and personnel, particularly in relation to the French fleet.

The war may be termed one between empires because it was very largely within the French imperial territories that the fighting took place. Neither of the homelands of the antagonists was the object of attack – except in some British raids aimed at German forces in France. In fact, it was not the empire which was the issue. The issue was the French fleet, how it would be used, and who would control it. So this was in fact a naval war.

The story must begin, therefore, with the messy end of the alliance which had been formed to fight Nazi Germany, and it will end with the simultaneous invasion of southern France by Germany and of North Africa by Britain and the United States, and the final scuttling of the French fleet – which brought to an end the major object of contention. The other final result was to be the triumph of de Gaulle, though that will be alluded to only briefly. In the end the general proved himself as cunning a politician as any man on any side in the war, but that was an internal French matter, not really by then part of Britain's conflict with France.

This conflict between Britain and France is not generally termed a war, but by any objective view that is what it was. It involved the two sides firing at each other, interfering with their trade, being rude to each other, and Britain conquering French territory. But neither actually declared war on the other, and it suited both sides, conscious of the looming power of a Germany energized beyond the norm by the inspiration of Nazism, and of the developing and overwhelming power of the explicitly democratic United States, to refuse to acknowledge the reality.

The war was, of course, a political nonsense and should never have happened. Faced with the realities of German and United States power (and that of Soviet Russia and, briefly, Japan), it was clearly self-indulgent for Britain and France to fight each other. One might easily see it as a reversion to an earlier time, when, in the eighteenth century, the two powers fought each other by land and sea to gain colonies, almost as though the two took refuge in the past in the face of the unpalatable present. In that sense it could be characterized as both countries deliberately ignoring the real danger, which was Nazi Germany. It was clear to all who looked at the situation that after 1940 Britain could not tackle Germany, but she could deal with Germany's allies and Germany's naval power. So it was more than a head-in-the-sand attitude; rather than a reversion to the past it was, as Churchill knew was necessary, a revival of the old British eighteenth century wartime method of enlisting allies and recruiting foreign soldiers to do as much of the fighting on Britain's behalf as possible. In the end, of course, Churchill's greatest recruits were Soviet Russia and the United States, but until they were dragged into the fighting the prospect of securing control over the French Empire would clearly help to increase the resources Britain needed to fight Germany.

Chapter 1

The Falling Out

On 10 May 1940 the German army invaded the Netherlands, Belgium, Luxembourg, and France. Within days it had broken through the positions of the French army at Sedan on the Meuse, and within two weeks had reached the coast of the English Channel, encircling and pressing in on the whole of the British Expeditionary Force, the whole of the Belgian army, and the French First Army. To the south, German forces had established bridgeheads over the river Somme at three places, so preventing any relief of the encircled Allied forces.

For Germany this was how it should have been a quarter of a century earlier; for France this was what had been feared all along. For both of these powers the actions of Britain had been all-too familiar, arriving late, in inadequate strength (as in 1914), and this time its army was about to be thrown into the sea, as should have happened, at least according to German hopes and wishes, in 1914 or 1918.

By the end of May, these trapped forces had been squashed into a small area in and around the port of Dunkirk, the Belgian army had surrendered, and the British were beginning the hazardous process of taking their army home in an armada of small boats organised by the Royal Navy and commanded from Dover Castle. After a time the French insisted that their men should also be taken off, at which point equal numbers were moved.[1] Most of the French soldiers were soon returned to France, hopefully to fight on, and some British were also landed further south. It was not, at the time of the Dunkirk evacuation, intended to stop fighting in France.

So by early June the British army had only a relatively few scattered units on the continental mainland, mainly in or heading for the ports. This was always what the French had feared: that the British would put themselves first, leaving France in the lurch. Why this should have surprised or shocked them is not clear, since that was what every nation state did without much conscious thought, but the French always seemed to expect everyone to come to their aid, neglecting their own interests for those of France. After all, it had been in the self-interest of France to have an alliance with Britain in the first place.

The alliance of Britain and France had technically existed since 1914, but from 1919 onwards, when the United States cancelled its guarantee of the Versailles settlement, Britain had effectively reneged similarly. The alliance was only returned to effectiveness in 1939 and 1940, in several slow stages. There were joint Franco-British staff talks on how to combat a German invasion from March 1939 onwards and a guarantee was given by both powers to Poland a month later. This seemed to be a bluff, and so it was ignored by Germany until too late, for it then became clear it was not a bluff, rather to the consternation of everyone involved – the British and French found they were at war, the Germans had not expected this outcome either, and, of course, the Poles got no help in their agony.

The declarations of war, when Germany did invade Poland in defiance of the guarantee, were characteristically uncoordinated by the Allies, coming from Britain at 11.00 am on September 3, in the face of a threatened House of Commons rebellion against the government of Prime Minister Neville Chamberlain, while France's ultimatum put her declaration of war at 5.00 pm.[2] It was a clear lack of Allied co-ordination which was hardly lost on Adolf Hitler. The reluctance of both governments to enter the war had been all too obvious.

The commitment of the two countries to the alliance nevertheless produced the next stage in the revival of co-operation, the transfer to France of the British Expeditionary Force almost as soon as war was declared. The number of British troops in France was steadily increased during the period between October 1939 and May 1940 – the 'Phoney War', as impatient American correspondents called it. And the French made a serious effort to tighten the military and political bonds of the alliance in March 1940 by asking for a joint declaration that the two would make neither an armistice nor a peace treaty separately from the other. This was a document produced by the French government and signed without argument by the British.[3] Indeed at the meeting in Britain where it was presented there was no discussion on the subject and it seems likely that some of those who attended scarcely noticed it. No doubt it was generally assumed that the existence of the alliance covered these points already, and that the French were being merely fussy.

However, despite the alliance and the declaration that neither would desert the other, the destruction of the joint military front of the allies in May by the German attack was preceded by the unravelling of the political front in both states. The basic problem, in both countries, was that the governments in power when the war began were quite unable to adjust to a condition of warfare, yet at the same time they were incapable of realizing their incapacity and were quite unwilling to surrender their power. The French government had succumbed first, even before any serious fighting had taken place. Edmond Daladier, the French Premier since 1938, had been the fourth man at the table at Munich, along with Hitler, Mussolini, and Chamberlain. He was vigorously anti-Communist, and had advocated Allied help for Finland in its war with Russia. None of the promised help ever arrived, and when Finland, acting like any other country from motives of self-interest and self-preservation, reached peace terms with the enemy in March 1940, Daladier was left high and dry. Having advocated sending help he was accused of not doing so, of an inability to plan sensibly, or to act decisively. All of these accusations were perfectly accurate.

This result was also, however, an outcome of the nonsense of the policy – why help a distant minor country against a great power when already at war with another great power, Germany? Russia may well have been aligned with Germany in the partition of Poland, and was supplying Germany with needed raw materials, and there may well have been sympathy for the Finns, but if the British and French contrived to assist Finland militarily they might well find themselves fighting both Germany and Russia. The stupidity of the policy does not seem to have dawned on either the British or the French, but at least the British were fairly reluctant to join in. They were also even more divided over the past and the future than the French, recriminations over the previous appeasement policy being rife, so that full governmental concentration on the German war was difficult.

Daladier was not defeated in the French Parliament, but he was subject to powerful and cutting attacks from those who resented the very existence of the war with Germany, from men who were clearly near-traitors, from the defeatists, who did not see any way of winning that war, and from those who were over-friendly towards Communism, or Russia, or Finland. That is to say, Daladier went down before a coalition of disparate enemies who had little or nothing in common, and could not provide any coherent governmental alternative, other than a new concentration on the German war – which many of his opponents actively disliked. The vote in the Chamber of Deputies on a no-confidence motion gave him the parliamentary version of a Pyrrhic victory: 239 deputies supported him, and only one voted against him; but 300 abstained. It was an effective defeat, especially in time of war when a wide base of support was clearly required if the government was to be effective. He resigned on 21 March, and was replaced by Paul Reynaud, his Foreign Minister, though Daladier himself now became, for a month or so, the new Foreign Minister. The lack of a coherent alternative government meant that the opposition to the war by large numbers of Deputies simply continued. It was hardly a change which would boost anyone's confidence.[4]

Reynaud was in favour of fighting the war against Germany with vigour. He was more energetic, but perhaps rather less in tune with French public opinion, than his erstwhile chief. His new government was approved in the Chamber on 22 March by a majority of just one. He quickly accepted the project of mining Norwegian waters and of seizing control of the Norwegian town of Narvik, both of which were intended to reduce drastically the supplies of Swedish iron ore reaching Germany. (This, again, was badly timed, since the Baltic/Gulf of Bothnia sea route would soon be re-opened as the ice in the Baltic melted. The Norwegian measures would have had little effect on German supplies for at least the next six months, during which stocks would have been built up – and might well have brought declarations of war from the Scandinavians.) But Reynaud's single-vote measure of approval in the Chamber compelled him into an activist phase in the hope of attracting supporters among the lukewarm.

The result, therefore, was that the new government, brought into power in part by a temporary coalition of those who opposed the war, those who supported Finland against Russia, and those who supported Russia and/or Communism, adopted none of the policies of those who had a majority in the Chamber of Deputies, but pushed ahead more energetically with Daladier's policies against Germany, such as they were, which did not command much of a majority. It was clear that much of France was lukewarm towards the war, if not downright unwilling to wage it.

The British government of Neville Chamberlain, late of Munich and of the surprised and hurt tones of a man feeling betrayed by his country's enemy, survived only a little longer than had Daladier's. He had been one of those responsible for the destruction of Czechoslovakia by the Munich agreement in 1938 and this was an albatross which constantly weighed him down. His pre-war responsibility for the policies which had led to the war left him open to constant criticism, both from the parliamentary Opposition, and increasingly from MPs of his own party. He fell from power for the same reasons that Daladier fell – lack of war-waging – and held on that much longer – just six weeks – only because any British Prime Minister has a firmer grip on the House of Commons than Daladier had on the Chamber of Deputies.

Chamberlain's war policy had been similar to that which he imagined had defeated Germany in 1914–1918: blockade leading to starvation. This was reinforced by a distaste, amounting to revulsion, for the prospect of a repeat of the trench warfare of that war. But this time Germany had access to all the raw materials and food produced in Eastern Europe, and had agreements with Russia to supply any deficiencies. Further, the blockade of Germany in the previous war had been only slowly successful, and had been accompanied by constant military battering at the German military positions all around Europe, but especially on the western front, and this was not happening in early 1940. Blockade and not-fighting was scarcely a policy likely to win the war in less than a generation. Activity was needed, but Chamberlain was not capable of developing an activist war policy.

The campaign in Norway was designed to enforce and improve the blockade, but it was overtaken by a German invasion of the country, not just its seas. As a campaign it was mismanaged at every level, disorganized, subject to repeated delays and changes, and generally misdirected, above all by the army command, though the navy was hardly inspiring either. When this became clear to the House of Commons, in part by letters to Members from officers who had returned from Norway angry at the mismanagement, Chamberlain was shocked to find that he was not wanted any more. He survived a vote of confidence, just as had Daladier, and with a reasonable majority, but he was opposed not just by the two parties in Opposition, but also by a large fraction of his own party which voted against him, and there were a large number of abstainers, which was as clear a declaration of no confidence as those voting against.[5]

Chamberlain's House of Commons victory, like Daladier's in the Chamber of Deputies, was Pyrrhic. He resigned and was quickly replaced by Winston Churchill, who as First Lord of the Admiralty had been in charge in some way of the Norwegian expedition, and whose interferences had significantly contributed to its failure. But the difference was that Churchill wished to fight, like Reynaud, and there had been a strong suspicion that Chamberlain did not, just as Daladier's energies had been directed elsewhere. It was not accidental that both men fell from power as a result of war policies which were apparently designed not to fight Germany. Daladier fell because he looked to help Finland against Russia, Chamberlain because of Norway – but both were in effect attacked for not fighting the main enemy. But there was also an important difference: Daladier's opponents included a large group who did not wish to fight Germany at all as well as a large group who objected to the prospect of fighting Soviet Russia; on the other hand, Chamberlain's opponents did want to fight, and some had no objection to fighting both Germany and Russia at the same time. Here was one of the major elements in the divisions between the two countries which soon developed. It had become clear by May, even before the Germans attacked in the west that Chamberlain's policy of the blockade and isolation of Germany would not work. The war would have to be fought actively. And that was what Churchill would do.

So both countries now had governments headed by men who were willing and intending to fight. Germany obliged by attacking first. The French army was beaten in battle, the British army beaten and expelled from the continent. By 5 June the evacuation from Dunkirk of about 200,000 British troops and about 140,000 French left the rest of the beaten and demoralized French army facing the victorious Germans on a front line stretching across northern France from the Somme to Luxembourg. And on that day the front also became active once more – that is, the Germans began a new attack.

In Britain the evacuation from Dunkirk paradoxically produced great relief. In some dim-witted quarters it was even seen as a victory. Churchill called it a 'miracle of deliverance', an attitude even shared by the King, though that was hardly a claim to victory. It is indicative of the fraught inter-Allied relations that even the evacuation produced constant bickering, with the French claiming that the British favoured lifting British troops, which had certainly been the case at first, but once the French had agreed to take part, equality in evacuation numbers was achieved. Now that the new German offensive towards the south had begun there were more serious matters to argue over, but the atmosphere was inevitably poisoned by the earlier defeats. The French fixed on air power as the only means by which the German offensive could be stopped, and demanded that the RAF should be the instrument. Churchill, on the other hand, rather more clear-sightedly, understood that it was most unlikely that the French would be able to continue the fight for long in metropolitan France, and was determined to reserve the major part of the RAF for the defence of Britain, which would be necessary once France succumbed. So the bickering over the evacuation from Dunkirk was replaced by bickering over the number of squadrons of aircraft which should be sent to France and over where and how France would continue the fight.[6]

The renewed German offensive in the north produced instant despair among both the British and the French. By 7 June, only two days after the initial German attacks, the French Chief of Staff, General Maxime Weygand, stated that he believed the army had already lost the battle.[7] He was already talking of asking for an armistice, and behind him and influencing him was the gloomy presence and voice of Marshal Philippe Pétain, hero of the last German war, anti-democrat, anti-British, and defeatist. The British sent a new division, the 52nd, across to France on 6 June,[8] promised to despatch the Canadian Division on the 11th, and another division later, while a large proportion of the French evacuees from Dunkirk had already been returned to France through Brest.[9] But on the 9th the only British division actually fighting, the 51st Highland, was cut off north of Rouen. Another evacuation by sea was begun, but the last survivors were forced into surrender by the 12th at St Valery, after less than 4,000 men had been evacuated.[10] By that date also the Germans were across the Seine and the Marne, and the French government and the Command Headquarters had been evacuated as far as Briare near Tours.

At a meeting of the War Council there on 11 June – when the British had found out where to go – the two Prime Ministers heard Weygand deliver an immensely gloomy assessment of the military situation. Churchill had his Secretary of State for War, Anthony Eden, and three generals with him, Reynaud had Pétain and Weygand and his new Under-Secretary for the War Department, Brigadier General Charles de Gaulle, but the active protagonists were Churchill and Weygand, the one looking for hope and optimism, the other sunk in despair and defeatism.[11]

Both Prime Ministers were burdened by Cabinets which included the men whom they had replaced and who advocated either surrender or negotiation. Churchill had Chamberlain at his Lord President of the Council, and Lord Halifax was there too, as Foreign Secretary – Halifax had been the other possible successor to Chamberlain, and was an advocate of a negotiated peace with Germany. His War Cabinet of five therefore contained at least two men who were actively considering that they should accept peace terms dictated by Adolf Hitler, and Halifax came perilously close to an active conspiracy to achieve this.[12] Churchill was not even the head of the majority party in the House of Commons, for that post had been retained by Chamberlain, whose own main aim was to return to power as Prime Minister presumably once Churchill had failed. Reynaud had got rid of Daladier on 5 June, but he now had Pétain, a defeatist from the start of the war, as his Vice Chairman of the Council – his deputy Prime Minister – and as his personal military adviser. He and Churchill were both Ministers of Defence as well as Prime Minister, but Churchill had thought through the implications of that post (new to the British constitution) while Reynaud had not really had time to do so – hence the presence at the meeting of de Gaulle, who was used by Reynaud for difficult or dangerous or awkward tasks. So neither man was yet thoroughly or firmly seated in power, and both of them liable to be ousted by the reaction to a military defeat. The despair and defeatism of Weygand and Pétain was in part a threat to overthrow the government. The absence of Chamberlain and Halifax from the meeting was perhaps a sign that Churchill did not trust them though, to be sure, they did not have direct military responsibilities.

One of the main results of the meeting at Briare was that both of the Allies had come to accept that the 'Battle of France', which had begun only a few days before, was already virtually over. Various suggestions for continuing the fight, mainly coming from Churchill, were raised only to be shot down. One was to fight street by street for Paris in order to absorb the whole German army in street fighting, a suggestion which visibly shocked every Frenchman present[13] – the city was declared an open city the next day in accordance with a decision made by Weygand and Reynaud two days earlier. Churchill had also talked about the creation of a 'Breton Redoubt' to be supported by the British by sea and air, something which had long been suggested and simultaneously either ridiculed or ignored by both General Staffs, who had a clearer idea of the difficulties than many of the politicians.

Weygand disdained the idea of a Breton Redoubt, seeing only the difficulties, and all the French refused to contemplate fighting for Paris. Weygand saw only one hope, though, given his hopeless exposition earlier, it was scarcely more than an attempt to cast the blame for the current French defeat on the British. He wanted every British fighter plane to be sent to France, claiming that 'this is the decisive moment'. This was nonsense, and he and Pétain must have known it. The decisive moment had been the German breakthrough at the Meuse a month before, and then at Forges-les-Eaux on 7 June. Churchill refused, remarking that the (future) decisive moment would come when the Luftwaffe attacked Britain. In other words, he recognized that France was beaten, just as clearly as did Weygand, but by holding on to one of his main weapons he made it clear he aimed to go on fighting.

The discussion went on, looking at what to do when the present fighting ended in the French defeat. Churchill's fertile mind threw up suggestions, old and new: a Breton Redoubt, guerrilla warfare, fighting on from the empire, none of which appealed to the French in any way. Indeed the very notion of guerrilla warfare was a touchy subject in France, where it had been tried in 1870 and where one of the results was the Paris Commune, a horror story which such right wingers as Pétain and Weygand and others recoiled from almost physically. (At one point at this time a rumour spread of a Communist *coup d'état* in Paris, exactly the sort of rumour which grew out of the situation and out of French political memories and fears.)

But if the whole of metropolitan France was conquered there was still the empire. Weygand obligingly raised the issue by characteristically commenting that he did not see how the war could continue if France itself was occupied. He was stopped at that point by Reynaud, who made it clear that this was a political, not a military matter – but Pétain was also there, and he was both a military man and a politician by now. De Gaulle was also there, another man bestriding the two spheres. Weygand had just about reached the point at which he would allow his disaffection to override his loyalty and his duty to the elected government.

Churchill, however, also raised the issue, a little tentatively, for it was after all necessarily a French decision. He made it clear that his and his government's policy was to fight on even if metropolitan France was occupied – his decision on the aircraft had already shown that. It was clear from what he said that he hoped the French government would similarly fight on, based in North Africa, where there was, in fact, a considerable army, which could probably be augmented by troops from France. He touched then also on what the French Navy would do in such a situation. Reynaud headed that off by commenting vaguely that France would fight on, though how and where he did not say. Clearly the French had not yet seriously considered the matter.

Before the conference dispersed, but after the formal discussions were over, Churchill went into the issue of the French fleet again. He buttonholed Admiral François Darlan, Chief of Staff of the French Navy (that is, its effective commander), and sounded him out on the prospect of the Navy's survival under French command even after the defeat on land. Churchill asked Darlan directly that he never surrender the fleet to Germany, thereby making it clear that he expected it to be necessary to make a decision on its future soon. Darlan was clear also: it would not be allowed to fall into German hands, and if it came to desperate measures, he would send it to Canada (or to the empire, or to the United States – reports of the conversation vary).[14] Churchill took some comfort from this but even as he flew back to Britain the French defensive lines in the north broke, and Weygand ordered a general retreat. This, of course, only confirmed what had been clear to those at the meeting, but now it was public. France was beaten and the issues which had been raised hypothetically at the meeting – an armistice, peace, fighting on somewhere and somehow, and the French fleet – were now matters of immediate concern.

The two Allies thus diverged. The French government, having retreated to the Loire valley, now went further south, to Bordeaux. Defeats continued, and it was clear that the occupation of all France by the German army was imminent. The question of an armistice was at last discussed frequently by the French Cabinet at their meeting after Churchill had left. It was forced on the ministers by Weygand, who was not actually a Cabinet minister, but could certainly make himself heard, and was insinuated into the agenda for the future by Camille Chautemps, a former Premier and now a Vice-Premier under Reynaud. But it was clear that the Cabinet was divided on the issue. The majority were in favour of fighting on, and at this stage only Pétain and one other minister wished to ask for an armistice. But that belligerent majority was shaky. All of them could see that continuing defeat would mean the occupation of all France by enemy forces, but no-one could produce a credible plan for fighting on, and neither the Breton Redoubt nor the North African ideas were received with any favour. That is, if an armistice became possible, it was clear that several ministers who had said they were in favour of fighting on would clearly go for it.[15]

Another meeting with Churchill, who had Halifax with him this time, was held on 13 June, but came to no clear conclusion. Churchill was now wholly appraised of the desperate position in France. After the British left there was another French cabinet meeting at which the defeatists scented blood, and the waverers began to shift their ground in favour of an armistice. Weygand, now being accepted as almost a full member of the meeting, again demanded an armistice. Pétain supported him, and denigrated any idea of the government leaving metropolitan France. This, indeed, was a most unpopular idea with all the ministers.[16]

Weygand was already evading taking action on orders from his government, using the confusion as his excuse. On the British side Lieutenant-General Alan Brooke, the new commander-in-chief of the reconstituted British Expeditionary Force, thought he had been ordered to prepare to hold on to Brittany, but found no French support for this nor any interest in it when he consulted with Weygand. It was clear to him that the only result of the British forces fighting on would be their defeat and capture. He sent a message to General Sir John Dill, Chief of the Imperial General Staff, to the effect that he should order the evacuation of all British forces before they fell into German hands. Dill referred the decision to Churchill, who came on to the phone to Brooke, did not like the idea of another evacuation, pointing out that the BEF was in France in order to provide the French with support to help them go on fighting, not to help them give up. But by the end of the conversation, just before Brooke exploded with rage, he had been persuaded that he was needlessly risking another British army, and Brooke was ordered to evacuate his troops.[17] This process began the next day. The 52nd Division went to Britain by way of Cherbourg, the Canadian Division through St Malo, and other troops out of Brest, Nantes, and St Nazaire. (These two divisions had in fact only just arrived in France.) In four days (15–18 June) over 140,000 British, Canadians, and assorted allies were evacuated, almost as many soldiers as at Dunkirk.[18]

This order was the effective end of the Franco-British Alliance. The RAF bomber force in France went back to Britain at the same time, and five squadrons of RAF fighters remained only long enough to provide air cover for the evacuations. Brooke had been told on 14 June that he was released from having to obey orders from Weygand, and Weygand henceforth conspicuously failed to pass on any information, apparently preferring to see the British forces in France destroyed. Weygand's Anglophobia, never really concealed, became open. He is said to have predicted that England would only last three weeks, and would 'have her neck wrung like a chicken'. (He later disavowed this, but it was clearly a reflection of his feelings at the time, and he was in a sufficiently unpleasant mood to have said it.)[19]

The permission given to Brooke to evacuate the army was obviously the slightly delayed result of the accumulating evidence leaking from the French government that an armistice was being actively discussed by the French Cabinet. At the same time the project of continuing the war from North Africa was also under active discussion. Under-Secretary de Gaulle was sent to London to arrange for shipping to be made available to assist in transporting the French army across the Mediterranean. This would involve the French fleet as well, but on 15 June Admiral Darlan refused even to consider it, describing the idea of fighting on from North Africa as 'preposterous', though this was partly because the task he was given was impossible.[20] Pétain, Weygand, Darlan, and two other men, met separately, possibly in effect planning a *coup*, though in the event they did not need to carry one out, for they were handed power instead of having to take it.

The fleet cropped up every now and again in the discussions. Churchill had made it clear to Darlan that he considered it a vital matter that it should not fall under German control. In each discussion in the French Cabinet one or more ministers had mentioned it, though it was not in the context of British fears and wishes. Now Darlan in effect refused the use of the fleet in moving the army to North Africa, just as Weygand had refused even to consider either the Breton or the North African ideas, and had begun to ignore the orders coming from the government. That is, just as the alliance with Britain had been effectively dissolved by the British decision to remove their forces from France, so the French government's authority over its own forces was dissolving.[21]

At another meeting of the Cabinet at Bordeaux on 15 June the Premier found himself in a minority over the question of fighting on: the waverers had now clearly shifted towards the armistice camp. Pétain threatened resignation, and it looked as though the Cabinet would break up. Pétain had been consistently defeatist, but he had great prestige with the French public, who had not been enlightened to his defeatism or to his political views. He was known to be right wing, as were virtually all the army officers, so this was hardly unexpected. But if he resigned it would probably mean that the government itself would fall, so the resignation tactic was probably designed to promote his own appointment as the replacement for Reynaud. The private meeting he had had earlier had lined up Weygand and Darlan, both

popular figures more by virtue of their posts than because anyone outside
government circles knew much about them. The other two present were
Paul Baudouin, Reynaud's Under-Secretary for Foreign affairs and a former
Secretary to the War Council, who had already been clearly identified by
Churchill as defeatist, and Yves Bouthillier, the Finance Minister. Pétain
had therefore lined up on his side the commanders of the forces and the
crucial ministers, including one man, Baudouin, who could put his fingers
on the means of communication.

Before Pétain could do anything decisive, however, there came a new proposal, which was probably unexpected by anyone, which at least temporarily
spiked Pétain's guns – which indeed may have been its purpose, but which
is generally seen as being helpful in the end to the Marshal's aims. The
cracks in the Cabinet were papered over by the proposal which came from
Camille Chautemps that the Germans should be asked what their terms for
an armistice were. Everyone understood this in his own way, but in fact it
favoured the seeking of armistice terms from the Germans. What Chautemps
perhaps did not, or maybe chose not to, understand was that simply by
asking for terms the French would be accepting defeat and drastically limit-
ing their future options. It did mean that Pétain could scarcely resign over
the earlier refusal to seek an armistice.

Some of those who had agreed to Chautemps' proposal believed that
any proffered terms could still be rejected and the fight could then go on;
others thought they were asking for peace terms rather than an armistice;
Chautemps himself claimed that the probable severity of Germany's terms
would stimulate French resistance; still others thought in terms of a cease-
fire, during which armistice terms could be discussed. Chautemps' wording
skilfully covered all these possibilities, but the soldiers and sailors knew
perfectly well that simply by asking for terms of any sort the French government, after the defeats in the last month, was acknowledging the German
victory, and that once it became known in the army that terms had been
requested the morale of the soldiers and their willingness to go on fighting
would collapse. It would be extremely unlikely that any troops could be
persuaded to fight on again even if the terms the Germans were persuaded to
grant would destroy the country. Chautemps' proposal certainly papered over
the Cabinet's divisions, but at the cost of imminent, certain and decisive
national defeat. It is not sure, but this may well have been part of Chautemps'
purpose.[22]

It was, of course, by no means as easy as that to get out of the war.
Once he had seen the implications, and now being in a minority in his own
Cabinet, Reynaud wanted to resign, but President Lebrun would not let him.
And there was the question of Britain, to whom in theory France was still

indissolubly allied and with whom the French government had insisted on making an agreement that neither peace nor an armistice should be made without the agreement of both parties to the alliance. And that brought up, again, the issues of the empire and the fleet.

So the first thing to do was to get the British to consent to the request for an armistice. Reynaud, despite strong misgivings on his part, and despite personally wanting to go on fighting in France or in North Africa, managed to word the request, sent through the British ambassador, Sir Ronald Campbell, in such a way as to appear to be blackmailing the British into agreement. He pointed out that the only hope the French had – that the United States would join in against Germany – had been finally dashed by the refusal from President Roosevelt to assist in any way which would involve the United States in the fighting. Reynaud stated that the transfer of authority over the fleet would not be an issue in the armistice terms. This was, he said, out of the question altogether. But he also said that if Britain refused to allow France to stop fighting, Reynaud would resign – a curious statement from a man who professed to want to fight on. He then added the real threat, that any successor government would not necessarily be bound by the promise regarding the fleet, or by the agreement not to seek a unilateral armistice.[23]

This was all very much in the spirit of the Chautemps proposal, which Reynaud had disliked but whose ambiguity he had now clearly imbibed and accepted. He had attempted to resign over it, but had been stopped by the President. His request to the British can be seen, in part, as a new attempt by Reynaud to get out of his own personal dilemma. If the British refused to accept the armistice Reynaud could resign, as he had said. But if the British accepted, he could also resign, since he did not personally agree that an armistice was necessary. The obfuscation of the Chautemps proposal got him out of this problem; it was alive and well and had spread to all members of the Cabinet, even the Premier. Only those who had been defeatists all along could come out of this government crisis intact and content. Hence the suspicion that Chautemps was really acting as an ally of Pétain and his group.

For a time, based on the first British reaction, it seemed that the British would refuse to agree to the French seeking an armistice. But Reynaud's blackmail worked on them, and in the British War Cabinet it was the prospect of a government in Bordeaux headed by someone other than Reynaud which persuaded them to agree, but with conditions. The prime condition was that the French fleet must be safeguarded, and could not be permitted to come under even indirect German control. But the British now went further, clearly fearing that the disintegration in France had gone so far that no government, not even Reynaud's, would be able to stop the Germans from seizing the ships if they wished, with or without an armistice agreement. If the country was occupied any government which remained would be hostage to German wishes, and would have to accept German orders. So the new British demand was that not only should the fleet not become subject to any sort of German control, which had been the earlier requirement, but that it be 'sailed forthwith to British harbours pending negotiations'.[24]

This was not something any French government could agree to. Whether the French ministers realized that the British troops in France were being evacuated at that time is not clear, but some at least must have known it, and no doubt Weygand could have told them – if he had not by this time come to simply ignore the British. A new message from London amplified the earlier one, and argued that putting the French fleet definitively out of German reach would strengthen the French hand in the negotiations, and suggested, duplicitously in the circumstances, that British troops were still fighting alongside the French army and so Britain should be consulted on the terms of any armistice. No doubt some British troops were still fighting, but the message omitted to note that they were all in process of being evacuated.

But the same message made it clear, even if not in so many words, that the British now assumed that, whatever they said, an armistice would result. So that, besides demanding that the fleet be put out of German reach, the message wanted the French Air Force to fly its planes to North Africa, so that these planes could not be used against Britain, and that the troops of other allies which were still in France, Poles, Belgians, and Czechs, should be evacuated to Britain.[25]

The implication of this message was that the British government had already decided that the Franco-British Alliance was dead, even if its orders to General Brooke to evacuate his forces did not already mean that. The main object of British policy towards France was therefore aimed now at acquiring as much in the way of French military assets – the fleet, the Air Force, Allied soldiers, even French troops – as could be secured before the armistice went into effect. Of course, the French would regard this as British self-interest surfacing once more – an interpretation which is quite reasonable, and only to be expected – but they would then draw the conclusion that the defeat of France was someone else's fault – namely Britain's – which was a dangerous delusion. Belgium had already been blamed for surrendering when that country had been almost entirely conquered, and President Roosevelt's refusal to declare war on Germany was another example of a refusal to help France in its hour of need; now, with some relief because it was a normal French reaction, Britain could be blamed as well, for not sending the RAF, for evacuating its troops, for refusing to agree to an armistice. It all helped to evade the responsibility for defeat. All of these states, however, France included, were really only acting in their own interests all along. This was how nation states always behaved. But it was basically a stupid reaction to heap the blame on everyone else. What had happened to the boasted clarity of French thought?

It was, therefore, with much surprise, even shock, that a telephone message was received from General de Gaulle, at the time in London. He passed on a new proposal from the British War Cabinet to Reynaud in Bordeaux that Britain and France should unite into a single state. 'An Indissoluble Union' was the phrase used. It was an idea which had been floating about in both Britain and France since the war began, as much to provide mutual encouragement as anything. It only became worth serious political consideration in the depths of defeat – which, of course, made it most unlikely that it would be worthwhile. It was discussed at a British Cabinet meeting on 15 June, and again the next day.

More importantly, it was at this point that General de Gaulle became seriously involved in political affairs. He was in London to arrange for the ships which were supposed to transport French troops to North Africa, but when the issue of a union was broached he seized on it as a solution to everyone's problems. Reynaud's wilting will to go on fighting would be stiffened, the issue of the fleet would go away, and the fight would go on from bases in North Africa as well as Britain. The phone call to Reynaud was therefore to dictate the text of the 'Declaration of Union' which Reynaud would be able to present to his Cabinet later that day. De Gaulle's participation, however, was more decisive than merely as a messenger and transmitter. He was personally against the idea of an armistice. He did not like the British conditional approval which had been sent to France on 15 June. He had alerted Reynaud earlier on the 16th that a proposal for union was being discussed in Britain, but Reynaud needed something more than a discussion paper to present to his Cabinet, given the desperate situation in France, so de Gaulle reported to the British War Cabinet that Reynaud would require something concrete to present to his Cabinet colleagues. When this message reached the British Cabinet, that Reynaud could only go on with a definite plan to propose, the Declaration was quickly agreed. The text of this declaration was what de Gaulle telephoned through to Reynaud.[26]

This came soon after the earlier messages giving the British conditions for accepting the armistice proposal. Clearly the proposed union changed the position, although for the British it was really only another method of securing control of the French fleet and getting the French to fight on, for an obvious part of the consequences of the proposed union was that the united state would continue the war, with a single command. This would definitely put the French forces on the British side, men, planes and ships. For the

French ministers this new proposal completely superseded the earlier conditions which the British had imposed on the question of the armistice, in effect cancelling them, though that is not what the British intended. Reynaud in particular (and, perhaps, de Gaulle) saw the new situation as one in which the fight would simply go on.

The whole idea fell flat. When Reynaud presented it to the French Cabinet, reading the text through twice to his colleagues, there was no enthusiasm at all. A few ministers were interested, but the majority were simply dismissive. All realized that it was, or claimed to see it as, merely a ploy to get France to go on fighting – not, as it happens, an inaccurate assessment. All of them also fully realized that, in the circumstances of the moment, with the French army retreating everywhere, and with half of France under enemy occupation, any union with Britain would put France in a permanent subordinate position: as another dominion, some said. Some were offended at the idea of being united with a monarchy. Some of the objections were of this niggling and petty and unimportant type, but collectively they were a clear indication that the idea was unpalatable, even objectionable to most of the French ministers. Better a Nazi province than subject to George VI, was one reaction.

The defeatists were, as a result, strengthened again. The notion of a unilateral armistice gained ground. The Cabinet meeting dissolved into confusion, insults and recriminations, until Reynaud adjourned it. He went to the President and asked for permission to reconstruct his government, aiming to include only those who were willing to fight on, but Lebrun had worked out that the majority were in favour of an armistice and he refused. He asked Reynaud to follow the Chautemps line and ask the Germans for their armistice conditions, but Reynaud would not do it. He did not officially resign, for he was supposed to do so to the Council of Ministers itself, but Lebrun called on Pétain to form a new government without Reynaud. Pétain was thereby saved from the embarrassment of conducting a *coup*, though his aim, of reconstituting French society on 'conservative', that is, reactionary terms, remained.[27]

The British proposal of union had therefore brought about the final dissolution of the only government of France which was willing to continue fighting. But that government had been steadily weakening under the pressures of internal dissent, of its own defeatists, of external defeats, and of the disobedience of its senior military commanders. President Lebrun was quite correct in calling on Pétain to form a new government, since he had seen that the old government's policy had failed, and that therefore a new policy under a new Premier was required – and the only other policy on offer was to seek an armistice, which Pétain (and Weygand) had been advocating for days.

From the British point of view the worst case which had been presented by Reynaud earlier had now come to pass. The proposal for union, which was designed to keep France fighting, had been rejected, but the only French government willing to consider doing so had gone as well. In its place came a new government totally unwilling to pay any heed to British wishes, determined to seek an armistice – Pétain publicly announced that one was being sought the very next day – and the conditions under which the British had signified their acceptance of the idea of seeking an armistice – the transfer of the fleet – would now be ignored.

The new government in France was quickly in position, full of military men in the most important positions – Pétain as Premier, Weygand as Minister of National Defence and Darlan as Minister of Marine, with other generals in charge of the War and Air Ministries. These were the men with the real power, and the rest were a collection of Reynaud's former colleagues who would find it difficult in the circumstances of the moment to resist the military men. The first meeting of the new Cabinet agreed to ask what conditions Germany proposed for an armistice and that afternoon the new Foreign Minister, Paul Baudouin, asked the Spanish government to pass the message to Germany and the Papal Nuncio to do so to Rome. A difficult interview with the British ambassador, Sir Robert Campbell, followed, leaving Baudouin exhausted.

Nothing was said at any of these meetings about the French fleet, and this was to be an acrimonious subject for the next three weeks. It was the fate and use of that fleet which was to be the occasion for the beginning of the war which the French and British would wage against each other for the next two years.

Chapter 2

The French Fleet

The fleet which now became the subject for argument between Britain and France, and between France and Germany, was reckoned to be rather less than half the size of the Royal Navy. The two largest navies in the world were the Royal Navy and the US Navy. Japan came next. By 1939 Germany, France, and Italy were more or less equal in naval strength, though their fleets were composed differently. The Royal Navy could cope with any one of the European navies with little difficulty, especially since Germany and Italy, the two states which in June 1940 were active enemies, faced different seas, and the British held the gate between them at Gibraltar. But as France steadily fell under German control during June 1940, and the French Channel ports were successively conquered, and then those facing the Bay of Biscay, the prospect arose that all three of these fleets might come under German-Italian control. Much of the French fleet was concentrated in the Mediterranean, where a junction of it with the Italian fleet could well overwhelm the British Mediterranean fleet and open the way for the conquest of Malta and Egypt. And if Spain, under its right-wing fascist regime, actively joined in the war, there was no hope of holding Gibraltar. In such a case Britain's position would be desperate. Adding all these fleets together produced the nightmare scenario that the Royal Navy could be outnumbered and over-whelmed in the English Channel.

For the present, in early June the French Navy was actively fighting on the British side – on 12 June Admiral Darlan sent part of the Toulon fleet to bombard Genoa, and on the night of 20/21 June a joint bombardment by the French battleship *Lorraine* and part of the British Mediterranean fleet was mounted against the Italian Libyan port of Bardia.[1] But the repeated comments and requests and demands from the British not to let the fleet fall to Germany highlighted the fact that, with the army beaten and the air force defeated, the navy was the main military asset the French government now had, given the fact that the colonial army was required to hold on to the colonies.

The policy of the new Minister of Marine, Admiral Darlan, who retained his old post as Chief of Staff, was the key to the future of the fleet. He was torn over what to do. He was part of a government which had requested an armistice, but he personally could not contemplate relinquishing control of the ships to either Germany or Britain. On the day after the new Pétain government took office (that is, 18 June) he was bombarded with requests and demands. The US Ambassador to the exiled Polish government came to see him and invited him to send the fleet to the United States. Then a note was presented by the US Ambassador to France, Antony Drexel Biddle, sent by the US Secretary of State, Cordell Hull, insisting that the fleet be safeguarded and kept out of German hands. If it was allowed to fall to Germany then the integrity of the French Empire could not be guaranteed, Hull said – that is, the United States would feel itself entitled to seize strategic points of the empire for its own security.[2] This was much the same sort of indirect blackmail to which Reynaud had subjected the British government.

Darlan did not realize it, but this note had been instigated by the British, though the US government was equally bothered at the possible combination of the German, Italian, and French fleets. A US Navy assessment produced on 17 June showed that the combined European fleets would be considerably larger than either the Royal Navy or the US Navy.[3] In the background of all US naval thinking was the strong possibility that Japan would join Germany and Italy. In that case the combined Axis forces would be at least as strong as the Royal Navy and the US Navy combined and, since both of these navies would need to be divided between the Atlantic and Pacific (and Indian) Oceans, the combined Europeans at least would be able to obtain force superiority in the Atlantic and particularly in the eastern Atlantic, that is, the waters around the British Isles. The inclusion of the French fleet in that combination was the element which would tip the balance.

The next visitors to Darlan, still on 18 June, were the chiefs of the Royal Navy, the First Lord of the Admiralty, A.V. Alexander, and the First Sea Lord, Admiral Sir Dudley Pound. These were Darlan's precise equivalents in his two jobs, as Minister of Marine and as Chief of Naval Staff, but in the British government. Darlan scarcely needed to see them to know what they wanted, but he did his best in their conversations to evade the issue and at the same time to placate them. He would not agree that the fleet be sent to British harbours, and he professed to be hurt at the very suggestion. He knew full well that the fleet was virtually the last card in his government's hand. He stated that he would transfer the ships to African ports if they were in danger of capture and pointed out that the battleship *Richelieu*, not quite finished, had already left Brest for Dakar. He also added that he would order all merchant ships in danger of capture to go to British ports. This was a significant gesture, since this would in effect be considerable reinforcement to the British merchant marine. Beyond all this, which was moderately pleasing to the British, Darlan was adamant that the fleet would never be surrendered to anyone and that if the German armistice terms contained a provision for such a surrender, he and the fleet would go on fighting to the end. The ships which survived would then go to friendly ports, or they would be scuttled.[4]

Darlan was, as it happened, as good as his word. Even as these meetings and conversations were taking place at Bordeaux the German army, in the form of units of General Hoth's XV Panzer Corps, was approaching the ports of western France. On 18 June as the talks with Alexander and Pound were going on, the evacuation of British troops of the 52nd Division from Cherbourg was completed, in part under the protection of the French battleship *Courbet*. When the German 7th Armoured Division arrived at the town that day, the battleship sailed to Plymouth. The German 5th Armoured Division was heading for Brittany, and was at Rennes on the 18th. The Canadian Division had been evacuated from St Malo, and 30,000 troops or more were taken from Brest. The *Richelieu*, mentioned in particular by Darlan at Bordeaux, was sailed out of Brest that day. It was almost finished, but its guns were not yet operational and it needed to undergo trials and working up – and the detection and elimination of problems – before it was fit for service. It was directed to head for Dakar.

At Cherbourg and Brest there were several unfinished ships and some others undergoing repair. These were destroyed. At Cherbourg three incomplete submarines were blown up in the dockyard and the dockyard itself was sabotaged. At Brest, once *Richelieu* had gone with two destroyers as its escorts, four more submarines, all under repair, were blown up. The destroyer *Cyclone* and a sloop, *Etourdi*, both being repaired, were destroyed as well, and then the harbour was extensively damaged, as happened also at Cherbourg. The German forces were also approaching the French bases at the mouth of the Loire. At Lorient the sloop *Enseigne Henri* was scuttled; at St Nazaire and Nantes a large scale evacuation of almost 60,000 troops took place. The battleship *Jean Bart*, unfinished, without its guns, and barely able to move, was towed out of St Nazaire and, accompanied by two destroyers, headed for Casablanca.

All this was what might be expected of a state facing a catastrophic defeat on land and it did tend to support Darlan's repeated assurances to everyone who asked, that the French fleet would remain in French hands and under French control, though it was scarcely a sign that the country would go on fighting, since all the ships' movements had been in retreat. (A considerable number of French naval vessels had also escaped from other Channel ports and had taken refuge in various English Channel ports from Dover to Falmouth.)[5]

Meanwhile the armistice terms were being constructed by the Germans, with Hitler dominating the discussions. The French negotiators had no input and soon found that, whatever the terms, humiliation was to be their lot. Hitler had, not surprisingly, designed the ceremony to cancel the memory of the perceived humiliation of Germany in the similar event of 1918 – but at the same time the actual terms were, or seemed to be, comparatively lenient, when the actual military situation was taken into account.

The formation of the Pétain government on 16 June provoked more than one of the men in Reynaud's government to flee from Bordeaux. General de Gaulle flew from Bordeaux to London on 17 June, supposedly just escaping arrest. Daladier and Mandel, the former Minister of the Interior, and a group of Deputies were evacuated from Bordeaux on the cruiser *Massilia*, which finally left the Gironde on 21 June, against the orders of Pétain's government, but with his and Darlan's connivance, going to Morocco. The purposes of these men varied. The cargo of politicians on the *Massilia* might be numerous and prominent enough to set themselves up as an alternative government to that of Pétain if they chose, but they would need more support. For the present, however, they were immobilized in their ship.

On 18 June de Gaulle in London had broadcast an appeal over the BBC asking Frenchmen who wished to go on fighting to get in touch with him. How many heard him is not known, probably very few, but he had a considerable pool of potential recruits in Britain among refugees and evacuees. This was all somewhat vague and indeterminate for the present and the existence of a legally constituted French government permitted him to be branded a traitor. It also in the event blocked any moves by the *Massilia* men.[6] More troops, mainly Polish, but with some Czechs and a few Belgians, were evacuated from the southern ports of Bayonne and St Jean de Luz – 19,000 men in all – on 19 June, and next day a British demolition party was sent ashore at Bordeaux to sabotage the dockyard installations.[7]

The British had ceased to demand that the French fleet go to the British ports, since it was clear that to do so would only have the very opposite effect and simply annoy the French in general and Darlan in particular. But they did not withdraw the demand, and the French knew that this was what their ally really wanted. It was necessary to take Darlan at his word for the moment and to assume that he really could and would keep the fleet under French control, while the actions at Cherbourg and Brest and St Nazaire did imply he meant what he said and that the fleet had the appropriate orders.

The problem was that he might not always be in a position from which he would apply those orders. His position in Pétain's government was secure given the general loyalty to him personally in the fleet, so it would be difficult to replace him. But the basis of Pétain's government was very narrow: it could easily fall at any moment, and if the armistice terms stated that the fleet had to be given up to Germany he was ordered to arrange it by Pétain. Darlan, known as a man who would obey orders, would probably obey. Until the armistice terms emerged the British, the Americans, the French government and Darlan would simply have to wait. All had stated their positions and wishes, but all now depended on Hitler.

Pétain's government was, meanwhile, existing on even more uncomfortable foundations than its predecessor, and de Gaulle's appeal and his subsequent formation of a French National Committee – not to mention the shipload of politicos on the *Massilia* – showed that the political and military classes were fragmenting, and that the whole basis of Pétain's power was being called into question. German advances towards Bordeaux threatened to capture the whole government, and appeals through Spain for the Germans to halt were ignored – indeed, the city was bombed, which seemed to be a rude German reply to the request, though it was probably merely a coincidence.[8] A plan was formulated to shift the government even further south, to Perpignan and another was developed to give Chautemps delegated powers, and send him, with some other ministers, to North Africa – yet another group who could claim to be the French government. This would set up a twin government which could continue if that part of it in France became captive – and Pétain himself was adamant that he would not personally leave France, so his capture would be very likely. In North Africa Chautemps would recruit other men, and could form a fairly convincing government, but this idea was blocked by the civilians in the Cabinet, who did not like the potential for conflict between the two halves.

In turn this show of determination provoked a right-wing reaction. The military members among the ministers were against the move to Perpignan and they contrived first to delay and then to stop the move. President Lebrun was, however, still keen to go, and Pétain, having dithered over the issue for a time, determined to arrest him if he went. In other words, this was another stage in the progressive, continuing *coup d'état* by which Pétain and his group of right-wing military men seized power. The President was persuaded, or intimidated, or sidetracked and repeatedly put off his departure. The moving spirit in all this was Pierre Laval, yet another former Premier. The President had blocked Laval's appointment as Foreign Minister when Pétain's government was formed, but Laval had Pétain's ear, and he was a consummate intriguer. His and Pétain's moves in these two or three days thus completely subverted the Cabinet decision to move away from Bordeaux.[9]

The German armistice terms were telephoned through to Bordeaux on 21 June from the railway carriage at Compiègne where Hitler insisted that they be presented. The carriage had been the very one where the armistice of 1918 had been signed, brought out of a museum for the occasion – it was then burnt, all at Hitler's orders. This infantile gesture of humiliation for the French army was offset to a certain extent by the terms, which unexpectedly lenient; they contained all too many items lifted from the terms imposed on Germany in 1918, but, given that France was now under German occupation, this was lenient treatment. Of course, Hitler knew that there was still a considerable French Army overseas and that the fleet was as yet physically out of his reach. And, after all, this was only an armistice; it was presumed that the actual peace terms would come later and the French Empire and the fleet could be dealt with then. Meanwhile Hitler wanted the fighting in France to end so that he could persuade Britain also to stop fighting. So the terms were that three-fifths of France would be occupied, but the rest, the south, would not, and the government could stay in the unoccupied area; the army would be demobilized, but 100,000 volunteers could be enrolled; the Air Force would go. The French government would continue, as would the empire and the fleet. All this was, of course, a German version of the Versailles settlement – occupation, army numbers, no air force and all. The fleet, which was the subject of Article 8 of the Armistice terms, was to be disarmed and demobilized, except for a limited number of smaller vessels which were needed to patrol the empire, but the ships would remain under French control and command. The German government promised that it had no intention of using the French ships during the war, nor when peace resulted, but the demobilized and disarmed ships were to be put under German and Italian supervision by means of the Armistice Commissions. The location of the ships was to be their home bases, which in effect for many of them meant the ports on France's Atlantic coast, exactly the area which the Germans intended to occupy in order to continue the war with Britain.[10]

This would clearly be unacceptable to the British, but it was also unacceptable to the French. The French had a short time to propose changes and this was where they concentrated their main objections to the terms, proposing that the ships be sent to bases in Africa. One of their more persuasive points was that the ships sent to any of the Atlantic ports would be very vulnerable to British air raids. This was persuasive because the Germans also hoped to use their own air power against the Royal Navy in the continuing war, and the RAF could clearly do the same – indeed had already raided German naval bases in the North Sea more than once. In the meantime Darlan, who had disliked the German proposals, agreed to move his ships to the African bases which were being suggested by the French. The only French aircraft carrier, *Béarn*, was ordered to the West Indies. This was, of course, in full accord with what he had already ordered for the ships from Brest and St Nazaire. The counter-proposal produced an ambiguous reply from the Germans, but the Cabinet decided to shift the ships anyway, thus confirming the orders to Darlan of the previous day. As a result the Germans were left with a *fait accompli*.[11]

All this had no conciliatory effect on the British. The ambassador, Sir Ronald Campbell, left Bordeaux on the 22nd, taking with him his whole staff and he was accompanied by the Canadian and South African staffs. Churchill broadcast a strong criticism of the Pétain government, accusing it of desertion by asking for an armistice. De Gaulle broadcast again from London on the 22nd, hoping that the French would repudiate their government. Neither had any obvious effect. Indeed Pierre Laval was brought into Pétain's government the next day, as a Minister of State, which might be a partial reply. He had been perceived as being anti-British and pro-German for years and was remembered in Britain above all as one of the architects of the betrayal (as people now saw it) of Ethiopia when that country was attacked by Italy. His co-option into the government was as clear a signal as any that Pétain was uninterested in reviving or continuing the alliance with Britain, or even maintaining friendship. (It was also a sign of President Lebrun's failing influence.) Pétain replied to Churchill's broadcast with one of his own, dismissing his criticisms. Franco-British friendship was clearly as dead as their alliance.[12]

There followed a string of complaints, exhortations, and speeches from Britain over the next few days, in which insults were heaped on the Pétain government and its members and accusations of bad faith and lack of honour were made. The British now recognized as the only fit French governmental representative the French National Committee which had been set up by de Gaulle, and made it clear that the Pétain government was now regarded by London as no more than a tool of Germany. In reply de Gaulle was condemned as a traitor and a puppet of Britain.

This was a clear enough sign that the Franco-German armistice terms were not acceptable to Britain, and that meant in particular Article 8, concerning the future of the fleet. The prospect of an extra half a dozen battleships, a large array of cruisers and destroyers, plenty of submarines and an aircraft carrier positioned in ports on the Bay of Biscay and the English Channel and under effective German control, just at the time when the British Isles were threatened by a maritime invasion, was not something any British government could think of without a shudder and without doing something to prevent such a situation arising. The British government therefore felt it had to go further than simply complaining about the armistice terms.

On the other hand, a report by the First Sea Lord to the War Cabinet gave details of the disposition of the French ships, some at Dakar and Casablanca, a considerable number in English ports (and by implication under British guns), two battle-cruisers at Mers el-Kebir, other ships at Alexandria, again under British domination, with Toulon holding a large proportion of the rest. It does not appear to have been made clear that the *Richelieu* and the *Jean Bart* were unusable – Sir Dudley called the *Richelieu* 'the most powerful battleship in the world today' – and the account is clear that the ships were well scattered.[13]

In a decisive speech which should have been taken as a clear warning by both the Pétain government and Germany, Prime Minister Churchill in the House of Commons on the 25th explained that Article 8, concerning the demobilization of the French fleet, was worthless. He was convinced the fleet would soon be under German and Italian control, whatever was said in the armistice terms. He made it clear that there was to be no more negotiation on the issue, that the defence of Britain was his primary and overriding concern, and that all actions were acceptable in that cause. 'At all costs, at all risks,' he said, 'in one way or another … the French navy [must] not fall into the wrong hands.'[14] To anyone hearing or reading this it was as plain a warning as could be given without a clear declaration of war or revealing British plans.

The French Navy was in fact, as the First Sea Lord had shown, pretty well scattered, and relatively little of it was at the time in the Atlantic ports. Indeed, a large number of the ships were actually already in British ports. Two old but still powerful battleships, *Courbet* and *Paris*, were at Portsmouth and Plymouth respectively. Also at Portsmouth were the destroyer *Léopard*, six sloops, five torpedo boats and a supply ship. At Plymouth there were besides *Paris*, the destroyers *Triomphant*, *Mistral* and *Ouarganon*, a torpedo boat, three sloops, and three submarines, including the giant submersible *Surcouf*, the largest in the world. At Falmouth there were more ships: two submarines, three sloops, and a target ship, and at Dundee the submarine *Rubis*, a remarkable vessel which continued in operation under Free French command for the whole of the war. There were also numbers of minelayers, minesweepers, patrol vessels and tugs in several other ports – 186 ships in all.[15] Altogether in harbours in Britain there was a very large fraction of the French Navy, though only a very few of the better and more effective vessels, for these had been moved to the Mediterranean when Italy entered the war. (The Royal Navy, in another reprise of the Great War, had assumed responsibility in Atlantic waters.)

The real power of that Navy lay in its big modern ships. *Courbet* and *Paris* were old and slow, even if they were battleships. Elsewhere the other five French battleships were at various places, and in various stages of preparation. The two new ships taken out of Brest and St Nazaire were on their way to African ports, *Jean Bart* reaching Casablanca on the 23rd and *Richelieu* Dakar on the same day. *Jean Bart* was in no condition to fight anyone, being virtually unarmed, but *Richelieu* would be the most powerful battleship afloat when its guns were properly installed. Two others, *Bretagne* and *Provence*, also relatively old and slow, were at Mers el-Kebir, the new naval base close to Oran in North Africa, and the *Lorraine* was at Alexandria – so this one at least was under a certain degree of British control. There was also a destroyer at Gibraltar and a submarine at Malta. But *Bretagne* and *Provence* had with them at Mers el-Kebir two fast modern and powerful battle-cruisers, *Dunkerque* and *Strasbourg* and a group of modern fast super-destroyers and cruisers. ('Super-destroyers' were very fast and well-armed vessels, larger than the normal destroyers, which were later reclassified as light cruisers; they were the latest examples of the skill and inventiveness of French ship designers.) This was the French navy's most powerful concentration of ships, a group of vessels in many ways more powerful than their British equivalents. It lay very close to the British maritime communication route through the Mediterranean from Gibraltar to Malta and on to Egypt.

Also at Alexandria, besides *Lorraine*, there were four cruisers and more cruisers were at Algiers and Toulon. Beyond Europe there was the only French aircraft carrier, *Béarn*, which had been in the Mediterranean until recently and had been sent to the West Indies by Darlan as part of the programme to remove all of his major ships out of German reach. It was accompanied there by two cruisers and there was another cruiser in the Far East. All of these squadrons were accompanied by a retinue of destroyers and sloops and smaller vessels, as usual. There were more ships at Dakar with *Richelieu*, but the main weight of the French fleet was certainly in the Mediterranean, particularly at Mers el-Kebir and Toulon. This was in part the result of the division of responsibility between Britain and France at the start of the war and the fact that until 10 June Italy had been neutral, but it was also a result of the recent French decision to shift their main ships away from their European ports.[16]

For the British this concentration of force now posed a major problem, since if the French ships in the Mediterranean linked up with the Italian fleet – another six new and fast battleships – in whatever way, the British could well be driven out of that sea. Each of the concentrations of French ships was being observed by British ships, an irritant the French learned to live with. Another British priority was to prevent the French ships in

British ports and at Alexandria from leaving, since if they did so they would necessarily go to France or to one of the French North African ports. 'Procrastinating tactics' were to be used to keep them in harbour – but this would only work for a relatively short time, when a decision on letting them leave or seizing them would need to be made. The latter was under active planning as soon as the French armistice was agreed.

Meanwhile the British government had come to the conclusion that what-ever were the terms the Germans had proffered to the Pétain government it was not possible to believe that they would be honoured. It was, after all, only an armistice, not a peace treaty, whose eventual terms could well be considerably different. (Consider the differences between the 1918 armistice and the Versailles settlement.) Further, once implemented the armistice terms would be easy to change – for France would be in effect disarmed – or simply ignored and it would not be difficult to find instances where the terms had been broken by one side or another. For a government which, as had Nazi Germany, faked a Polish attack to give itself a reason for declaring war, such a procedure was second nature. Above all, the disarmament of France would leave it at Germany's mercy. In comparable conditions, the French army had occupied a large part of Germany in the 1920s.

On 24 June the War Cabinet when being told where the various French ships were, was informed that the Admiralty believed that the ships in British ports could be prevented from leaving, as could those at Alexandria and the vessels in Gibraltar and Malta. Those at Dakar and Casablanca could be watched – *Richelieu* and *Jean Bart* had been shadowed by British ships on their voyages. Mers el-Kebir was, however, described as a well-defended port.

So Mers el-Kebir – usually referred to by the British as 'Oran' from the town nearby – was the main problem. It held the most powerful concentra-tion of major French ships and was the best defended base. But an attack was not something to be undertaken without both preparation and a preliminary attempt at persuasion. (This sequence – persuasion, threat, force – became the regular process in each stage of the Franco-British war which was about to begin.) Contacts were made with the French colonial governors in Rabat, Algiers, Tunis, Beirut, and Dakar, in the hope that they could be persuaded to reject the Pétain government and the armistice terms, but without success. It was clear that the Pétain government, which was relocating to Vichy in central France at the time (chosen because, as a holiday resort, it had plenty of hotel space which could be commandeered for accommodation and office space), had asserted a certain control over its North African territories, though it was also clear that that control was by no means unshakable. The *Massilia* passengers had gone to Morocco, for instance, where they were first confined to the ship, and then confined onshore, clearly because their influence was feared. They were thus immobilized and unable to do much to affect the developing political situation in France.[17]

The British Admiralty was ordered to prepare plans for Mers el-Kebir and on 27 June Sir Dudley Pound reported that by 3 July a British force could be placed outside the French base in sufficient strength to intimidate or 'eliminate' the French ships. He was ordered to assemble a fleet to be prepared to do just that. The Admiralty transferred a substantial force from Scapa Flow, the Home Fleet base, to Gibraltar. When the ships arrived they were constituted as Force H, commanded by Admiral Sir James Somerville, brought out of semi-retirement for the post. He had the aircraft carrier *Ark Royal* (which just avoided being hit by a U-boat torpedo on the voyage south), the battle-cruiser *Hood*, and three battleships, *Valiant*, *Resolution*, and *Nelson*, plus cruisers and destroyers. Somerville and his ships were in position by 30 June at Gibraltar. It was a force roughly equivalent to the French ships which were in Mers el-Kebir.[18]

Any government which was alert would have taken to heart the repeated warnings about the French fleet which were voiced by various members of the British government, from the King and the Prime Minister down. But the Vichy government was not alert. It was preoccupied with its move to Vichy, with keeping and expanding its power within the French governmental and political system, with the armistice with Germany, with establishing its control in France and in the Empire, with the defiance of de Gaulle. The absence of direct diplomatic contact after the British ambassador and all his staff left did not help – he did not even leave a *chargé d'affaires* behind. It was certainly on shaky political ground, and the group of other former ministers, including Daladier and Mandel, which had reached Morocco in *Massilia*, might form themselves into another alternative government. While they were still confined to the ship they had arrived in, a high-powered British government delegation, headed by the Colonies Minister Lord Lloyd, which tried to meet them was confined to its hotel, refused access and had to leave without doing so. There is no doubt but that the Pétain government had enough to preoccupy it, but it is also clear that it was derelict in its duty to watch for danger from outside, possibly imagining that the armistice with Nazi Germany gave it some sort of immunity or protection. So when the threats from the British government, which were obvious enough in all conscience, emerged into reality they were completely taken aback.

The basic problem was probably that the Vichy regime, self-satisfied with having reached power, now assumed that the British would cave in as well – the attitude articulated by a Weygand's 'neck wrung like a chicken' comment. The quality of resistance and determination which the Prime Minister was able to summon escaped them, as did the sheer quality of Churchill himself. Weygand had expected that 'England' would last no more than three weeks, but this was army thinking. In 1940, the British resistance to invasion depended, as it had in 1914 and 1779, 1797, 1805 and 1588 and often in between, on the Royal Navy. Only Admiral Darlan in the new French government might have appreciated this, but he does not seem to have done so, preoccupied as he was with his own fleet. But until the Royal Navy was eliminated the prospects of any invasion of the British Isles were minimal. Hence, once again, the need for the British to ensure that the French navy did not take part in such an attack.

If invasion was threatened the Royal Navy would be used to prevent it, assisted by the RAF, and it was clear to the British that the prospect of the French Navy being available to Britain's enemies in the English Channel was one which would have to be scotched. It would not do to wait to see if Germany honoured its armistice terms. These armistice terms, the British agreed, did not remove the French fleet from the board and unless the Pétain government could guarantee that its fleet could not be involved in any attack on Britain, then the British would need to act as though the threat of French participation, existed either as an ally of Germany, or when its ships had been seized, in reality. The Vichy regime had been warned as clearly as diplomatic and political practice and language allowed without an explicit threat being voiced. When attacks happened they had only themselves to blame if they were surprised and unprepared.

At the same time a certain sympathy for them and for Darlan in particular, can be felt. In the midst of the collapse of their whole social and political world, their exclusion from Paris, and the demolition of the powerful French army, they scarcely could expect that their navy would be attacked by their ally, even if they had already reneged on more than one of the agreements made with that ally – by agreeing to the armistice, for example. As German troops settled in to occupy most of their country, and as the members of this new government hunted for places to live in and a place from which to govern, and began to have ideas on what to do with the power they had so unexpectedly acquired, the fact that their Navy was largely out of the Germans' reach was perhaps the limit of their maritime concerns. Putting themselves in the British position in their imaginations was scarcely a priority, nor was it a practice they were capable of. And yet, that is what a Foreign Office is for and the new French Foreign Minister, Paul Baudouin, should have picked up the strong signals emanating from Britain. Again it is a failure of imagination that he failed to understand them.

Chapter 3

Mers el-Kebir

The British commander of Force H, Vice-Admiral James Somerville, was unhappy at what he had been ordered to do but, like Darlan, a lifetime in the Navy had habituated him to obey. He had been told, when he was appointed to the command that his first task would be to remove the threat of the French force at Mers el-Kebir. It had been made clear to him that this might involve the use of force against Britain's erstwhile allies. This was, after all, why he had been given an aircraft carrier, a battle-cruiser and three battle-ships as his force. He might be unhappy at what he had to do, and he certainly regretted it all his life, and considered it a mistake, but he clearly understood well enough that the elimination of the threat implied by the French battle-cruisers and battleships was necessary and he was prepared to see it done.

The operation against Mers el-Kebir was just one of a series of actions designed to seize control of all the French warships within British reach – in Alexandria and in Britain as well as the battle fleet at Oran. All these tasks and operations had to be undertaken at the same time, since attempting to secure one ship would clearly alert all the rest. The date set for the operation to secure the ships at Mers el-Kebir was 3 July, because this was the earliest date Somerville's fleet could reach the place, so that became the date for the actions at all the other places as well. This also allowed time for the necessary planning to take place. Force H sailed from Gibraltar to Oran late on the afternoon of 2 July.[1]

At Alexandria talks about the French ships attached to the Mediter-ranean Fleet, Force X had been going on for some time. On 25 June Admiral René Godfroy, in command of the battleship *Lorraine*, three heavy cruisers, a light cruiser, three destroyers and a sloop, was refused permission to leave Alexandria to sail to Beirut. The British Commander-in-Chief of the Mediterranean fleet, Admiral Andrew Cunningham, had friendly relations with Godfroy, and gained the strong impression that the admiral and his captains were perfectly content to claim to their government that they were unable to sail, citing *force majeure*. Godfroy even went so far as to offer to discharge his fuel oil, which would render the ships immobile and reduce the need for Cunningham to keep a substantial force at Alexandria to watch them. Cunningham did not think this necessary. All this had happened before the decision by the War Cabinet that it was necessary to eliminate any possible threat to Britain by these ships was transmitted to Cunningham.[2]

The possibility of reducing the French crews to skeleton, or caretaker, size or status was being suggested by Cunningham by 29 June, when he also commented to the Admiralty on the undesirability of using force to secure the French ships. Next day, however, the Admiralty demanded that the ships at Alexandria should be seized; making the point that it should be done simultaneously with the operation at Oran. Cunningham's opinion on how to do this was requested.

Cunningham had been in office as Commander-in-Chief of the Mediterranean Fleet for a year by this time, and he was quite able to resist or ignore inconvenient or inappropriate orders from London, and not averse from doing so if it conflicted with his own judgment. The Admiralty also appreciated that the prospect of a full-scale battle between French and British ships in Alexandria harbour was not to be borne. So Cunningham had considerable scope for initiative and negotiation, which he was fully prepared to use. The result was a slow and erratic progress, which never did reach a situation which was considered satisfactory at the Admiralty. But at least it avoided any fighting.

The operation to take control of the French ships in Britain was relatively straightforward, but neither easy nor bloodless. It was hoped that the French were off guard, for some officers had dined with their British counterparts on the evening before the planned seizure. The raids, in the best clandestine style, took place at dawn on or before 3 July and most of the French succumbed straight away. They had, after all, been effectively imprisoned in their ships for two or three weeks and some of the men, certainly some of the officers at least, must have expected some sort of British action to take place. A visit by Vice-Admiral Sir M. E. Dunbar-Naismith, in command of the Plymouth naval base to several ships at Plymouth, had raised French suspicions at least on the big submarine *Surcouf*, where several officers felt that a British attempt at seizure was imminent.

In two ships at Plymouth, there was resistance and fighting. On the destroyer *Mistral* and the submarine *Surcouf* some of the French seized weapons and fought back. This did not last long, but four men died. In all the other ships the French accepted the British action with no more than a protest, if that. At Portsmouth and Falmouth and the other ports the seizure was accompanied by no greater French resistance than verbal complaints.[3]

In the result the British gained control of the two old battleships, four destroyers (including *Mistral*), twelve sloops, six submarines (including *Surcouf*), thirteen torpedo boats, three minelayers and sixteen submarine chasers. All of these, even the battleships, would be very useful in the sort of anti-submarine, convoy war which was developing in the Atlantic. In addition there were 160 smaller craft, the type of ships (tugs, trawlers, mine-sweepers, and patrol craft) which had been specifically noted in the French armistice terms as being available for German use for the prospective invasion of Britain. These were now available to be used by Britain instead of against her. And all these were acquired without any violence except in *Mistral* and *Surcouf*.

It was in the Mediterranean that the real difficulty came, for that was where the main strength of the French navy was. At Gibraltar there had been a great deal of discussion both among the British officers and between the newly-appointed Somerville and the Admiralty as to exactly what Somerville was to do and the more Somerville asked for clarification and instructions the less leeway he found he had. He may not have realized it, but the general purpose of his mission had a much wider scope than simply removing a possibly hostile naval threat to British sea supremacy in the Mediterranean. It seems clear that the Admiralty, and behind it Churchill and the War Cabinet, was determined that the French ships should be eliminated where they were – that is, sunk, one way or another – though their surrender and transfer to British control would also be acceptable.

The US Navy, in its private assessment, had already noted that the combination of the three European Continental navies, if it took place, would produce a very powerful force indeed. It might be enough to accomplish an invasion of Britain even against the determination of the Royal Navy, given as well the apparent German strength in the air. Therefore, it followed that preventing such a combination by eliminating one possible element of it made sense. The French Navy was the most vulnerable to attack, and therefore the easiest to deal with. Further, its strength in the western Mediterranean would make Gibraltar vulnerable. It was only a day's sail from Mers el-Kebir.

But beyond all that it was necessary to persuade anyone who was paying attention – that is, every military man, every sailor, every airman and every politician in the world – that Britain was capable of fighting on and had the will and determination, the ruthlessness and the unscrupulousness, to do so. Above all, Hitler, Mussolini, Stalin, and Roosevelt had to be convinced of this. It would also help if the Vichy French could be persuaded, though no one had any illusions that this would be seen as anything but a hostile act.

There was no better way of doing so than to throw the weight of the traditional British weapon, the Royal Navy, at their pusillanimous ex-Ally's ships. So when Admiral Somerville cavilled at the use of force, and expressed the hope that he would be able to persuade the French commander at Oran, Admiral Marcel-Bruno Gensoul, to disarm his ships, he was steadily brought into a position where he was compelled, by the instructions he operated under, to be prepared to use force. In the event the French admiral fully cooperated with Somerville's instructions and virtually forced him to do so. But Gensoul was also in effect, boxed in by the limited alternatives presented to him.

The real problem was not using force – that is what navies and admirals are for – but to do so in such a way that the immediate naval threat in the western Mediterranean was removed and yet that the Vichy government did not respond with active hostility. It was clearly a strong possibility that Pétain, pushed by an outraged Darlan, would declare war. He was already Anglophobic and this feeling was bound to spread. The danger was real, but on the side of peace was the fact that Germany, by disarming France and demobilizing its ships, was operating on the British side.

If Somerville was unhappy and rather puzzled by his instructions, Admiral Cunningham at Alexandria was angry. 'Am most strongly opposed to proposal for forcible seizure of ships in Alexandria, nor can I see what benefit is to be derived from it', he signalled almost as soon as he learned of the Admiralty's instructions.[4] His established position as Commander-in-Chief gave him much greater leeway than the newly appointed Somerville, as did the fact that he knew and liked his French counterpart Admiral Godfroy, whereas Somerville had never met Gensoul at Mers el-Kebir – not to mention the fact that Godfroy's ships were under Cunningham's guns. So while Somerville was asking for clarification and being steadily moved to a situation in which he would be compelled to fire on the French ships, Cunningham success-fully argued that the use of force at Alexandria would be disastrous. And as it happened it was the personal relations, or absence of them, which were to be crucial to the events of both at Mers el-Kebir and at Alexandria.

No one really knew how the French in Mers el-Kebir would react to the appearance of a powerful British force on their maritime doorstep. After a good deal of discussion it had finally been settled that they should be offered four alternatives – to join the British in fighting on, to sail to a British port and be demilitarized, to sail to the West Indies, also to be demilitarized, or to sink themselves.[5] It was highly unlikely that any of these other alternatives would be acceptable to any of the French admirals, certainly not to Gensoul, and in effect a fifth alternative, to stay in Mers el-Kebir in a demilitarized state but under direct British supervision (and thus ultimate control), also existed, though it was unlikely to be any more acceptable than the others. (It would put the Mers el-Kebir ships in the same situation as those at Toulon, but with British rather than German or Italian supervisors.) In a French port it was probably no more enforceable than in a French port under German supervision. Churchill used the ease with which the British were able to seize the French ships in British ports to claim that the Germans would be able to do the same if the ships had been in French ports which were under German occupation. In a French port, the British supervisors would have been quite unable to control French actions – just as the Germans proved unable to control the French ships at Toulon in the end; none of these alternatives would work and it is probable that both Somerville and Gensoul knew it. So, if none of the various British alternatives were accepted by the French, Force H was to destroy the French ships, especially the battle cruisers *Dunkerque* and *Strasbourg*.

These alternatives, it must be emphasized, existed only as cover for the British determination that the French naval force at Mers el-Kebir should cease to exist. The only alternatives really acceptable to the British were surrender or sinking. If the French ships surrendered they would become available to the Royal Navy; if they sank they would cease to be a problem. Anything in between would leave them still a threat, and shepherding them across the Atlantic then watching and supervising them at Martinique would preoccupy too many British ships which were needed close to home and in the Mediterranean.

These supposed alternatives were detailed in a signal from the Admiralty to Somerville on 2 July and even the form of words to be used in presenting these alternatives to Gensoul was laid out. Finally, Somerville was told that he had just the daylight hours on 3 July to accomplish the work. This meant that the effective time limit for a decision by Gensoul was sometime in the afternoon – darkness arriving at about 7.00 pm, for Somerville would need time to carry out the destruction if the several alternatives of surrender were refused.

For most of 3 July Somerville's messenger, Captain Cedric 'Hooky' Holland, the captain of the aircraft carrier *Ark Royal* and formerly the naval attaché in Paris and a fluent French speaker, went back and forth in Oran harbour sending messages to Admiral Gensoul in his flagship the battle-cruiser *Dunkerque*, one of the ships the Admiralty was most anxious to eliminate (the other was her sister ship *Strasbourg*). For a long time Gensoul refused to see Holland, using the excuse that he was not of sufficient rank, though quite probably this was only a delaying tactic. When Holland finally did get to speak directly to the admiral, late in the afternoon, he was unable to get past Gensoul's reiterated assurances that he would abide by the armistice terms. Gensoul even gave Holland a copy of the order he had been given by Darlan, marked 'secret and personal', in which Darlan insisted that the ships should remain French and that if the armistice terms were not adhered to by the Germans or not strictly carried out, Gensoul should take his ships to the United States.[6]

This was not enough for the British. There was no guarantee that Gensoul would continue in command of the ships at Oran, nor that Darlan would continue in office in Vichy when the regime succumbed to Nazi control, as the British expected it would, nor even that Gensoul's orders would not be changed, though his obduracy suggested that he would obey them if it came to it. Gensoul had been informed of all the alternatives as presented by Somerville through Holland, but he appears not to have believed that a refusal would have any consequences. His ships had steam up, but the boom across the harbour entrance was closed. Somerville had sent aircraft from *Ark Royal* to lay mines at the harbour entrance to try to prevent the ships from escaping if that is what Gensoul wanted them to do; this provoked a hurt complaint from Gensoul.

Meanwhile Gensoul reported his situation to Darlan, but in such a way that none of the less unpalatable alternatives were presented – his signal stated that the British had ordered him to sink his ships or be sunk. This, of course, was the essence of the issue, and he was not wrong in his summary, which stripped away most effectively all the decorative wrapping the British had put round their own message. The French communications system, however, left something to be desired in this crisis. Gensoul sent his signal at 9.45 am, but Darlan did not get to know of it until early in the afternoon.

Gensoul stonewalled for hours, perhaps in hopes of specific orders from France, perhaps hoping the British fleet would go away, perhaps hoping to be able to slip out of Mers el-Kebir in darkness. At one point he was informed that the ships at Alexandria had agreed to be demilitarized, though this had no obvious effect and in fact it was only a temporary opinion of Godfroy's which changed fairly quickly. At Mers el-Kebir the long delays had brought the hours of darkness ever closer, when it would be impossible for the British to ensure that the French ships were sunk. Finally, at 4.45 pm, with dusk due by about 7.00 pm, a signal was received from the Admiralty which suggested that French reinforcements were on their way. This was the result of the interception of French signals and cruisers had been sent out from Algiers (fairly close to Mers el-Kebir), and from Toulon. Somerville could not afford to be trapped between Gensoul's ships and others out at sea, and so could wait no longer. He signalled to Gensoul that he would open fire at 5.30 pm unless his terms were accepted.

Gensoul finally appreciated the position he was in and at last he ordered his ships to go to action stations. Holland proposed yet another alternative, 'but as it did not comply with any of the conditions laid down', as Somerville said later, the order was given to fire. This last message was received only one minute before the 5.30 pm deadline and was no doubt interpreted on the British ships as yet another device to gain more time – as indeed it probably was.

There was, in fact, a delay of another twenty-five minutes before actual fire was begun, but then within three minutes a hit was obtained on *Bretagne* which caused her to blow up. Over 900 of her crew died. The battle-cruiser *Dunkerque* was badly hit and had to be run aground to save her. *Provence*, *Bretagne*'s sister, was also beached and set on fire. The destroyer *Mogador* was severely damaged, much of her stern blown off, and the seaplane carrier *Commandante Teste* was damaged. All this happened in little more than ten minutes.

Gensoul had ordered 'action stations' as Captain Holland scrambled to leave his flagship. The shore batteries had been manned and prepared and the entrance to the harbour was now open once more with a swept channel. Such ships as could do so returned fire and the shore batteries also fired, though none of the British ships were hit. The noise and smoke in the harbour concealed what was happening from the view of the British out at sea. *Strasbourg*, without the British realizing it, had avoided receiving any damage and now got away through that swept channel. This was noted and reported to Somerville by 6.20 pm, but he waited for confirmation since there had been a number of false alarms already. By that time his force was steaming westwards towards Gibraltar, but at 6.30 pm the escape of *Strasbourg* was confirmed. He sent *Hood*, his fastest big ship, with a destroyer screen, in chase, but that extra ten minutes steaming westward had made all the difference. A flight of Swordfish from *Ark Royal* made an attack, thought to have been partly successful, though no hits were actually obtained. Another air attack was made just as the last light faded, but by then the cruisers and destroyers which had come out of Algiers had joined *Strasbourg*, which was intent on reaching Toulon. In the dark *Strasbourg* and these ships amounted to a more powerful force than *Hood* and its attendants. Somerville ordered the chase discontinued.[7]

Meanwhile at Alexandria Godfroy had been presented with a slightly different set of alternatives than were given to Gensoul. He could hand the ships over to the British, demilitarize them at Alexandria under skeleton crews, or sink them at sea. Cunningham was able to put these to Godfroy personally, whereas Somerville could not go into Mers el-Kebir to speak directly to Gensoul (the Admiralty would have forbidden it even if he had considered it). Godfroy refused absolutely to hand his ships over, nor was he any more enthusiastic about scuttling them, though for a time he did incline that way, so that the demilitarization alternative was the one favoured but without any enthusiasm, not surprisingly.

Cunningham had left him to think about the options, which in this case were genuine alternatives, not mere camouflage hiding the British intention to open fire. Godfroy then decided after all that sinking the ships at sea was the least objectionable of the alternatives, though he was still waiting for instructions from Darlan – a man he did not like. Cunningham persuaded him to start discharging his fuel and to begin disarming his weapons. But then came news of Gensoul's confrontation with Somerville at Mers el-Kebir and he received orders from Darlan to sail. Godfroy knew that this was impossible and he delayed matters by requesting authentication of the order. Meanwhile he stopped discharging his fuel.

Godfroy heard of the firing at Mers el-Kebir – the two French forces must have been in radio contact – and he became very angry. He withdrew all his undertakings and this time it looked as though the situation at Alexandria would descend into a battle in the harbour, just as it had at Mers el-Kebir.

Cunningham, however, brought in another friend, the French liaison officer Captain Amboyeau, and set about 'sowing dissension' as he put it, among the French crews. He also sent his own captains to visit their French opposite numbers to exercise their persuasive powers. He had already, long before this, encouraged fraternization and repeated friendly contact between the two sets of captains. (It is scarcely to be imagined what his own reaction would have been had another admiral attempted to 'sow dissension' among his own crews.) He also made it clear that he was prepared to sink the French ships at their moorings if he felt it necessary and he had carefully positioned his own ships to be able to do this. So, a day after Somerville, Cunningham had reached the same position.

Violence proved, in this case however, to be unnecessary. The crucial element in defusing the situation, apart from the proximity of the two forces within the harbour at Alexandria, was the meetings between the French and British officers and perhaps apprehension among the sailors in the French ships, who knew of the heavy casualties at Mers el-Kebir and were in effect looking directly into the mouths of the British guns. After the persuasive efforts of the British officers, and conscious of the apprehensions of his men, Godfroy and his captains had lunch together on 4 July. Post-prandially, as Cunningham put it, the captains persuaded the admiral to accept the British proposals.[8] This was a pleasantly French way of reaching a solution and it was a sensible way of allowing the admiral to save face, for consulting with other senior officers was a well–established naval tradition. Godfroy then agreed to resume discharging his fuel and to demilitarize his ships.

During all this Cunningham had been under as much pressure from the Admiralty as Godfroy was from the British. On at least two occasions Cunningham had ignored peremptory orders from London, in one case almost certainly dictated by Churchill himself, in order to give Godfroy time to cool down and for his own measures of persuasion and subversion to have their effect. The result was scarcely what the British government wanted, for the French ships stayed immobile in Alexandria harbour for the next three years, until freed by the Allied victories in Africa and the German conquest of the unoccupied part of France. But Cunningham had avoided a debilitating battle in Alexandria harbour, which would have damaged his own ships as well as sinking the French. (The French would scarcely have missed at such a short range, any more than the British.) Such a fight would have caused heavy casualties to both sides. Even the Admiralty had agreed that such a fight would be a disaster. The result was that the French ships remained unavailable to Britain's enemies and Franco–British relations were not further inflamed.

The result of all these events, in Britain, at Mers el–Kebir and at Alexandria, was a good deal of bitterness all round. Somerville made his repugnance at what he had been ordered to do perfectly clear and he had the vocal sympathy of his colleagues. There had almost been another battle at Alexandria, but there Admiral Godfroy was clearly over–matched and was not the suicidal type, though he was liable like Gensoul, to stand too much on his 'honour', a self–defined concept which has too often distracted military thinking. Cunningham had been almost too direct in his replies to Admiralty messages and had ignored orders. There were ruffled feathers all round.

The French reaction to Mers el–Kebir came almost at once. As Force H sailed back towards Gibraltar the gunboat *Rigault de Genouilly* came out of the harbour and launched a torpedo attack, which missed, as did the return fire from the British ships.[9] Two days later an aerial attack was made on Gibraltar, when mines landed in the harbour, though it was little more than a defiant gesture.[10] Air reconnaissance made it clear that *Dunkerque* was not as badly damaged as had been thought, so Somerville was ordered to try again. A full-scale repeat bombardment was intended at first, but this was changed to an air attack launched from *Ark Royal*. This time several hits were made and *Dunkerque* was deemed sufficiently damaged as to no longer be a threat (though it was able to get to Toulon a year later).[11]

The British ships watching Casablanca and Dakar had been warned in advance to be extra vigilant on 3 July, but there was no obvious French reaction. At Dakar there was the apparently formidable *Richelieu* and, until he was directed to make the second attack on *Dunkerque*, it had been intended that Somerville should sail to attack her. Instead a small force was collected off Dakar consisting of the small aircraft carrier *Hermes* from Freetown, the cruiser *Dorsetshire*, which had been watching *Richelieu* since it left Brest, and the Australian cruiser *Australia*, also coming up from Freetown. On 7 July Captain Onslow of *Hermes* sent in a message to the captain of *Richelieu* demanding that he either surrender, demilitarize, or scuttle his ship – or be sunk. The sloop *Milford* was supposed to deliver this, but was not permitted to enter the harbour – no doubt the French knew what was coming and anyway the ultimatum could be delivered just as easily and rather more safely from *Milford*'s point of view, by radio.

It was rejected, of course. After Mers el-Kebir it could scarcely be otherwise. *Richelieu* was given only six hours' warning, but it was not until the next day that the British took action, and this was carefully limited in scope. In the face of *Richelieu*'s 15-inch guns the British options were restricted to subtlety and the air. During the night a launch from *Hermes* sneaked past the harbour boom and dropped depth charges beneath *Richelieu*'s keel. The launch escaped. At dawn a flight of Swordfish from *Hermes* launched an air attack. In combination these attacks caused sufficient damage to the ship to immobilize it for the present.[12]

Other French ships were gradually mopped up, in Canada, at Singapore, in the Suez Canal. The aircraft carrier *Béarn* and its attendant cruisers were at Martinique and, in a straw in the wind which was almost as significant as the later 'destroyers-for-bases' deal, the United States intervened to ensure that the ships were detained there. Eventually an agreement was reached that the ships must stay in the Caribbean area; later still, after the USA was in the war, they were immobilized and disarmed. This intervention was a most significant anti-German move by the USA. The presence of the ships did have an effect on the political situation in the French islands and the senior naval officer, Admiral Georges Robert, became in effect Vichy's viceroy in the region.[13]

These various events had not destroyed the French Navy, but they had resulted in its surviving active ships being concentrated mainly at Toulon. The most significant units were, however, largely eliminated. Of the seven battleships and battle-cruisers in service at the beginning of June only one, *Strasbourg*, remained operational, though two, *Provence* and *Dunkerque*, were repairable. *Courbet* and *Paris* were under British control in Britain and *Lorraine* was under British guns at Alexandria, *Bretagne* had blown up at Mers el-Kebir, while the United States had blocked any action by the aircraft carrier *Béarn*. Further, the squadrons at Algiers and Oran were mainly removed to Toulon along with *Strasbourg*, where they became subject to demobilization under the armistice terms. The result was the removal of French naval power from most of the Mediterranean. Admirals Cunningham and Somerville therefore did not have to worry too much about the French ships – so long as the Pétain government did not declare war.

This was certainly a strong French impulse, not surprisingly, a feeling which was redoubled in the Navy. The officers of *Dunkerque* returned to Admiral Somerville, with an icily polite note all the memorials they had acquired from their association with British ships.[14] Darlan fizzed with ideas for revenge attacks, each of which he abandoned under persuasion from colleagues in the government. In the event, despite his outrage, the Vichy regime had no wish to be at war with Britain, an event which would have thrown them even more decisively into the arms of Germany and might well have resulted in the loss of the only significant armed force left to them – the ships at Toulon. Neutrality was their aim now and the naval humiliation would not deflect them, any more than did the earlier military defeat. The one reaction by the Vichy government was to break off diplomatic relations with London, but since the British envoys had been withdrawn from France since 22 June, this was a fairly pointless gesture – but doing it must have meant that there would be no declaration of war.[15]

The Germans did their best to exploit the situation, setting free numbers of French naval prisoners of war, releasing the Navy from navigational restrictions imposed in the armistice, and clearly hoping that French naval recklessness would produce a Franco-British war. Their scope for pushing the French in that direction was, however, limited by Darlan's determination to be independent of German influence. He did take several hostile measures, either by his own authority or by agreement with his governmental colleagues. The air raid on Gibraltar on 5 July was one and he ordered his ships to stop and search British merchantmen. French warships escorting French convoys were ordered to open fire if the British looked to be about to intercept. He particularly wanted to mount a major air raid on Gibraltar. In the result few of these measures were fully instituted, for, just as the British did not want to hear a French declaration of war, neither did the French want a formal war with Britain and some of these measures might well have pushed the British into it. The government took refuge in a legal opinion and pulled back from open conflict.

The alternatives were to shelter more comfortably under the wings of the Axis. There was a momentary scheme for establishing Italian air bases in Algeria to protect the French naval bases and another for a joint expedition to release the French ships at Alexandria. Neither got further than that. Perhaps the French distaste for fighting alongside their former enemies was even greater than their detestation at British actions, but they were also intent on preventing the establishment of either an Italian or a German presence within their empire.[16]

The Vichy regime, of course, profited considerably in an internal political sense, quite apart from the relaxation of some of the armistice conditions. Support for the new government solidified in the face of yet another enemy and the uneasiness in many of the colonies at the Pétain government partly died down. De Gaulle's Free French movement (or the 'Fighting French' as it was at first) had acquired considerable influence within France until Mers el-Kebir, but that now subsided. Vichy could be well content with the political results, though the loss of the ships was no doubt irksome.

Churchill's report to the House of Commons on 4 July produced a great roar of approval from the Members. It was a scene that was a mirror image of the support generated for Vichy in France. Churchill was hugely relieved at the reaction. The action had been driven by him, he had pushed the Admiralty on to undertake it and had even at one point dictated one of the signals. Yet he could have been wrong. The House of Commons was not yet under his control; it could have turned on him for betraying a beaten ally. Amid the cheers he sat and wept, something which came easily to him – but what was the source of the tears is not clear, though it was very likely tears of relief. But certainly, like Vichy, he had survived and had found support where it counted.[17]

The whole sets of events, in Britain, in Algeria, at Dakar and at Alexandria, were 'Operation Catapult'. It had been intended to eliminate the French navy from the political calculations of both Germany and Britain. In this it was clearly successful. The French navy was now in no condition to be used by anyone against the British Isles except in minor actions. The US Navy was also relieved at the reduction of European naval power and the President had been impressed by the ruthlessness involved. The message – that Britain would fight on – was received loud and clear all round the world.

Chapter 4

The French Empire

In reaction to a series of aborted schemes of revenge floated by Admiral Darlan, the legal counsellor at the Ministry of Foreign Affairs at Vichy commented that if carried out they would have created an immediate state of war. This is a most curious, narrow-visioned point of view – if I may say, typical of a lawyer – for if anything had created a state of war it was the actions of the British government at Oran, Alexandria, Plymouth, Portsmouth and Dakar. But neither Britain nor France had declared war. This was clearly the result of careful thought on each side. Both governments were all too conscious of the elephant in the room, Nazi Germany, its army and its air force.

Nevertheless declarations of war were rather going out of fashion and it was becoming quite normal to wage war without a declaration and that is what Britain and France did over the next two years and more, when they fought each other on a fairly major scale at least three times, perhaps four. There was another good reason for France to refrain from an overt declaration: the presence on British soil, under British protection and sponsored by the British government, of General de Gaulle and the French National Committee. He was convicted by a Vichy court on 2 August of treason and sentenced to death – *in absentia*, of course. The Vichy regime could usually blame de Gaulle and his followers for any fighting and so could avoid an open war with Britain.

De Gaulle's support among the French, however, at home and overseas, was as uncertain as his political position and the affair at Mers el-Kebir caused serious damage to his cause, though as time passed the wound tended to heal.[1] More immediately important was the fact that, partly as a result, the governors of many of the French African territories came fairly quickly to accept the Pétain government's authority and with them so did the armed forces in Africa, the *Armée d'Afrique*. This was an established force of over a quarter of a million men, and once it was clear that the men would not have to go to France and become involved in the fighting there, that army sank back into its normal colonial role, which was largely to maintain order by the intimidation of the local population. But it was also expected to defend the colonies against any outside attack.[2]

The British laid a blockade on France from the beginning of July 1940, thereby drastically reducing the possibility of the country acquiring imports, and at the end of July it was extended to all of French North Africa. This obviously affected the communications and trade between France and its colonies, though it appears to have been very difficult to enforce, since British ships in the Mediterranean were subject to Italian hostility, even if not French. This was a dangerous situation since any British interference with French shipping might well reopen actual hostilities in the light of Darlan's immediate reaction to Mers el-Kebir, though the rigour of the order to aggressively protect French convoys was soon relaxed, largely because of the very possibility of open fighting. So both sides pulled back from a fight, the British because they had no intention, and never had, of declaring war, and had quite enough on their hands with the Italian navy, the French because it became clear that the British would only enforce the blockade if provoked.

Neither the British nor the Vichy French, therefore, had any desire to go to war with each other. For Vichy an all-out war would clearly be disastrous. Quite apart from lining the new regime up too close to Germany, the fighting would clearly be at sea and perhaps in the air, and the French navy, badly weakened and scattered, would obviously lose. The condition of un-declared war was therefore of particular advantage to the British, who might not wish to find themselves at war with Vichy France, but if they were it would make little actual difference, given that Vichy France was hostile already and was largely disarmed. But the Vichy regime had gained power with a programme of acceptance of the armistice and an end to fighting. This had been achieved, if at considerable cost, and now to find themselves at war with Britain, even before a peace treaty had been made with Germany, would clearly undermine their credibility at home. Hence Britain was able to go much further and be more assertive than the Vichy regime without suffering very much in the way of consequences, while the Vichy regime was restricted to perhaps fighting back if attacked, or evading conflict if it could. It was a case of a careless, heedless aggressor against a fearful defender, and in such a conflict the defensive will always lose in the long term.

So, once the dust of Mers el-Kebir had settled, the new French government began the process of what it eventually called its 'national revolution'. On 10 July a meeting of the Chamber of Deputies in effect extinguished the

Third Republic and entrusted power and authority to Marshal Pétain as Head of State. He and his group thereupon set about aping the corporatist state which Mussolini had been producing in Italy. This was a muddled idea even in Italy, and in France it was difficult to impose because neither the Marshal nor the French people were at all enamoured by it. But the Vichy government was formed of a group of right-wing officers and controlling civil servants, most of whom were interested above all in 'order', that is, in being obeyed. It was, to their view, best to be able to govern through groups of people who were expected to do as they were told and to pass all this further down the chain. Needless to say, the notion of consulting the people, in elections or in any other way, was anathema. The government knew best.[3]

The result was a shambling, inefficient, corrupt and dim dictatorship. It was all too vulnerable to German pressure, in large part because it had no popular support to speak of and disdained it. For a regime which included a large proportion of senior officers, it was also surprisingly timid in its relations with its enemies. This was, of course, in part due to its disarmed state, but mainly to the sense of defeat which infected the whole body of the government. In its international relations the Vichy government was almost entirely reactive. It never took the initiative in relations with Germany or Britain, but always had to react to their demands and/or encroachments. Of course, it soon became clear to both of those countries that Vichy was like that. Neither had anything to fear from the government of Marshal Pétain, the great soldier.

This did not apply, however, in the empire, which had not been seriously involved in the fighting in 1940 and so had not been defeated. There had been much doubt and consternation in the colonies, of course, and the Pétainist *coup* was clearly confusing to those who did not directly experience the defeats and chaos and arguments in the *metropole*. But the high concentration of the military in the new government included men who had spent considerable parts of their careers in the empire and they knew that the holders of power in the colonies were essentially military men, which gave Vichy a clear edge in gaining their allegiance.

The empire consisted largely of African territories, grouped in four sets: North Africa (the Muslim lands of Tunisia, Algeria and Morocco), West Africa, stretching east through the savannah and desert lands from the Atlantic Ocean to Lake Chad, and including the tropical colonies of the West African coast, Ivory Coast, Guinea, Senegal, Dahomey and so on; Equatorial Africa spread north from the mouth of the Congo River to the deserts of Chad. Largely separate were Madagascar, off the east coast, and the small colony of Djibouti at the mouth of the Red Sea. Each of these groups had a governor-general and each individual colony – there were 16 in all – had its governor. In Tunisia and Morocco, which were technically protectorates, authority was wielded by a resident-general in the name of the Dey and the Sultan respectively.

In the Middle East there were two colonies, Syria and Lebanon, acquired at the end of the Great War from Turkey. They were therefore mandates of the League of Nations and technically subject to league inspection, not that the French had ever taken the mandate idea seriously. But these were very troublesome colonies, erupting in revolt very seriously more than once. Again the main authority was that of the governor-general, based usually in Beirut.

Elsewhere there were several islands in the Caribbean, principally Martinique and Guadeloupe and more in the South Pacific, which were grouped as another governor-generalate centred on Tahiti, as the French Oceanic territories. Finally there was Indo-China, three colonies grouped into another governor-generalate, though they were actually three protectorates, Tonkin, Cambodia and Laos.[4]

This was a world empire, in the sense that it was spread widely. Each colony had its own armed forces, but outside North Africa these were not large. It was the French practice to use soldiers recruited in one colony to garrison a different one. West Africa was a major source of such soldiers, usually referred to as 'Senegalese' – it was these Senegalese which had been used to put down the revolts in Syria, for example. In addition there was the Foreign Legion, largely recruited from other Europeans, Germans, Russians and Spaniards principally. These were men who had cut their ties to their homelands and found a new home in the Legion; it was a formidable professional force, very proud of its work and with a strong and inspiring military tradition.

When the Vichy regime turned to securing its control of the empire, the top-down system (uncannily like that imposed on France itself by the Marshal and his men) facilitated the process. It was only necessary to secure the allegiance of a fairly small group of men, the governors-general and perhaps the colonial governors and the rest would follow with little difficulty. If these men did not accept the new regime, it would be relatively easy to replace the recalcitrants, since it was being done in the name of the legal French government and there would be plenty of men who would disapprove of any lack of loyalty. But first it was necessary to gain the allegiance of the main players.

Vichy's success in securing control of the French North African territories, therefore, largely depended on the decision of the Resident-General in Morocco, General Charles Auguste Noguès. Noguès was also commander of the French forces in the whole region and when he gave his support to Pétain and his regime this led the other governors, in Algeria, Tunisia, and Syria, to follow him. In turn this led to the general suppression of de Gaulle's supporters in those areas as well as a number of other near-insurrections. A considerable purge was needed to remove the Gaullists, but this was accomplished during the latter part of 1940; there were, however, others whose support for de Gaulle had not been vocal and so who remained in post, a potential fifth column. Just to make sure Vichy appointed new governors in many of the territories and most of these governors were military men – notably Admiral Esteva in Tunisia. General Weygand was soon appointed overall commander in North Africa, with the title of Delegate-General. The Vichy regime very much looked like the product of a military *coup d'état*, not a wholly misleading impression.[5]

Outside his area, however, Noguès' decision either had no real influence, or it was undermined by others, or events took place without reference to North Africa. He had some influence in West Africa, where the governor of Congo was replaced by General Pierre Boisson, who was soon moved to be Governor-General at Dakar. Boisson was Pétain's personal choice, and a determined Vichy loyalist to the end. But far away in the Pacific Islands the Resident Commissioner in the islands of the New Hebrides (now Vanuatu) Henri Sautot, declared for de Gaulle as early as 24 June, which must have been as soon as he heard of de Gaulle's move into opposition. (The 'Appel' was only on 18 June.) He was summoned to explain himself by his superior the governor of New Caledonia, Georges Pélicier, but ignored the message. Pélicier himself was uncertain how to respond to the situation, obviously trying to avoid committing himself while waiting to see who came out on top in France. The Assembly on his island voted on 24 June to continue the war with Germany, but did not decide to join de Gaulle. In Tahiti the Governor Chasteret de Gery also attempted to sit on the fence. This indecisiveness was a mistake, for it left the making of decisions open to more determined forces.

These straddlers were, of course, in an awkward position, for they were trapped between the feelings of their subjects and their personal need to ascertain the views of the government, and in this situation they were uncertain as to just who the government was. There was much popular sympathy for the Free French and in Tahiti an unofficial referendum came out decisively on the side of de Gaulle. This precipitated the overthrow of Governor Chasteret de Gery in September, but it did not lead to any sort of stability, for the administrators who remained in office tended to favour Vichy and so were opposed to popular attitudes; the result was a see-saw of power between factions. In New Caledonia Pélicier resigned, unable to stand the strain, and was replaced by an army Colonel, called Denis, who came out unequivocally for Vichy. This provoked those who favoured the Free French and threatened the position of Henri Sautot in the New Hebrides. In what was evidently a co-ordinated move the French settlers in the interior of the island staged a march on the capital, Nouméa, and Henry Sautot landed on the island from the New Hebrides.

Sautot arrived in an Australian cruiser, HMAS *Adelaide*, an action which made it suddenly clear to the French just who was the local great power. It was evident that Australia was taking a leaf out of the British book, though in fact *Adelaide* had been sent at the suggestion of the War Cabinet in London. But exercising power is addictive and Australia was in fact now using its naval power to ensure that there was no possibility of an enemy base, or even one sympathetic to Germany, being established near its shores, even so ambiguous an enemy as Vichy. Australian resistance to the use of *Adelaide* had at first been based on the fear of provoking Japan, which was already a major economic player in the region.[6]

One of the elements in this complexity of *coups* and counter-*coups* in the Pacific had been the presence at Tahiti and later at Nouméa on New Caledonia of the French Navy sloop *Dumont d'Urville*. Its captain, Commander de Quieyrecourt, strongly favoured Vichy, especially after news arrived of the events at Mers el-Kebir, and when his ship was present in the harbours of Papeete and Nouméa he held the preponderance of power and authority. So it was only when this ship left Tahiti that the governor could be overthrown; and its presence at Nouméa helped Colonel Denis to power. The *Adelaide* proved the decisive card in the pack, however, for a cruiser clearly over-topped a sloop, even when another French ship, *Amiral Charner*, was sent to support de Quiyerecourt from Indo-China. The net result was the removal of *Dumont d'Urville* (and *Amiral Charner*) to Indo-China and the decisive establishment of Free French control in the New Hebrides and New Caledonia; there remained, however, a confused instability in Tahiti, the seat of the governor-general.[7]

Elsewhere in the empire the navy was more successful in holding the line for Vichy. In the Caribbean the ships of Admiral Georges Robert gave crucial support to the governor in Martinique and the arrival of the cruiser *Jeanne d'Arc* brought Guadeloupe into line. The presence of the aircraft carrier *Béarn* in Admiral Robert's squadron was a major local factor. At the Canadian islands of St Pierre and Miquelon in the Gulf of St Lawrence, the presence of a single naval vessel, the sloop *Ville d'Ys*, kept the Gaullists out of power. The Vichy presence so close to its shores was a considerable annoyance to the Canadian government, which had difficulties with its French Canadian population over participation in the war. But here, as in the Pacific, it was an outsider who made the crucial decisions. The United States persuaded the other American states, at a meeting at Havana in Cuba in July 1940, to agree that there should be no change in the European colonies in the American continents.[8] This was clearly aimed at Germany, which were rumoured to want to re-enter the colonial game, and the French islands were clearly an obvious prey – as the British islands would be in the event of Britain's defeat – but it was held to apply to the contest between Frenchman as well, so that Vichy, technically still the legal government of France, was able to retain control. The real decision, of course, lay with the United States, which was concerned above all with local stability and the exclusion of Germany.

These *coups* and counter-*coups*, and ultimatums and purges, make it clear that there was already considerable support in all the colonies for the Free French, but that the Vichy regime held the military and naval power and that this was decisive. It is however also clear that the Vichy regime had considerable support amongst the populations, but that this was especially so among the governors and administrators. The early successes the Gaullists had were in the Pacific, which was hardly a vital place, at least in 1940.

The problems of General Paul Legentilhomme, the commander of the garrison in Djibouti (French Somaliland) give a flavour of the difficulties the Gaullists faced in these early months. Legentilhomme declared for de Gaulle as soon as the question arose, in June 1940, and was apparently followed by his Governor, Hubert Deschamps. He then found himself faced by the possibility of being attacked by the large Italian army based in Ethiopia, though the Franco–Italian war actually lasted only about two weeks (10–22 July). He refused to allow the Italian Armistice Commission entry into Djibouti, but they outflanked him by simply getting Weygand to appoint a higher-ranking French general, Germain, to supplant him. Sensibly Legentilhomme then left the colony and after surviving the sinking of the liner *Empress of Britain* north of Ireland on his way to Britain, he joined de Gaulle in London.[9]

The only major French colony in the east was Indo-China and there the defeat of France in Europe caused major changes. The Governor-General, General Georges Catroux, was a Free French supporter from the start. But he was immediately entangled in Japanese aggressions, which he tried to appease by large concessions. He also had friendly contacts with the British in the person of the admiral in command of the Royal Navy's China Squadron, Admiral Sir Percy Noble. The Japanese pressure briefly brought the settlers to support Catroux, but the news of Mers el-Kebir swung opinion towards Vichy. As a result it proved possible for Vichy to order the replacement of Catroux by the French naval commander in the region, Admiral Jean Decoux. Catroux's dismissal was ascribed in Vichy to his concessions to Japan, but it is likely that it was really his pro-British and pro-Free French sympathies which, after Mers el-Kebir, were seen as the more heinous. Both Catroux and Decoux were handicapped in doing anything by the virtual demilitarization of their colonies. Most of the local French forces had been sent to France in 1939. The Japanese therefore had a virtual free run and Decoux could not stop them any more than Catroux had been able to. Their tactics were a piece-by-piece advance, beginning with the insertion of a Japanese control commission to supervise the border between French territory and China. Catroux had been compelled to accept this and Decoux had to do so as well.[10]

General de Gaulle's organization could only gain influence, both in Britain and amongst the French, if he could show some success in acquiring recruits to his own forces and in gaining control over some French territory. Until late August, only Djibouti and the New Hebrides were inclining to the Free French and the ousting of Legentilhomme meant that they soon lost all influence in Djibouti. In the last few days of that month, however, four of the colonies of Equatorial Africa came over. Their reasons were various. In Chad there were a number of Corsican officers who feared that their home island would be ceded by Vichy to Italy, but it also had a governor, Félix Eboué, a Guyanese, who, like Henri Sautot in the Pacific, was Gaullist from the very start; in the French Congo the British blockade cut the planters off from their continental European markets and made them dependent on British Nigeria for supplies and for a market for their products.

As in the Vichy clampdown in other areas the main focus of decision lay with the governors. Some of them, like Eboué in Chad, accepted de Gaulle from the start, while others were persuaded, by one means or another. In Cameroun (a mandated territory of the League, like Syria) two officers landed, subverted the local army garrison and travelled to the capital, Yaoundé, where the governor succumbed to their persuasiveness and their forces. These two were Captain Hettier de Boislambert and Captain Philippe de Hautecloque, the latter now calling himself 'Major Leclerc'. (Rapid promotion was one result of, and surely an inducement for, individual officers' adherence to the Free French.) In the French Congo the news persuaded the governor to leave by crossing the Congo River to the Belgian Congo at Leopoldville. His ship crossed with that of Colonel Edgard de Larminat, the designated Free French Governor-General of the whole of French Equatorial Africa. The interior colony of Ubangui-Chari followed, though with some difficulty and after a good deal of argument. The last of the Equatorial colonies, however, Gabon, held to Vichy through the influence of the local bishop and a group of naval officers, whose power held the governor in thrall, assisted by the opportune arrival of the submarine *Sidi Ferruch*.[11]

The city of Dakar, already subjected to the British attack on the naval vessels in the harbour early in July, was constantly a problem in London after that. It was the most notable place in French Africa, a city of over 100,000 people but it was, above all, an important naval base with a capacious harbour and its geographical position on the westernmost point of the continent made it a prize to be sought after by all. From there it would be possible for an active enemy to interrupt the British convoy route which ran parallel to the African coast from South Africa and the Gulf of Guinea by way of Freetown and on towards Gibraltar. The German Navy wanted it, or at least access to its facilities, though Admiral Raeder could not convince Hitler to be interested. The United States was concerned about it and reactivated its consulate there in August, after having suspended it for reasons of cost for the past nine years. Above all the British were vitally concerned. They feared that it would become a base for German submarines – this was a fear for the USA also – from which the British convoy route could be menaced and the central part of the Atlantic become hostile territory. Already German and Italian submarines were active out of French Atlantic coastal bases such as Brest and St Nazaire, and they were ranging south as far as the Atlantic islands of the Canaries and the Azores, whose intricacies could shelter supply ships, enabling the submarines to stay in the area much longer. Italian submarines were beginning to use a base near Bordeaux, and if both Germany and Italy could use bases in France they might soon be using bases in Africa – Casablanca, say, or Rabat, or Dakar, or Conakry, or Cotonou or Libreville – from which they could range over the whole Atlantic. This was the next British naval nightmare scenario, to succeed that banished by Operation Catapult.[12]

There were also rumours and assumptions that there were Germans in Dakar. The American consul said afterwards that there were none, but it is evident that he was mistaken, for he had only been there a few weeks and the local French were certainly not going to flaunt the presence of their German guests. On the other hand, though there seem to have been a few Germans there, they had no influence on events and they were not active in either a military or a naval way. Vichy was not willing in any way to cede to Germany any power in its colonies. What was certain was that the Vichy regime had secured full local control, in part by replacing the former governor with the loyalist General Pierre Boisson. Boisson himself was as fiercely anti-German as he was anti-British, so any Germans in Dakar would have no influence. But it remained a general assumption in Britain that Germany would be able to use Dakar, even if that was not the case yet. The steady German pressure on the regime, it was assumed, would force a series of concessions and when the Germans controlled it, Dakar would be available.

The Vichy regime was, however, determined to exclude Germans and Italians from the empire as much as possible. General Weygand was appointed as a sort of super-viceroy in North Africa – called the Delegate-General – to command the armed forces there. The German and Italian Armistice Commissions had little to do, because the French detested them, and in Syria and North Africa the local French forces hid equipment from them and maintained forces whose existence they did not declare. The German Armistice Commission was for a long time kept out of Morocco and when the officers were finally allowed in, the French insisted that they wear civilian clothes. So the British (and later American) suspicions that Axis penetration of the empire was active were generally wrong, but only in a degree. And it was, as it happened, the second British expedition against Dakar in 1940 which gave the Vichy authorities the confidence to insist on excluding Germans from the empire.

The effects of Mers el-Kebir, at home and in the empire, had been to solidify support for the Vichy regime. The supporters of the Free French had been purged, if they had already disclosed themselves, or had learnt to keep quiet. Yet they were numerous enough to make it clear that Vichy support remained to a degree uncertain. The defection, as Vichy would put it, of the Equatorial and Pacific territories was a sign of that uncertainty.

The loyal colonies – loyal to Vichy, that is – were held by the military presence. Tough generals and admirals – Weygand in North Africa, Boisson in West Africa, Decoux in Indo-China, Robert in the West Indies – were put in place to reinforce the regime. But this meant that the colonial regimes became all the more openly militaristic and that the military were bearing down as much on the French in the colonies as on the indigenous population. This was a situation which could not possibly result in continued Vichy popularity.

Another, more slow acting but insidious, effect of Mers el-Kebir was that the Navy had become less able to hold the empire together. The presence of naval vessels at St Pierre-et-Miquelon and at Martinique and Guadeloupe were decisive in holding these possessions for Vichy. But the ability of the Navy to be everywhere in the Pacific territories allowed the basic sentiments of the local settlers in favour of the Free French to surface. It was a paradigm of the whole Vichy-colonial problem – the Navy knit the empire together, but there were no longer enough ships to do the job now that much of the naval force of the Vichy regime had been concentrated, disarmed, at Toulon. Already, within a couple of months of the Vichy regime's emplacement, it had lost control of a substantial part of the empire and only gripped the rest by main force.

Chapter 5

Dakar

Dakar may have been a marginal worry for the Admiralty, but the first suggestion for seizing it seems to have come from de Gaulle. It was quickly seized on by Churchill, who pushed the London planners to produce a scheme quickly. This mixed parentage, combined with the pressure to act quickly, led to changes and confusion which significantly affected the outcome. It began as a Free French expedition with British naval cover, on the assumption that the city would welcome de Gaulle's troops, and evolved steadily into a British expedition intended to seize the city and hand it over to de Gaulle to govern. Along the way the Prime Minister bullied and intimidated a whole string of army and naval officers into providing information, making a plan and allocating the forces. The Chiefs of Staff, the Joint Planning Staff, and almost every man involved in producing the plan disliked it, and argued that it was a mistake. What they did not do was to work to make it successful.[1]

From having become a primarily British expedition the plan changed back to being one in which the Free French forces would be supported by British equipment and British ships. The plan as it was eventually produced, therefore, was for the Free French forces to be carried from the ships to Dakar, preceded by a launch bearing a white flag and a tricolor with a message asking the governor to come over to Free France. All this was based on the twin assumptions that the Free French would be welcomed by the French administration and inhabitants and that there was very little in the way of Vichy French armed force in the city. If the Free French landing force was resisted then the British forces, ships and troops would be able to back them up.

Three possible scenarios for the events were sketched out, conceived as possibly succeeding one another: 'Happy' would be the condition where there was no resistance to de Gaulle's forces, the governor accepted de Gaulle's authority and his forces and they were welcomed to the city; 'Sticky' envisaged some resistance which might have to be dealt with by a naval bombardment of specific and restricted targets; 'Nasty' envisaged strong resistance which would require landings by British troops.

Meanwhile the Vichy government had made a discreet contact with Britain through their respective diplomats in Spain. It had been possible to establish Vichy governmental control in most of the African colonies, but the British blockade was clearly causing serious economic damage, and both the colonies and the metropolis required to be able to trade. The contacts in Madrid were instigated by the Vichy Foreign Minister Baudouin and brokered by American diplomats (Robert Murphy at Vichy and Commander Ben H. Wyatt, the US Naval attaché in Madrid). They took place in Wyatt's home and were therefore at naval attaché level (between Captain Alan Hillgarth, the British attaché and Captain Jean-Roger Delaye for Vichy), and were concerned primarily with naval affairs. The British promised nothing, but Darlan decided that it was worth testing their intentions by sending a trial convoy consisting of the tug *Pescagel*, escorted by a single sloop, *Elan*, through the Strait of Gibraltar from Casablanca to Oran. The passage took place on 7 September. The British did not react, partly because they were at the time preoccupied with the operation against Dakar, but they had made no promises about future passages, neither did they relax the blockade – it was available for British use as and when required.[2]

The loss of four of the colonies of Equatorial Africa by Vichy at the end of August led Darlan to take another chance. The continued Vichy control of Gabon meant that access was still available through Libreville and if force could be applied he felt that the four lost colonies could be recovered. They had been lost, after all, to a very small expedition; a counter expedition a little larger could well reverse matters. He sent a squadron of ships out from Toulon – three light cruisers and three super-destroyers – on 9 September. They were not seen by any British ship until they were less than 50 miles from Gibraltar on the morning of 11 September, where they were spotted by the destroyer *Hotspur* – though the French naval attaché in Madrid had warned his British counterpart of the approach of the ships the day before and Captain Hillgarth had sent the information both to Gibraltar and to the Admiralty. The whole squadron went through the Strait at high speed before the British could react. The British naval authorities in Gibraltar were clearly caught within their own ambiguities since any attempt to stop the French would need to be agreed from London and London gave no instructions, having fallen into a muddle over communications, divided authorities and slow decipherment. The ships went on to Casablanca to refuel; Force H was eventually given the order to stop them, but by then it was far too late, provoking memorably scornful explosions from Admiral Somerville. What the British did not know was what the French ships were intended to do after Casablanca, but the passage of the six ships did happen at a particularly awkward moment.[3]

The expedition to Dakar, after several accidents and delays, finally sailed in sections over a period of several days; all were at sea by 1 September. It was clear from the start that things were going wrong. There was first of all a fear that security had been breached on a massive scale. The destination was widely known in certain restricted circles in Britain: Free French officers and men, British naval officers, dock workers at the ports. The Free French officers had loudly toasted each other in restaurants in London, shouting '*à Dakar*', among other revealing toasts. De Gaulle himself had publicly ordered tropical kit in a shop in London, remarking that he was going to West Africa, though that scarcely pinpointed Dakar, since he could have meant Equatorial Africa. Cases of leaflets burst open, one in London, one at Liverpool, and red-white-and-blue leaflets appealing to the Frenchman of Dakar blew around Euston station and the Liverpool docks before being collected, or otherwise dispersed and used.

In fact, though the Vichy authorities knew that an expedition was on its way, they did not know where to and a deception programme had been set up by the British to mislead them into believing that it was heading to Egypt. (Churchill wanted to add Martinique to the deception, but this would have been less than convincing, since the Havana agreement was that no European colonies in America should change hands and it was known that Churchill would not tread on American toes in such a way.) There were, in the end, so many stories and rumours and guesses that the security leaks merely caused even more confusion and the precise information about the destination which did get out probably did no damage. Certainly the authorities at Dakar had no inkling that an expedition was headed their way until it appeared offshore.

More serious were the consequences of the rushed loading of the ships, which meant that much of the material in the transports was mixed up and no one knew where everything was. Moreover, it had not been loaded with the actual operation in mind – a method called 'tactical loading', by which items needed at the start of an operation were to be the first to be unloaded. The normal way to load was of course to make the most economical use of space, but this was no good at the landing place. An officer from Combined Operations in London went up to Liverpool to try to sort out the loading system, but by then it was too late to do more than move a few items around. This is exactly what had gone wrong in the Norwegian campaign six months before and the reason was much the same: a lack of detailed forward planning, leaving the loading to men who did not know what was going on, usually the dockers, and an assumption that everything would be all right. This muddle was clearly the result of the haste with which the expedition was planned.

Then there were the other assumptions: that the French in Dakar would welcome de Gaulle, and that they had only very few troops on hand. These assumptions had guided the planners all along, but were dented just as the expedition began. The day before the expedition was to sail, two Royal Navy officers, Commander Jermyn Rushbrooke and Captain John Poulter, who had been liaison officers at Dakar until expelled by the French at the end of June, finally arrived in London, having been summoned almost three weeks earlier, though the message had indicated no urgency, and then a chapter of accidents had delayed them. They were the only men who had any recent first-hand knowledge of Dakar and also had the military eye – not even the Free French could produce any men who knew Dakar, it seems. Rushbrooke and Poulter reported that both basic assumptions underlying the expedition were mistaken. They insisted that the officials and troops were loyal to Vichy and that any landing would be vigorously resisted by the governor and the garrison. They also described the fortifications of the city, which were clearly much more formidable than the planners had thought (or assumed – they had been working on information dating from the Great War, since when things had changed somewhat). Poulter also produced documentary evidence that rather than a garrison of 1,400 men, Dakar had one of 7,000, mainly Senegalese infantry under French officers. One problem with this information – apart from the fact that it turned up at the last moment – was that it was greeted with a good deal of scepticism. The earlier assumptions had become so fixed in the minds of the commanders and planners that these now got in the way of accepting the new information. It was pointed out that there was a lack of confirmation from other sources, even though there were no other sources, except the out-of-date ones used in the planning. These did, however, provide a good excuse for ignoring or downplaying the new material.

A further problem was that there were, in effect, three commanders: for the Navy Vice-Admiral Sir John Cunningham, for the British troops Lieutenant-General Noel Irwin, and for the French forces General de Gaulle. In a fairly typical ham-fisted approach the British had originally intended that Cunningham and Irwin should command the whole force, until de Gaulle made it clear that he would personally command the French. He was supported in this insistence by his liaison officer Major-General Sir Edward Spears. In the end the command was tripartite, an arrangement which was remarkably clumsy, required repeated conferences, and was bedevilled by poor communications.

Despite the puncturing of assumptions inflicted by the news from Poulter and Rushbrooke, de Gaulle was wholly optimistic. While the expedition was at sea the news arrived of the progressive Gaullist takeovers of the Equatorial African colonies and this tended to support de Gaulle's contention that he would be welcomed at Dakar. Captain Poulter's evidence was therefore still further discounted.

The expedition sailed from several origins: Scapa Flow, the Clyde, Liverpool, Gibraltar and Freetown, with the various contingents joining on the way. It eventually consisted of two battleships, *Barham* and *Resolution*, the aircraft carrier *Ark Royal*, three cruisers, ten destroyers and two sloops; the Free French naval contribution was three sloops and an armed trawler. The men and equipment were carried on four troop transports and twenty other vessels. The troops included a British Marine brigade and other units, 4,270 men; the Free French forces included a Foreign Legion battalion, a marine company, a machine-gun company and some other soldiers – about 2,400 men. The news that there were 7,000 soldiers in garrison at Dakar was, given these numbers, somewhat disconcerting and there was also the presence of the *Richelieu* to consider. Immobile though the ship was, it did have 15-inch guns, which may or may not be usable. There was also the fact that the fixed defences of any fortified port have the advantage over the guns of a fleet at sea, since they fired from a firm position, while the ships were constantly changing their positions, their situations and their ranges. On the other hand, there had seemed to be little in the way of mobile naval forces at Dakar which would threaten the British fleet, though this was another assumption about to be proved wrong.

The news of the passage of three French cruisers and three super-destroyers through the Strait of Gibraltar and their refuelling at Casablanca was therefore a most unwelcome surprise. Admiral Somerville with the battlecruiser *Renown* and half a dozen destroyers (all that was available of Force H, many of whose ships, including *Ark Royal*, had gone to join the Dakar force) went after them, intending to block them up in Casablanca, but eventually it was found that they had left Casablanca also. This news reached the expedition on 14 September. The French squadron had clearly gone on to Dakar and its presence completely changed the balance of power as between the expedition and the garrison. Not only that, but these were ships clearly loyal to Vichy and along with the appointment of Boisson as Governor-General, their arrival obviously meant that the Vichy authorities would be in firm control in the city and that they had at their disposal a naval force more nearly equal to that which the expedition could bring to bear than had been expected and planned for.

The expedition was ordered to intercept the French cruisers, but again either the orders came too late or the squadron was too quick, and they had reached Dakar before the expedition could find them. An air reconnaissance found them in the harbour during the day. And yet while the expedition was already nearby, and was heading to Freetown for water and final arrangements, it was clear that Dakar had no suspicions even as to the expedition's very existence, still less its intentions. The French ships still had their tropical sun-awnings up and were in positions in the harbour which restricted their ability to fire towards the sea. The expedition went on to moor off Freetown to replenish with supplies and above all with fresh water.

The news of the presence of the French ships at Dakar was signalled to London and phoned through to the Chiefs of Staff, who were spending the weekend with Churchill at Chequers. Within ten minutes the message came back that in view of this news, the operation should be cancelled and that the Joint Planners would meet the next day. By that time Churchill had suggested that the expedition could revert to an older idea, that the troops should land at Conakry in French Guinea and travel overland to attack Dakar and that meanwhile the ships would blockade Dakar from the sea. The various staffs in London were all against this. They pointed out that they could not afford to tie up even more ships so far from Britain while invasion of Britain itself was threatened. (This was mid-September 1940, the height of the Battle of Britain, the very time when it later appeared that the air battle was on a knife-edge.) They also pointed out that the distance from Conakry to Dakar was well over 1,200 miles, and at least 230 miles of it would have to be covered by marching. (Presumably Churchill had been using a small-scale map.) The suggestion was made that the Free French troops should go on to land at Duala in Cameroon and take control of Gabon and then move north to Chad, which was Gaullist but was now under threat from a Vichy force which was known to be assembling to the north of Nigeria. The ships would then be brought back to Gibraltar to return Force H to its proper strength, or to Britain.

This was agreed by the War Cabinet when Churchill reported to it on the 17th and the cancellation was transmitted to the expedition, which was then approaching Freetown. The expedition commanders passed the message on to de Gaulle, but replied to London that they did not agree that cancellation was necessary. They pointed out that Dakar was clearly still unaware of the expedition's presence and that the arrival of the six new ships made no real difference. Churchill replied that he would reconsider if they could make a good case for continuing.

De Gaulle was just as upset at the cancellation as the British commanders and he and Spears both sent strong protests about it to London. When all the commanders met together they came up with a new plan, by which a landing would be made at Rufisque, to the east of the city and outside the range of the batteries, should the initial summons ('Happy') fail to bring about the city's surrender. De Gaulle was frank that he could no longer be certain of the state of morale at Dakar, given the arrival of the Vichy naval reinforcements, but he declared himself willing to accept the risk and responsibility of initiating fighting between two French forces.

It was the question of morale in Dakar and the issue of whether the Free French forces would be welcomed which had meanwhile preoccupied the War Cabinet in London. The Chiefs of Staff had effectively removed the landing at Conakry from the plans by a cold douche of facts and common sense, so the only question for the members of the Cabinet to decide was whether an attempt on Dakar was still feasible. They agreed to discuss the matter again the next day and in the meantime enquired of the expedition their opinion of Dakar's morale. In the evening, before a reply to this had been received, the telegram from the commanders arrived dealing with that very point and expressing a strong desire to go ahead with the operation.

So here there had occurred several curious reversals. Those in Britain who had been keen on the expedition originally – Churchill and the War Cabinet – had now become cool to the idea; those who had been doubtful originally – the Chiefs of Staff and the commanders of the expedition – had now become, at least among the commanders, keen to go on, while the Chiefs of Staff were clearly less opposed than they had been. De Gaulle, originally confident about being able to persuade the Dakarians to join him, was now much less sure. Above all, the decisions as to whether to attack Dakar had now effectively been left to the commanders of the expedition, for the War Cabinet accepted their assessment of the possibility of success.

Then, before a final decision was made, the French squadron of cruisers came out of Dakar, heading south to run past Freetown and into the Gulf of Guinea. Their plan involved sending the tanker *Tarn*, escorted by the cruiser *Primauguet*, ahead so that the three cruisers (and *Primauguet*) would have a supply of fuel available at Libreville when they got there. These two ships had left Dakar on the 14th, before the British found their companions at Dakar. The cruisers' aim, as it had been all along, was to enforce the recovery of Cameroon and French Congo to Vichy and probably thereby also the inland colonies. Their presence may well also have affected the control of the Belgian Congo and, since there were British ships in area, it could well have resulted in a naval fight. *Primauguet* and *Tarn* were well on their way when the other cruisers, *Georges Leygues*, *Gloire* and *Montcalm*, under the command still of Vice-Admiral Celestin Bourrague, moving much faster than *Tarn* could, came out from Dakar. None of the French ships had any idea that a major British force was in the area. Nor did the British have any idea of the cruisers' intentions. It seems to have been assumed that their arrival was mainly a coincidence and that their destination had been Dakar all along.

Another French ship, and the merchantmen *Poitiers*, had meanwhile turned up. It had left Dakar for Libreville on the 15th and was intercepted next day by the cruiser *Cumberland* not far from Freetown. It may have been carrying ammunition for the Vichy forces in Gabon or, as it was also said, sand, railway sleepers and assorted cargo. The captain scuttled his ship before *Cumberland* could inspect it, which rather suggests a cargo less innocent than sand and railway equipment. The crew were made prisoner by *Cumberland* as they attempted to row to the shore and *Poitiers* was sunk by gunfire as it was settling only slowly. The whole episode rather shocked the expedition commanders. They did not expect a French ship to be scuttled (though German ships usually did so to avoid capture), and perhaps they were also shocked that the ship turned up so unexpectedly.[4]

Then *Tarn* and *Primauguet* were discovered by the cruisers *Cornwall* and *Delhi*, in the Gulf of Guinea, further on than *Poitiers*. *Primauguet* was compelled to stop and *Tarn* necessarily stopped as well. The captains of *Primauguet* and *Cornwall*, as it happened, knew each other from joint peacetime duty in Shanghai. Captain Ford Hammill of *Cornwall* explained his orders to Captain Henri Goybet, and reminded him of better days, but he also insisted that the French ships must turn around and go back to Casablanca (not Dakar). Equally persuasive, if not more so, were the fourteen guns of the two Royal Navy ships pointing at *Primauguet*, which had only eight guns. After a delay while Goybet contacted his headquarters, he agreed to go back to Casablanca.

This confrontation happened on the 19th, by which time the other French cruisers had encountered the main British force off Freetown, and were being shadowed by a steadily increasing number of Royal Navy ships, first by *Australia*, which was joined by *Cumberland* (both cruisers) while the cruiser *Devonshire* (in which Admiral Cunningham had his headquarters) and some destroyers were following on, as was the formidable battleship *Barham*. Then Bourrague heard of the stopping and reversal of the *Tarn* and the *Primauguet*. This deprived his squadron of any possibility of success, since he would soon be immobilized by lack of fuel if he went on, so he had to abandon his mission. Suddenly turning round and speeding up, and taking the British ships by surprise by this manoeuvre, he headed back to Dakar at high speed. He was followed by the British ships, which were unable to gain on him, though he was bombarded with radio messages. He managed to get into harbour at Dakar without coming within range of any of the British guns.

One of the cruisers, *Gloire*, slowed down because it had developed engine trouble and was 'persuaded' by Admiral Cunningham to go to Casablanca, under escort. These two interceptions, off Freetown and in the Gulf of Guinea, had effectively halved the French naval strength at Dakar, though there were still the guns of *Richelieu*, two cruisers, the destroyers and the submarines and the shore batteries.

Darlan, faced by yet more examples of the British foiling his plans, replaced Bourrague with Vice-Admiral Emile Lacroix, who was flown out to Dakar at once, arriving on the 21st. Darlan also asked the Armistice Commission that he be allowed to rearm *Strasbourg*, now at Toulon, and to send this formidable ship, with three more cruisers and some super-destroyers, to West Africa. Fortunately for the British, the Germans were suspicious of Darlan's motives, which were no doubt mixed, and refused his request. The arrival of *Strasbourg*, faster than either of the two British battleships, would have posed serious difficulties for Cunningham. No operation could have continued at Dakar with that ship present and available to interfere with the landings. Further, Darlan might then have been persuaded to revive an earlier plan to attack Freetown, followed by the revival of the original Vichy plan to recover Equatorial Africa.

The encounter of the French cruisers with Cunningham's fleet meant that the Vichy authorities in Dakar were now warned, at the least that a major British force was in the area, and there could be no more attractive target for it than Dakar itself. An assault and landing were not expected, as Admiral Lacroix said the next day, but he did assume that a blockade was intended. Perhaps this was because only the warships of the British force had been noticed by the cruisers, but not the transports, which had travelled by a slightly more seaward route than the Gibraltar ships.

Dakar is situated on the southern side of a narrow peninsula which projects from the continent to form the westernmost point of the African mainland, Cape Verde. The city actually faces east, looking into the wide bay which is formed by the neck of the peninsula to its north. The peninsula has a projection to the south and this forms the bay and the site of the city. It is an exceptionally useful site, being well sheltered from the westerly gales, and without surf or even a serious swell (though these are problems on the northern and western coasts and further south). In the bay was the fortified island of Gorée, which had also been one of the settlements of European merchants since the original first voyages of the Portuguese explorers and pioneers. Dakar had been a French settlement for ninety years, though Rufisque, a small port a little way to the east, had been so for much longer. Dakar in fact had been founded as a French town, and its strategic location in an age of steam power had steadily increased its importance.

The city's situation on the peninsula made it easily defensible in the face of a land attack. In the face of an attack from the sea, a far more likely contingency, it was ringed by several coastal batteries, which dominated the approaches to the city, the peninsula and the bay. The batteries on Gorée Island and those on Cape Manuel, south of the city, were especially well sited to block the seaward approaches to the city, reinforced by batteries on the island of La Madeleine, on the Atlantic side. There were also fighter, bomber, and seaplane bases around the city, notably at Thiès, some miles inland, but there was also an airfield close to the city, at Ouakam. In the harbour, rather clogging it up so far as the naval forces were concerned, were over fifty merchant ships. The *Richelieu* was moored in the inner harbour, protected by a breakwater from torpedo attack. Since her arrival one of the 15-inch gun turrets had been completed, though not yet test-fired. This in effect made the ship yet another stationary gun battery.

Two of the cruisers which had been chased into the harbour, *Georges Leygues* and *Montcalm* were present, as were the three super destroyers, *L'Audacieux*, *Fantasque* and *Le Malin*, which had come from Toulon with them; there was also another destroyer, *Le Hardi*, and there were in addition three submarines, *Ajax*, *Bévéziers* and *Persée*. (*Bévéziers* had arrived, unnoticed by the British, during the previous few days, and it had been in the Mediterranean two weeks before; the Armistice Commission had given special permission for it to be moved to West Africa; two others, *Sidi Ferruch* and *Poncelet*, had come south at the same time and were now at Conakry in Guinea and Libreville in Gabon respectively.) The fact that these submarines were not known to the British to be present at Dakar turned out to be important.

The attempt to persuade, or perhaps rather to intimidate, the city and its garrison into rapidly joining the Free French side (situation 'Happy') failed ignominiously. There were several strands to this plot – sabotage of the communications by an infiltration party, a landing by air at Ouakam airfield, close to Cape Verde, to persuade the airmen to defect, the arrival in the inner harbour of an emissary from de Gaulle with letters for the army and naval commanders, a scattering of leaflets in various places and addressed to different groups and the approach of two of the Free French sloops. All these approaches failed. The infiltration group, headed by Commandant Hettier de Boislambert, who had done much the same thing at Duala in Cameroon, failed to persuade any of the army officers he contacted and the men went into hiding. They did cut some of the internal communications, which affected the local response later in the day.

The airmen who landed at Ouakam airfield captured the airfield commander when he came out to see who they were, but he was quickly released by his men, who then captured the captors. They found on one of the invaders a list of the Gaullist sympathizers in the city, which suggests either incompetence or a staggering lack of imagination – or perhaps just over-confidence. It would be disastrous for some of those on the list. The scattering of leaflets was successfully accomplished, but few seem to have been read by those they were addressed to, while they did let the military know what was being attempted.

The arrival in the harbour of two launches flying flags of truce sent in from the Free French sloop *Savorgnan de Brazza* was similarly ineffective. The bearer of the letters, Commander Georges d'Argenlieu, got no further than the harbour mole; he was stopped by a lieutenant pointing a revolver at him, and when he saw a group of armed men running toward him he and his men swiftly returned to his launch and left, pursued by machine-gun fire from Gorée which wounded him (so permitting the later Gaullist propaganda claim that the Vichyites had fired on a flag of truce). The other two Free French sloops, *Commandant Ducros* and *Commandant Domine*, had meanwhile approached the boom, intending to land special forces who were to try to persuade the crew of *Richelieu* to join the Free French, but they were seen and driven off by fire from *Richelieu* and from Gorée Island.

All this took place in the morning fog, which shifted and opened and at times shrouded the view. This was also a phenomenon which was completely unexpected by the expedition and by its meteorologist. It has been blamed for these early failures, in that it hid the menacing presence of the British battleships from the eyes of those in the city. It had been hoped that this would be a helpfully intimidating factor, though in fact it probably had little effect on the result. It is clear that there was no support in Dakar for de Gaulle and the Free French, beyond those few whose names were now all-too well known to the Vichy authorities, thanks to the security lapse at the airfield. Governor-General Boisson ordered the arrest of just fourteen men who were known Gaullist sympathizers, which would be a sign of the absence of Gaullist support. There was a demonstration by Africans, dispersed with some force. And that was all. The city remained quiet, though it was heavily patrolled – only to be expected in the circumstances. When the two sloops were driven off under fire, it was clear that the 'Happy' scenario had been a complete failure.

De Gaulle had been broadcasting to Dakar all morning, increasingly threateningly. The only effect of this was to alert the authorities to make preparations to repel some sort of attack. An air reconnaissance finally revealed the size of the fleet outside the harbour, hidden until then by the fog. The big ships, *Barham* and *Resolution*, moved into the bay and were fired on by the *Richelieu* and by the batteries of Fort Manuel and Gorée

Island. For an hour a sporadic duel between ships and the shore went on in the fog. The British sank the submarine *Persée* as it attempted to get out of the harbour to reach the waters off Cape Verde. Some damage was done to the docks and to some of the houses and a general panic resulted in the native town, when some British shells overshot those targets. On the other hand the cruiser *Cumberland* was severely damaged by a shell from the Cape Manuel batteries and the destroyers *Foresight* and *Inglefield* were also hit. At about 11.30 am the fleet withdrew, and soon afterwards Boisson broadcast a reply to de Gaulle's last message. It was defiant and promised that any landings would be opposed.

The bombardment of the city had in effect brought the British forces into the conflict, well before this had been intended. The next stage – situation 'Sticky' – called for a landing, possibly opposed, which was to be supported by the British ships. The fog complicated everything, and communications between the ships and the commanders were slow and erratic. (The British commanders were both in *Devonshire*, but de Gaulle was on one of the transports, *Westernland*.) The landing was intended to take place at Rufisque, out of range of the batteries around the city, but co-ordination between the transports and the warships, and between the advance force and the follow-up force, proved to be quite impossible. Eventually, just after 5.00 pm, the three Free French sloops approached Rufisque and launched their landing craft and two of them went right up to the jetties, intending to land their Marines and provide covering fire if needed.

Meanwhile, as the three Free French sloops headed towards Rufisque, out of Dakar came a naval sortie. The cruisers *Georges Leygues* and *Montcalm* and the destroyer *Le Malin* headed east along the coast in the direction of Rufisque and the destroyer *L'Audacieux* came out through a gap in the boom near Gorée. *L'Audacieux* was seen at once by the cruiser *Australia* and the destroyers *Greyhound* and *Fury* and was instantly bombarded by all three. She was rapidly reduced to a blazing floating wreck, which drifted slowly across the bay during the rest of the day to beach eventually south of Rufisque. The French cruisers and the other destroyer, however, were hidden by the fog, though their sortie was reported by aircraft from *Ark Royal*.

The Free French sloops were thus approaching Rufisque from the south as the Vichy French cruisers were approaching it from the west. The supporting craft for the sloops, intended to bring reinforcements and to provide covering fire were now a long way off, largely because no one knew where they were in the fog, but the sloops went in to land the marines they carried, less than 200 men. As it happened, the Vichy cruisers and the Free French sloops remained completely ignorant of each others' presence and the cruisers turned back more or less at the time the sloops were attempting to land the soldiers. But it turned out that there was a coastal battery at Rufisque – another surprise – which fired almost point-blank at the sloops and drove them off from the jetties they were trying to use. They moved south to an open beach but there they were fired at by Senegalese riflemen from the shore. Knowing that they had no immediate support, either from reinforcements or by ships, they abandoned the landing. More or less at that moment, de Gaulle cancelled the operation for that day. It was said later that had they landed at the beach, the Senegalese would have retired – but this was only one of several similar stories designed to suggest that a bit more determination would have won the day – not an unreasonable supposition. But what it does emphasize is that the whole conflict between the different groups of Frenchman was very tentative. Neither group wanted to gain the reputation of shedding French blood, or at least being the first to do so.

This was not an attitude which affected the conflict between the British and the French. It was decided that the situation 'Nasty' had now been reached. At a commanders' conference that evening, a new plan was made. The British fleet would go into the bay and bombard the city's fortifications into ruin the next day and then land the troops. This intention was conveyed to Governor-General Boisson as an ultimatum at 11.00 pm; he replied defiantly at 4.00 am, 'France has entrusted Dakar to me. I shall defend Dakar to the bitter end.' (This actually represented second thoughts on the contents of the message. The first impulse of Boisson's council had been to reply with the single word '*Merde*'.)

So at last the British had come to the Mers el-Kebir position once more, in which a British fleet would bombard a French city and the ships in its harbour, not in their own defence only, as on the first morning, but intending to destroy and sink from the start. This time there was to be less concern about civilian casualties than there had been at Mers el-Kebir, nor was the operation to be anything like so limited. The ultimatum from Cunningham and Irwin stated that 'once our fire has begun it will continue until the fortifications of Dakar are completely destroyed and the place occupied ...'

This was not actually what happened. The bombardment began with three air attacks, each by six aircraft from *Ark Royal*, directed at the ships in the harbour, at Fort Manuel on the tip of the peninsula overlooking the harbour and at the battleship *Richelieu*. Hits were claimed on all of these, but only near misses were actually obtained – and six of the aircraft taking part were shot down. From one of these the French recovered a notebook giving radio frequencies, from which they were able to jam British radio traffic for the next few days – yet another careless security lapse. During all this the destroyer *Fortune* detected and fired at the Vichy submarine *Ajax* which was preparing to attack the battleships; *Ajax* was damaged, the crew surrendered, and the submarine was then sunk.

At about 9.30 am the battleships began firing at *Richelieu* and the forts on Gorée Island and at Cape Manuel. The batteries replied, as did *Richelieu*. The cruisers *Australia* and *Devonshire* meanwhile fired on the ships in the harbour including the cruisers and super-destroyers, which also replied. They manoeuvred successfully to avoid the British shells. No results on either side were obtained and firing ceased not long after 10.00 am. The fog was much thinner this time, but the destroyer *Le Hardi* laid a smokescreen which spoiled the British aim. There was a pause in the bombardment to allow the visibility to improve and for the sailors to eat and then it restarted. The result was no better than before, though *Barham* was hit more than once, suffering only minor damage. The British ships pulled out at about 1.30 pm. An air raid at 3.00 pm by a dozen aircraft produced only the shooting down of two more of *Ark Royal*'s planes.

Another commanders' conference that evening reached the gloomy conclusion that they should abandon the whole enterprise; de Gaulle would go on to Equatorial Africa and gain control of Gabon from the local Vichy authorities. This decision, however, soon changed. The British commanders reconsidered. This may have been partly as a result of a misleading report that several of the French ships were beached and burning, which was an exaggeration based on the condition of *L'Audacieux*. A more likely explanation of the change of mind is that they had considered the contrast between a signal from Churchill which had come in earlier saying 'having begun we must go on to the end, stop at nothing', and the minimal damage their ships had sustained. To have received only minor damage to several ships was scarcely 'stopping at nothing', especially when no landing had been made, nor even really seriously attempted. By 7.30 pm the British commanders had decided to try again. (They finally told de Gaulle this four hours later.) It was perhaps just as well that they did so decide, for another signal from the Prime Minister made clear his strong dissatisfaction with what little they had achieved so far.

Their new intention seems to have been another bombardment aimed at reducing the forts and the ships in the harbour to ruin, followed by a landing, presumably at leisure. But the commanders' renewed determination was of no avail. Next day was clear, with maximum visibility. But the French Air Force, which had been absent on the first day, and annoying on the second day, was now fully active and highly effective. (No doubt de Boislambert's interference with communications had been responsible for the slow Air Force response to the bombardments on the first day.) The spotting planes for the fall of shot from the battleships were driven off, and the French bombers were again a nuisance even if, like the British planes, they did not hit anything.

The battleships came to their bombardment courses about 9.00 am, but the submarine *Bévéziers* had been lying in wait for just such an opportunity. A spread of four torpedoes was fired; *Barham* evaded them, but one struck *Resolution* near the stern, forcing her to reduce speed and turn away. *Barham* and the cruisers continued firing and were themselves bombarded by the French ships. (The shore batteries were out of range this time.) But the damage to *Resolution* was decisive. After only ten minutes *Barham* turned away to cover her fellow battleship and by 9.20 am both had ceased firing and withdrew. A report was sent to London that yet another attempt had failed. And in London the damage to *Resolution* convinced all, even the Prime Minister, that the game was up. Confirmation that the expedition should withdraw was sent at 2.30 pm.

Chapter 6

Harassments and Conversations

The ships of the Dakar expedition limped away from Dakar, heading back south to Freetown. *Resolution* needed care and attention and *Barham* took the ship in tow, moving at only six or seven knots. The fleet was still under threat of attack and aircraft from *Ark Royal* patrolled in search of any submarines in the area. One plane did find a submarine, the *Sidi Ferruch*, which was able to approach no nearer than ten miles from any of the ships, being forced to submerge by the aircraft.

Apart from the need to repair *Resolution* and *Cumberland*, two major other issues followed from the defeat at Dakar: what de Gaulle should do now to recover and what lessons, military and political, needed to be learned from the events. There was also the possibility of Vichy French retaliation, as after Mers el-Kebir. This had already happened again at Gibraltar. On 24 September sixty French bombers from Morocco carried out an air raid on the naval base and the town and a second attack was made by eighty-one bombers the next day. One anti-submarine trawler, *Stella Sirius*, was sunk, and some damage was done on shore. At sea four French destroyers came out of Casablanca heading for Oran; they fired on the destroyer *Hotspur*, which was on patrol in the Strait, and which fired back, but no one hit anything.[1]

Darlan was angry once more, hardly surprisingly. He had asked that *Strasbourg* be released, of course, and at Gibraltar Admiral Somerville was alerted by Captain Hillgarth from Madrid that Minister Laval had asked the German Armistice Commission to release the whole French fleet; Somerville was thus warned that it might arrive on his doorstep. He did see two of the French destroyers which had passed earlier, *Epée* and *Frondeur*. They were heading west this time and sped up to twenty-eight knots when they saw the battle-cruiser *Renown* coming out. He was also shadowed all day by French aircraft from Morocco, but Darlan had been refused *Strasbourg*, as was Laval the whole fleet – the Admiralty did not take this idea seriously – and the withdrawal of the expedition from Dakar, and its failure, let everyone cool down.[2]

The other French reaction that reached Britain was in the form of messages through the French and British ambassadors in Madrid. One came from the Ministry of Marine by way of the French naval attaché and the British attaché, Captain Hillgarth, but which obviously originated with Admiral Darlan. He bitterly complained of still another British attack on a French colony and threatened reprisals which would make the Mediterranean untenable to the British fleet. But the message also demanded the suspension of British attacks, a relaxation of the blockade to allow food supplies to reach the French free zone and the abandonment of British support for de Gaulle's civil warfare. It therefore went well beyond the issue of Dakar or Mers el-Kebir. At the same time, a less belligerent message came from the French Foreign Minister, Baudouin, who concentrated on the issue of the blockade of food supplies. The way these somewhat contradictory messages were dealt with was to ignore the loud one, from Darlan, but reply to that from Baudouin, and in it to address Darlan's complaints, which were all, of course, rejected.[3]

So was set the basic pattern of relations between Britain and Vichy France for the next nine months or so. The British blockade was officially maintained but was not enforced in most cases, so long as the French convoys were escorted by warships – but it was always possible to use the blockade against specific French convoys, particularly if there was a strong supposition that there was an attempt to run specific contraband, such as rubber or oil, items which were likely to reach the Germans. This, as will be seen, was what happened. The British support for the Free French movement also continued. Many of the British who brushed up against General de Gaulle came away thoroughly annoyed at him, but a general understanding of his position was maintained. At the same time, indirect contact continued with the Vichy government, not only through Madrid, but also through Washington, and in other, even more clandestine, ways.[4]

There were also more purely naval and military lessons which were to be learned from the Dakar business – 'defeat' and 'fiasco' were the usual descriptions employed. It followed on the same sort of problems which had been encountered in the campaign in Norway and the failure to eliminate all the French ships at Mers el-Kebir. These were all relatively small expeditions but all of them in their particular ways pointed out the same problems.

The blame for the Dakar defeat was variously awarded to the weather, the supposed presence of Germans, the arrival of the French cruisers with supposed reinforcements, the lack of security at the embarkation stage. When the whole affair was studied carefully, however, it was evident that the expedition may have had problems with all these issues, though the idea of German involvement was quite wrong, and yet none of them was adequate to explain the defeat, not even taking them all together. Indeed, the fog, which certainly made aiming the guns difficult, could well have been of considerable assistance if the landings had gone in at the beginning. A full consideration could put all these aside as mere excuses; the basic reason for the defeat was that the defence fought better than the attack, with better spirit and was better organized. There were virtually no reinforcements delivered to Dakar, though the extra ships were obviously useful; the garrison was tougher and better motivated (again, as at Mers el-Kebir) than the attackers. And any careful consideration of the events made it clear that the basic military problem was that neither the Free French nor the British were really happy at the thought that they were trying to kill Frenchmen. It was the same reaction as had been felt by Admiral Somerville, when ordered to fire at the French ships, and was the main reason Admiral Cunningham in his reluctance to attack in Alexandria.

Once a proper study was done in the Admiralty and elsewhere some fundamentally important lessons were drawn.[5] It was recognized that the whole planning process was rushed and inadequate and that the planners should have been the men who actually went to sea. Similarly, overseeing the loading of the ships needed to be done by men conversant with the intent of the operation. The separation of French and British commanders was a constant hindrance, as was the slowness of the communications between them. There had not been enough training for the troops, which was in part the fault of the rushed initial stages again. So the major lesson was that adequate time for planning and training was required.

At a practical military and naval level it was now recognized that a ship designated and equipped as a headquarters vessel was needed so that orders could be delivered, information co-ordinated and events controlled more directly. The difficulties the French forces had in landing their troops needed to be addressed by investigating the beaches and the sites chosen for landings more closely and in advance. The expedition had carried tanks, but no opportunity had existed for landing them; a specialized type of ship – eventually the 'Landing Ship (Tank)' – was clearly required, and this eventually spawned a whole elaborate series of landing craft. To anyone familiar with the histories of the later landings on hostile shores – Dieppe, Sicily, Anzio, Normandy and the Pacific Islands – it will be obvious that the lessons of Norway and Dakar were well learned, at last.

The fundamental error, at the basis of the whole failure, lay with the wholly inadequate information that the planners and the expedition possessed about the defences, the geography, the climate and the garrison of Dakar.

Clearly a longer preparation time would have allowed the information brought by Commander Rushbrooke and Captain Poulter to be properly assimilated. But there was also always the issue of the 'morale' of the garrison. The Free French naturally assumed it was low, as a result of the defeat in France. But the Dakar troops had not been involved in the fighting in France, and so had not actually been defeated. No allowance was made for the invigorating effect of what was seen as the treacherous attack at Mers el-Kebir by the British. What was clearly also needed, along with better planning, better equipment, more troops, and better information, was a better imagination, an ability to see the situation from the viewpoint of the defendants.

In the usual paradoxical way of such events, some of the results were unexpected. The British failure at Dakar stiffened the Vichy government in its relations with its German conqueror, for they had won a victory. Yet it also led to an amelioration of its relations with Britain, even though its members remained strongly anti British, as though the victory at Dakar balanced out the defeat at Mers el-Kebir. The French could now turn to the Germans and point to their successful defence of Dakar, so when Germany asked – demanded – access to the French Empire for air and sea bases, the French could blandly say that they were perfectly capable of defending themselves. Already on 24 September, the second day of the attack, a German 'economic' mission, headed by a colonel in the German army, had set off for Dakar. A second plane with their staff was supposed to follow, but when the first plane landed at Casablanca, General Noguès detained it and the Vichy Foreign Office refused permission for the delegation to go on to Dakar.[6] The Vichy French wished to stand by themselves and since they always denied that there had been any German presence of involvement in the Dakar business they did not intend to be forsworn. It was assumed, no doubt rightly, that the Germans, once present, would establish themselves permanently as the first infiltrators into the French Empire. They had already boosted their numbers in French North Africa to over 600 men and shipments of raw materials to Germany had greatly increased. Preventing Germans reaching Dakar was thus seen in Vichy as self-defence.[7]

Marshal Pétain's government developed an effective technique of countering German demands by pointing to the terms of the armistice and by submitting long lists of demands for reciprocal concessions. For a time Pierre Laval, Vice-Premier, and the real power in the government from 10 July, was prepared to go a considerable distance towards collaborating with Germany, even to the extent of making a final peace treaty and joining in the war against Britain, but this was not a policy acceptable to Pétain or to most of the other Vichy government members and eventually they organized a *coup* which removed Laval from power in December.

The British, through the ambassador in Madrid, were fairly well-informed about all this, and were able to intervene here and there with some effect. Their most effective technique, however, was to instigate a heavy message from Washington, usually including a veiled threat to seize the French Caribbean islands and the ships there. This again strengthened the Vichy hand against Germany, though gradually the sheer weight of the German presence in France prevailed.

The conflict between Britain and Vichy would not, however, go away, even if neither government was at all interested in developing that conflict into open warfare. At the end of September the British thought that the two French battleships in Dakar and Casablanca (*Richelieu* and *Jean Bart*) might be coming out to go to Toulon. Admiral Somerville was warned to watch for *Richelieu* especially, and was instructed that if the ship headed north (that is, towards the French Atlantic ports, or perhaps to Germany) rather than east into the Mediterranean he must stop her. In fact, the French seem to have had no intention of moving either *Richelieu* or *Jean Bart*, but the same fear sent Somerville out again at the beginning of November.[8]

The Vichy threat to make the Mediterranean untenable for British ships was a very credible one. To reach Malta from Gibraltar British warships and convoys had to sail past the long stretch of the coast of French-controlled North Africa, while to the north for much of the same distance there were the hostile Italian forces based in Sardinia and Sicily. Somerville raided these places, their airfields and bases, every now and again, and he fought a battle against the Italians soon after Mers el-Kebir. It was usually difficult enough to survive Italian attacks without having to face French hostility and their ships as well. Had the Vichy regime been actively hostile, fighting the convoys through would have been impossible and it is probable that Malta would have fallen quickly and possibly Gibraltar as well. The Admiralty, for one, was acutely and actively conscious of the threat, and pointed this out to the Foreign Office on 30 September in a memorandum, recommending an approach to Vichy which would involve as few calls on the Royal Navy as possible.[9]

It seems probable that both the British and the Vichy French realized just how closely they had come to declarations of open warfare as a result of Mers el-Kebir and Dakar. One result of Dakar was therefore that both were thereafter much more circumspect and became more careful to avoid a too-painful trampling on each other's toes. In this the French had to be the more careful, trapped as they were between Britain and Germany and with Germany in occupation of three-fifths of France itself, able to turn the screw much more unpleasantly than Britain ever could. The British were able to adopt a much more robust approach and were able to continue a policy of needling Vichy, fairly certain that nothing much would come in reply, though some caution was necessary to avoid pushing the victim too far and it was not the most important problem they were facing. Above all, the British were able to continue their support for General de Gaulle without Vichy being able to do much about it, and to some extent Britain could use their Free French forces to carry out operations which British forces themselves could not. The Free French were thus useful to both sides: the British could use them when employing their own forces was too provocative; the Vichy French could blame de Gaulle when a direct accusation against the British might result in even more serious conflicts.

General de Gaulle had only had a relatively minor role at Dakar and that had been a failure – but then so had been the much greater involvement of the British. Now the British force was dispersed, *Barham* went to Gibraltar for repairs and then into the Mediterranean. *Resolution* had to be patched up at Freetown and then she went to Gibraltar also for repairs, *Ark Royal*, having lost a fair number of her aircraft, went to Britain for more, then both to the Mediterranean. After some thought de Gaulle decided to take his forces to Equatorial Africa. There he would be on 'French' soil, amid a population (French, not African) which had become fairly enthusiastically Free French now that the British Empire and oceans were available to the planters as markets and they could make money. He would have troops under his own command, and would also be to a degree separated from the British. It was in many ways a gesture of independence, a separation from his British sponsors just as his flight from Bordeaux had been a separation from the failing French government.

For the British also this was a sensible move since de Gaulle's presence would ensure a firmer Free French grip on Equatorial Africa, so they themselves would not need to worry about it, and they could perhaps bring out some of their ships from the Gulf of Guinea. So the remaining naval force which had been left at Freetown and the cruiser *Devonshire*, four destroyers, and the three Free French sloops which had been at Dakar sailed into the Gulf of Guinea. They arrived at Duala in Cameroon on 9 October and de Gaulle received a cheering welcome.

It was obvious that de Gaulle would soon mount an attempt to take over Gabon, the only local colony still loyal to Vichy France. The British were prepared to assist with ships, but he was going to use his own land forces, both those he had brought to Dakar, and others which he collected in the Equatorial colonies. Darlan in reply dispatched four submarines, one from Toulon and three from Oran, to Casablanca and then on to Dakar, where they arrived on 26 October; meanwhile he moved two others from Beirut to Toulon. The Dakar vessels did not, however, go any further for the present, possibly deterred by the considerable British naval forces which had gathered in the Gulf of Guinea.

By early November the battleship *Provence* at Mers el-Kebir had been sufficiently repaired to be returned to Toulon. Darlan organized a display of French naval strength for the voyage. The *Provence* sailed from Oran accompanied by an escort of five destroyers, and was met by the battlecruiser *Strasbourg*, five cruisers and five more destroyers for the last part of the voyage into Toulon. It was a considerable display of naval power and a clear warning to Somerville and the British generally.[10]

Admiral Somerville with Force H, however, does not refer to this in his reports, though he was concerned at exactly that time, for the second time in a month, that *Richelieu* and *Jean Bart* might be coming out to get to Toulon – which may well have been a Vichy French disinformation exploit, designed to draw Force H to the west just in case Somerville was told to make another attempt to eliminate the Oran ships.

As though waiting for such an event in order to puncture Darlan's achievement, it was immediately after the transfer of *Provence* to Toulon that General de Gaulle began his operation to gain control of Gabon. He gave command of the operation to Colonel Leclerc (promoted from captain to colonel in a month and soon to be a general), who organized the landing at Mondah Bay north of Libreville on 7 November, the Free French troops going ashore from three Free French transport ships. The British warships confined themselves to acting as a distant covering force and the landing force was covered more closely by the Free French sloops *Commandant Domine* and *Savorgnan de Brazza*. The landing was accomplished success-fully. In Libreville harbour the sloop *Bougainville* (sent to Gabon sometime earlier by Darlan) was bombed by Free French aircraft and then fought a gun duel with *Savorgnan de Brazza*. *Bougainville* was set on fire and sunk. Outside the harbour the British sloop *Milford* was attacked by the submarine *Poncelet*, but the torpedo it fired failed to explode. *Milford* replied with gunfire. *Poncelet* was damaged, surrendered and was then scuttled. By 14 November Gabon had been conquered; the governor, trapped between the bishop, de Gaulle, Vichy and finally defeated, committed suicide.[11]

The significance of this little campaign was that de Gaulle had now apparently overcome any scruples he had had earlier about 'shedding French blood', and so had his troops. He had also succeeded to some extent in expunging the memory of failure at Dakar and since his forces had done the job themselves, his standing with the British – and with the Vichy French – was considerably enhanced. He now had an independent geographical, military and naval base.

The removal of Vichy rule from these areas meant, of course, that their products, timber, rubber, some minerals, were now available to the Allies and not to Germany or Italy. Metropolitan France could have had access to them because the French convoys were rarely stopped and it is probable that a good deal of these goods eventually went to Germany, if not to Italy. But now little would get to Europe outside Britain, whose policy of buying up such resources was thoroughly popular with the planters and farmers. The sheer extent of Equatorial territory was also a useful asset. A supply line, particularly for aircraft, was developed from the British Gold Coast colony at Takoradi through to Egypt, with Chad as an intermediary refuelling stop. And later it was possible for a Free French force under Leclerc, by then a general, to operate northwards out of Chad against the Italians in Libya and eastwards through the Sudan to fight other Italians in Ethiopia.

The British contacts with the French ambassador in Madrid continued. An unofficial emissary from Marshal Pétain, Professor Louis Rougier, turned up in Britain in October, but he could not really offer anything the British wanted. It was suggested he contact General Weygand, now the effective viceroy of French North Africa, but either Rougier could not or he would not, and no other approaches to Weygand, even through the ambassador in Madrid, had any effect. The British, in other words, having caught one French general, looked to collect more (and perhaps they were testing Rougier), especially since the Pétainist regime tended to look very militaristic, and military defections would be especially wounding.[12]

Pétain himself meanwhile had a meeting with Hitler in October at Montoire. Hitler had a hard time. He had already failed to recruit General Franco, the Spanish dictator, into joining in the war with Britain and now Pétain proved to be recalcitrant as well. It was also to prove impossible to make a definitive peace agreement with France, since Italy wanted Tunisia and Corsica, but had hardly earned them on the battlefield. Franco's price for joining in the war had also been a slice of French North Africa. Neither could be awarded prizes at the cost of French territory, for unrest in France was not something the Germans wanted to see – and Pétain and Vichy had shown clearly that they were willing to defend their empire – a lesson of the British attacks. Also, it went against the grain to award territory in advance. Hitler himself soon annexed Alsace and Lorraine, but at least his army had beaten the French army to be able to do so. After these bruising meetings, Hitler in effect gave up attempting to sort out his western allies and 'friends'.

Meanwhile, incidents at sea continued to irritate relations between Britain and Vichy. One aspect of this was the German and Italian use of France's Atlantic ports, which was now attracting the attention of the RAF. The demolition work at these ports when the army withdrew had only delayed

German use for a few months. By late July Bordeaux was in use as a base for Italian and German submarines and by late August Lorient was also being used by U-boats. The collection of barges, motorboats and various other vessels which were gathered for the invasion of Britain, provided a regular target for RAF bombers in September, and a month later Brest and Cherbourg were being bombed because they had become bases for destroyers and *schnellboote*. Late in December the heavy cruiser *Admiral Hipper* was able to dock at Brest, after a commerce raiding cruise in the Atlantic. The bombing campaign against these ports was not something the French could complain about, but they were necessarily conscious that their metropolitan territory had now become a battleground for two countries with which they were both technically at peace – though with Germany they were in the state of armistice and with Britain they were in a state of undeclared war.[13]

French overseas trade was also an area which was becoming one of contention between Britain and Germany. Britain's blockade of France was scarcely being enforced, partly because it would take up the time and energy of too many British ships which would be better employed against German submarines or Italian battleships. This had allowed Vichy to develop an Atlantic import system which was centred on, of all places, Dakar, where ships gathered from West African ports and from Martinique and the rest of the Caribbean, whence they were then convoyed through the Strait and on to North Africa; also the French trade across the Mediterranean between North Africa and the South of France was proceeding almost as in peacetime. It was assumed by the British that a good deal of these French imports went on through the free zone to German-occupied territory and on to Germany. When the War Cabinet discussed the matter on 18 November it was agreed that it would be best to begin enforcing the blockade, but the lack of ships delayed matters and even then enforcement was only occasional. In the end it was not until 1 January of the New Year that real action was taken.[14]

The original order to enforce the blockade had gone to Admiral Somerville on 19 November (the day after the War Cabinet's decision), but he was about to begin a new operation to pass a convoy through to Alexandria. He pointed this out but all the same he was able to send out three destroyers under a commodore to intercept the merchant ship *Charles Plumier* on the 23rd.[15] No other interruptions to French traffic took place until 13 December, when four destroyers brought into Gibraltar the *Avant Garde*, a trawler which had been acting as convoy escort and whose convoy had separated off before the destroyers arrived. Next day Force H was ordered to the Azores and the interceptions – classified as Operation 'Ration', presumably by someone of the Admiralty with a sense of humour – were suspended again.[16]

Somerville was very conscious, being the man on the spot that nothing he did should stir up still more local hostility. (He was, after all, the man who had ordered the bombardment at Mers el-Kebir.) The French convoys along the North African coast tended to stay within territorial waters when they could, both French and Spanish, and any too-obvious violations of these international rules might bring Spanish and/or French retaliation – and it was generally reckoned that Gibraltar could not be defended for more than a day or so in the event of a Spanish attack. Somerville was finally ordered to carry out interceptions as far as possible in late December, but again he avoided doing so by taking all his destroyers to sea on an operation, so leaving none available to carry out the interceptions. But he was given new orders on 30 December to start interceptions 'to prevent the French making a hole in our blockade', as he quoted in his report. He also pointed out that it was difficult to reconcile the necessity of infringing territorial waters in order to intercept French trade with a policy of not annoying neutrals and he asked for more information – another delaying tactic.[17]

Nevertheless, having some destroyers available he sent out a cruiser and five destroyers on 1 January to collect a convoy of four merchant ships escorted by another trawler, *La Tourlonaise*. As he had feared, the largest ship, a Messageries Maritime vessel, *Chantilly*, put up a resistance to the armed party attempting to board from the destroyer *Jaguar*. A burst of machine-gun fire, supposedly into the sea, killed two passengers and wounded four more, apparently from ricochets (so Somerville assumed). The trawler was allowed to go on to Oran; the convoy was brought into Gibraltar. Two of the ships were tankers and so were clearly violating the blockade.[18]

One result was a resumption of flights by French reconnaissance aircraft over the Strait and over Gibraltar, which Somerville assumed would result in his dispositions being known to the French Admiralty and therefore to the German and Italian sea commands as well. He may well have been wrong about this last assertion, but the French would certainly know of his movements and if retaliation was intended he would obviously be vulnerable. (It might also be that the aim was to find out when it was safest to run convoys through the Strait.) He asked that operations under 'Ration' be stopped, and rather to his surprise the Admiralty agreed for the moment. The governor of Gibraltar, General Viscount Dillon, went off to Britain to put the case on 'the French business', for which Somerville gladly supplied him with information and an argument.[19] 'Ration', however, was left in place and was occasionally enforced, more as harassment and an irritant and a reminder to Vichy of British annoyance than for any serious purpose in rigorously enforcing the blockade. It was a policy which could be turned on or off at will and so was particularly useful as a means of exerting pressure, or of gaining Vichy's attention.

But this did not always work for, after all, it was essentially a very blunt weapon. In March the cruiser *Sheffield* with four destroyers attempted to bring out a convoy which was within French territorial waters. It included one vessel, *Bangkok*, which was believed to be carrying a cargo of rubber. (In fact the cargo had been unloaded at Casablanca.) The destroyer *Fearless* was sent in to cut out the ship, but came under fire from a formidable battery of 15-inch guns at Nemours in Algeria, and got involved in a fight with the battery. The result was that the captain of *Sheffield* was retired, presumably for having sent *Fearless* into danger, when it should have been *Sheffield* which went in, if any of the ships did.

What angered Somerville was that this all happened as a result of an unenforceable policy.[20] Somerville was rightly annoyed and though he did not think so, he was backed up in his complaints by the Admiralty. His reports to the Admiralty were more or less politely worded, but he let off a good deal of steam in his daily letters to his unfortunate wife. He blamed 'that bloody Winston' for the policy and detested having to be hostile to the French. He was especially bitter about Mers el-Kebir, of course, but the killing of the two passengers on *Chantilly*, one a small girl, pushed him to 'ask what we are fighting for', since Britain had become 'just as much a dictator country as either Germany or Italy'.[21]

It was not simply Somerville who had to undertake such unpleasant tasks, however, and it was not only in the Mediterranean that the blockade of France was enforced. In January the Vichy French merchant ship *Mendoza* was intercepted off Puerto Rico in the Caribbean by the auxiliary cruiser *Asturias*.[22] This was well within the area of American interest, but no fuss was made. It was the US Navy's practice to spot and follow any German ship at sea in American waters – which, of course, usually brought a British ship to the scene, resulting in the capture, or more usually, the scuttling of the German ship. This does not seem to have been their practice with French ships, but there could be absolutely no doubt which side United States favoured in the European war.

Meanwhile the four Vichy submarines at Dakar, *Vengeur*, *Monge*, *Pigas*, and *L'Espoir*, having failed to intervene at Gabon, went on to Madagascar, where their presence, and that of a couple of sloops which made the same journey, was something which had to be borne in mind by all British ships in the Indian Ocean – the main convoy route lay through the Mozambique passage, between Madagascar and the African continent. Two Italian ships which escaped from Mogadishu in Italian Somaliland in February, when that land was being conquered, took refuge at Diego Suarez at the northern tip of Madagascar.[23] It began to look as though Vichy, under Britain's maritime pressure, was leaning towards the Axis – after all, Italy was scarcely a friend to France even under normal conditions, so that giving refuge to Italian ships looked like a straw in the wind. On 15 February three French ships were intercepted coming out of Atlantic ports and were sunk by the British submarine *Tigris* in the Bay of Biscay on the reasonable assumption that they were operating under German auspices, if not under direct German orders.[24]

It is clear that over the winter of 1940–1941 Vichy France was coming under constant British pressure at sea and in the air, for the air raids on the Atlantic ports also continued. Visits to Vichy by the Canadian *chargé d'affaires*, Pierre Dupuy, between November 1940 and January 1941, in which he saw both Marshal Pétain and Admiral Darlan, produced no improvement in relations, nor even much of a dialogue. Pétain's replies to Dupuy's queries as to the French naval bases were ambiguous, partly because the Marshal was 'tired' and sleepy – Dupuy woke him up more than once by saying 'General de Gaulle' loudly, which had an instant effect. Darlan, however, was quite definite that the fleet would either be moved out of German reach or be scuttled if the bases were threatened – but again the British did not trust him, nor, even if he was trustworthy, could they be certain he would survive to give such orders. In view of the more active British prosecution of the blockade it is not surprising that most messages from Vichy were complaints about the interception and confiscation of merchant ships and their cargoes.[25]

The removal of Laval from power in December was, for the British, a good omen, but two months later Admiral Darlan himself was appointed Vice-Premier and collected a whole set of ministries, so reducing the number of Cabinet members at Vichy to only five. The result was that governing was actually being done by a group of technocrats appointed by Darlan. Darlan was acceptable to the German ambassador to France, Otto Abetz (whose power was much greater than his office), because of his apparent Anglophobia, but he was just as concerned as the Marshal to retain some freedom of action for France.[26] Yet the fact that his appointment required German approval was as ominous as the onerous economic conditions which had been imposed by the armistice, which were now beginning to have a serious effect on the French population and Darlan had little success in ameliorating them. The constant British pin-pricks were an aggravation of all this unpleasantness, but they were not the most important matter for Darlan's consideration.

The arrival of a new American ambassador to Vichy, Admiral William D. Leahy, enabled Darlan to work around the British blockade to some extent.

The United States was willing, even eager, to supply economic assistance to France under the US flag and it was assumed that the British would not interfere with the shipments. Food shipments were sent into France, and aid also went to French North Africa, along with economic advisers. The calculation was that the British would obviously want to avoid annoying the Americans by attacking either the shipments or that area, not that the British had showed any intention of doing so. What the British actually wanted was for the governors of North Africa to join them voluntarily. This was a pipe dream, however, for the colonial administrators had taken an oath of loyalty to the Marshal personally, the Delegate-General for all North Africa was General Weygand, wholly loyal to the Marshal (and completely impervious to British approaches), while General Noguès in Morocco was Darlan's friend and Admiral Esteva in Tunisia was his fellow seaman.

Despite the gradual immiseration of life in France, and the burden of the German occupation, there was little to attract the French towards Britain during the first half of 1941. Defeats of British forces in North Africa, Greece and Crete followed hard on one another in the spring, and German successes and pressures were such that Darlan was constrained to agree to supply fuel, trucks and other vehicles out of the French stocks and supplies held in Tunisia and Algeria, in return for unfulfilled German promises regarding the release of French prisoners of war, or reductions in the economic exploitation, and so on.[27] Given that General Rommel, the German commander in Libya, was always short of supplies due to British interference with Italian convoys in central Mediterranean, these supplies more or less on the spot were a significant help in his campaigns. And once he had succumbed to German pressure in the question of the fuel, Darlan found it impossible to resist later pressures.

Vichy France was thus sliding steadily further under German control and Pétain and Darlan and the other collaborationist ministers were being used, willingly, by the Germans as a cover for their policy of exploitation. Though the French ministers did not know it, German plans would soon involve even greater pressure, and the Vichy Empire would suffer a further amputation as a result.

Chapter 7

Syria: The Quarrel

The conflict between Britain and France which began in June and July of 1940 had been conducted in the main at sea and with naval forces. The British attacks on Mers el-Kebir and Dakar, and the intermittent enforcement of the British blockade, were all carried out by the Royal Navy. Even the conquest of Gabon by the Free French had been encouraged, even made possible, by the protection provided by British ships offshore and it was the presence of the navy in the Gulf of Guinea which had deterred the intervention of Vichy submarines and cruisers. The British army's contribution to the Dakar expedition had not been needed.

This had been inevitable, given the general strategic situation. The main enemy was Germany and the conflict between Britain and France was partly a product of the British aim of imposing a blockade on continental Europe in an attempt to strangle the German economy. There could be no question yet, or for many years, of Britain physically invading Germany and any conflict with any of Germany's satellites was, again, something which could not yet be conducted by land. So Britain's war against Germany, as against France and Italy, was largely a naval and air war. The humiliatingly easy expulsion of the British army from Greece in April 1941 was another demonstration of the current impossibility of any land attack on Germany.

There was still the Middle East, however. There, as in most of the Mediterranean, the present enemy was Italy. During late 1940 and early 1941 the Italian empire was subjected to an even greater and more destructive assault than France's. In the Mediterranean the Italian Navy found itself subject to frequent attacks and almost as frequent defeats, by the Royal Navy. In November 1940 the carrier-borne air raid on Taranto harbour by Admiral Cunningham's Mediterranean fleet had crippled the major units of the Italian fleet, and in March 1941 an Italian squadron had been destroyed off Cape Matapan; even Genoa, as far from the British naval bases as it was possible to get in Italy, had been bombarded from the sea in February by Admiral Somerville's Force H. By April 1941 the Italian Empire in Ethiopia and Somaliland had been destroyed and the remaining Italian troops there were about to surrender. In North Africa a large Italian army was defeated by a British force one sixth of its size.

This sequence of defeats, however, had brought in German air and land forces to assist their Italian allies and the British had been subjected to attacks in Greece and Libya by the German army and they were about to be attacked in Crete as well. The conquest of Ethiopia was no compensation for the ever closer Axis pressure moving towards Egypt, though it did remove the only Axis access to the Indian Ocean. And beneath this conflict between Europeans there was restlessness among the Arab populations of the several countries of the Middle East which was about to complicate matters even more.

The Suez Canal was one of the vital links in the communication system which held the British Empire's disparate sections together. To make sure of Suez, the British had first bought a controlling interest in the Suez Canal Company, and then had established their control over Egypt then had conquered the Sudan and Uganda to control the Nile Valley and then had taken control of Palestine. For the British Empire Egypt had become a citadel from which its enemies could be defied and out of which expeditions could be launched against any of the surrounding lands from which there seemed to be a threat. Thus the campaigns in Ethiopia and Libya and Greece were essentially a means of keeping the current enemies – German and Italian – at as great a distance from Suez and its vital canal as possible.

This priority, of course, was by no means congenial to the people of those lands which the British felt they needed to hold. Egypt had heaved with rebellion repeatedly since the British moved in. An adjustment to the relationship in 1922 by which Egypt gained, in effect, a limited internal self-government of a constitutional monarchic sort and a technical independence had scarcely helped, since the British continued in military occupation of much of the country and continued to control the Canal. In 1941 Egypt was technically a neutral country in the wider war, but none of the participants made any allusion to this inconvenient fact when they fought each other in its territory. Cairo continued to be the headquarters for the whole Middle East command, under General Archibald Wavell and Alexandria was the main naval base for the Mediterranean Fleet under Admiral Cunningham. It is scarcely surprising that Germany and Italy regarded Egypt as a species of enemy territory.[1]

Elsewhere in the region the British control of Palestine had been grievously endangered by mutual terrorism between the Palestinian Arab native population and the Zionist Jewish incomers between 1936 and 1939, and both of these communities were now virulently anti-British. Not even the anti-Jewish policies of Nazi Germany had reconciled the Jews in Palestine to British rule, and the leading Palestinian Arab cleric, the former Mufti of Jerusalem, from his exile in Iraq, was in contact with both the Nazis in Berlin and the Fascists in Rome with a view to securing the overthrow of the British occupation.

This hostility encompassed the French as well. As part of the booty of their victory in the Great War, in 1919 France had acquired Syria, seizing it from an independence movement which had gathered beneath the kingship of the British-sponsored Hashemite dynasty. King Faisal, installed by British arms, had ruled in Damascus for a time until expelled by the French in 1920. He had then been compensated with the kingdom of Iraq, courtesy again of the British, who in effect invented the country for him, and his brother had been given the land east of the Jordan River ('Transjordan') to rule. Both men ruled at first as British puppets, but both had, like Egypt, been awarded technical independence at the price of a continued British military presence, though in these cases this was relatively small.[2]

In Syria the result of French conquest and rule had been, as in Palestine, constant trouble. This had included a major two-year rebellion in the 1920s, and there had been dour opposition from the local politicians ever since. The French attempted to conciliate and defuse this opposition by favouring the numerous minority groups – Shi'ites, Druzes, Alawites, Greek Orthodox Christians, Greek Catholic Christians, Maronite Christians and others – rather than the majority Sunnis who were the heart of the independence movement. They had installed separate parliaments in Damascus and Beirut for the two main countries, Syria and Lebanon, and had redrawn the provincial boundaries to favour their policies. But all this had been only partly successful. As a result the country was held by a considerable garrison of 40,000 French troops (and this was well down on the pre-1939 total of 160,000), and was governed by a self-interested bureaucracy more concerned with its own perpetuation than with governing efficiently.[3]

A widespread Arab hankering for both independence and unity left both imperial powers open to the (fully justified) accusation that their policies were designed to 'divide and rule'. Their involvement in war from 1939, and their very public quarrel meant that their resentful subjects looked with favour on their enemies.

The result of the defeat of Britain and France in 1940, therefore, was that there was a general licking-of-the-chops among their enemies in the Middle

East. The Mufti of Jerusalem, Hajj Amin al-Hussein, was in contact with Rome and Berlin; there were even Zionist attempts to interest Nazi Germany in their cause, including even negotiations by a future Israeli Prime Minister, Yitzhak Shamir, who was secluded in a British prison camp in Kenya, as a result of his terrorist activities in Palestine. In Syria the Governor-General Gabriel Puaux and the army commander General Eugène Mittelhauser delayed for several days in June 1940 before deciding to accept the armistice and the new Vichy regime's authority. It had taken a direct order from General Weygand – the commander in Syria himself until 1940 – to bring about Mittelhauser's decision, and Puaux had then followed. Their hesitations had revealed a clear ambivalence in their political allegiance, and the Free French were encouraged to believe there was a considerable sentiment in their favour in Syria.

The British were also concerned about who held authority in the lands next to their own Arab territories, and they were also encouraged to hope that the French rulers of Syria might change their minds. Just in case they did not, and the Vichy regime turned out to be supportive of Nazi Germany, the flow of oil through the Iraqi-Syrian pipeline was stopped. It could be restarted if Syria proved friendly. This was, of course, a version of the on\off sea blockade policy, Operation 'Ration'. But the apparent ambivalence of the local French response to events in Europe also persuaded the British not to exert too much pressure; it was thought that a change of mind was more likely to happen without British interference.[4]

On the other hand, the French in Syria had always been suspicious of British intentions, ever since the original conquest from the Ottoman Empire had been accomplished largely by British imperial forces, and Faisal had been installed at Damascus by the British. When General Mittelhauser's Chief of Staff, Colonel Edgard de Larminat, publicly disagreed with the decision to support the Vichy regime and tried to persuade some of the French army units in the south of Syria to go to Palestine to continue the fight, he was rebuffed by them and then put under arrest.[5] He escaped soon after and joined de Gaulle (to become the Gaullist governor-general in Equatorial Africa). Again his action implied considerable ambiguity and a range of opinions about the armistice among the French in Syria.

Then came the British bombardment at Mers el-Kebir. Local sentiment among the French immediately hardened and became wholly anti-British. Yet at the same time it was also thoroughly anti-German. In reporting these developments in local attitudes to France, Puaux also made the point that Italian or German armistice commissioners would not be welcome, and the arrival of any such men might well lead to a new reversal of attitudes. It was clear that the French in Syria were thoroughly uncertain in their opinions and policies.

In Iraq, the British defeats in Libya and Greece in early 1941 encouraged the emergence of a wide conspiracy. It involved the Mufti of Jerusalem, a former Prime Minister of Iraq, Rashid Ali, and a cabal of Iraqi army colonels. It was this development which finally brought German attention to the region. A series of minor items now accumulated to provide them with the possibility of a cheap victory. And in the midst of everything was the uncertain and puzzled Vichy French regime in Syria.

When Vichy's authority was accepted by Puaux and Mittelhauser, the British reacted cautiously, hoping against hope that neutrality at least would be the result. They stated on 1 July 1940 that no part of Syria would be permitted to be used by 'a hostile power' as a base for attacks on Britain and its territories, and this was spelled out in detail to Puaux.[6] But the Mers el-Kebir fighting soon brought French hostility. The British cut some economic ties (such as the oil pipeline) and brought the Free French leader General Georges Catroux to the region. Catroux had been dismissed as Governor-General in French Indo-China and then had come west to join de Gaulle. He was of a higher military rank than de Gaulle, but deferred to him as the original Free French leader, and as a more politically astute man. A Gaullist *coup* in Syria was mooted, but even as Catroux arrived, those involved in it within Syria were arrested.[7] The failure at Dakar further reduced Free French potentialities in Syria.

In the circumstances Puaux's loyalty to Vichy became suspect. A commissar, General Bourget, was sent out from Vichy, and at the end of 1940 he carried out a purge.[8] Puaux and Mittelhauser were dismissed and a new governor, General Henri Dentz, was appointed – yet another of the military men who were given high administrative posts in the Vichy empire. He combined the position of Commander-in-Chief with his post as Governor-General.[9] This obviously toughened Vichy control and drastically reduced the possibility of Syria leaning towards the Free French, though there was still a residual Free French sentiment in the area. Given all the other military activity in the region, the British were unwilling to stir things up in Syria. General Wavell was quite clear that, with all his problems, a neutral Syria was the optimum situation.[10]

General Catroux, with British encouragement, contacted Dentz proposing that the Free French would be kept out if he promised to join the Allies should Germany approach too closely. This was not a position General de Gaulle could accept, and he was supported by General Spears. De Gaulle's optimism had rebounded from the Dakar disappointment, partly as a result of his own successes in Equatorial Africa, and he was confident of the appeal of the Free French to the French in Syria.

So the Syrian argument went on through the early months of 1941 while Rommel pushed the British out of most of Libya and Germany had conquered Greece, so coming apparently ever closer to Syria – though at the same time British forces were conquering the Italians in Ethiopia. The British could not decide on their policy toward Syria beyond rather hoping it would not become too troublesome, though they did not change their warning that it must not become an enemy base. There were three French possibilities before them, personified by the three Generals, Dentz, Catroux and de Gaulle – continued Vichy control, a promise to shift to the Allies if Germany approached, or join Free France right away. But, despite wishing everything to be quiet, it was in fact the British who detonated the trouble which led to their eventual intervention in Syria – and as usual they did so without intending it or wanting it.

In early March 1941 the Foreign Minister of Iraq, Tawfiq el-Suwaydi, met his British counterpart, Anthony Eden, in Cairo. He was pressed to make the gesture of breaking diplomatic relations with Italy – Iraq had already broken with Germany. In reply Tawfiq wanted more and more modern equipment for the Iraqi army; at the same time he proposed to remove those Iraqi officers who were anti-British, a group of colonels collectively called the 'Golden Square'. Eden did not really trust Tawfiq, and was not at all sure that what he had promised would actually happen, but Tawfiq did in fact persuade the Iraqi Prime Minister to move against the dissident officers. They responded to this by mounting a *coup*, expelling the Regent (the king was a minor) and the government, and installing once again Rashid Ali al-Gailani as Prime Minister.[11] Rashid Ali was known to be a nationalist, a friend of the Mufti of Jerusalem, and his programme was full independence and the removal of British troops from Iraq. Beyond that he was a proponent, like the Mufti, of Arab unity. But, since the British would not go voluntarily, he would need to use force. To do this he needed German help.

This *coup* happened on 3 April. For the next four weeks the new Iraqi government consolidated its position. At first there was little reaction from anyone. After all, two days earlier Rommel had begun his campaign into Cyrenaica which pushed the British forces back to the Egyptian frontier, and three days later the German invasion of Yugoslavia and Greece began. Despite these distractions British imperial troops were found to take early precautions. A troop convoy heading for Malaya was redirected to the Gulf and an Indian brigade was landed at Basra on 19 April, and another force of the same size ten days later.[12]

These were not necessarily directed against Rashid Ali and his government, but were more in the nature of protection for the oil fields nearby and above all for the great oil refinery at Abadan on the Persian coast close to Basra. Iraq was one of the main sources of oil to which Britain had access, but the other oil fields were in the north of the country, with pipelines leading across the Syrian Desert to Tripoli in Syria (currently closed to bring pressure on Vichy) and Haifa in Palestine. This was a vital war interest for Britain, and so Rashid Ali's *coup* was seen as a clear threat, once it was realized that it was strongly anti-British.

Meanwhile Rommel had been prevented from going beyond the Egyptian-Libyan frontier by the need to besiege Tobruk, and the conquest of Greece had produced another British evacuation, which paradoxically brought British forces back to Egypt and so increased the availability of forces for use in other parts of the Middle East. It was intended to hold on to both Tobruk and Crete, but the whole British position could collapse if Iraq turned into an Axis ally.

Back in October of the previous year Hitler and Mussolini had issued identical declarations claiming that the Arab cause was close to their hearts, though neither did anything concrete to follow up their words. This was taken more seriously by the Arab leaders than either dictator had perhaps intended. The conquest of Greece and Cyrenaica certainly encouraged the new Iraqi Government in its defiance of pressure from the British. A message by way of the Italian ambassador gave further encouragement and promised help in the form of weaponry. This was fine, but it turned out that the Italians did not have the capacity to deliver anything, and the only way for anyone to do so was by air. This meant that Iraq could only be reached by means of the Luftwaffe's long-range planes, which needed refuelling facilities on the way, and for the present the imminent German assault on Crete required the use of all possible German air power to be concentrated there.

Nevertheless here was an opportunity for a quick victory and a blow at the present enemy, Britain, exactly the sort of swift, sudden operation Hitler particularly liked. Iraq had oil, and its southern port of Basra fronted on the Persian Gulf, and therefore the Indian Ocean, and it was enticingly close to the great oil refinery at Abadan, which fuelled much of the British Empire. Strategically it would be a useful prize and in Hitler's mind, which was largely by now focused on his imminent attack on Russia, it might be a useful flank for another front from which to attack Russia. Mussolini was more to the point and more practical. He called Iraq 'the centre of the British empire with its oil wells', and suggested that its adhesion to the Axis cause would be a body blow to Britain as serious 'as a landing in the British Isles'.

The problem, as the Italians had noted when refusing to send help to Rashid Ali, was that Iraq was far away, that the British largely controlled the eastern Mediterranean, that the British territories around that sea included Cyprus, Egypt and Palestine, all of their military bases, and that Turkey was a neutral and fully determined to remain so. So German attention became fixed on Syria, which would provide two things if the Germans decided to intervene: landing fields for the long-distance planes they would need to use, and arms which could be supplied to the Iraqis out of the French stores which had been set aside as part of the armistice terms. Rashid Ali, on the other hand, pointed out, when sending a long list of weapons requirements, that captured British weapons were needed, such as Bren guns, Vickers machine guns, Boys armour-piercing rifles, and ammunition for these, since the Iraqi army was equipped with British weaponry and so familiar with these guns.

The need to use Syrian airfields required negotiations with Admiral Darlan, who was adamant that he would require considerable concessions in the way of the release of French prisoners of war still held in German camps, a reduction of occupation costs, and the relaxation of the rigidities of the demarcation line between the two parts of France. A German guarantee of the French Empire was also asked for, a requirement which was directed particularly at Italy and Spain, both of whom had staked out claims to bits of North Africa, but it could also be invoked presumably to deter British interventions. In exchange the Germans wanted the use of French airfields in Syria and that the military supplies already in Syria to be sent to Iraq. These negotiations took place in the aftermath of the Nemours fight between the British squadron of the *Sheffield* and its destroyers and the land battery at Nemours in Algeria; it was thus a good moment for the French to seek concessions, and a good moment for the Germans to give permission to use French power against a British colonial possession. Darlan agreed, and he and the Germans reached an agreement, but Darlan found that in the detailed negotiations which followed the Germans managed to wriggle out of a good deal of what they were thought to have agreed to, especially as their Syrian adventure had failed before the negotiations were completed.[13]

The Germans had got the main thing they wanted, which was immediate access to French airfields and arms supplies in Syria; the payment to the French could come later, if necessary – there were undoubtedly strong German mental reservations about the price they were asked to pay. The first German planes landed at Narab airfield near Aleppo in north Syria on 9 May, and two Heinkel He 111 bombers reached Mosul in northern Iraq on 10 May. By this time open warfare had been going on in Iraq between British and Iraqi forces for a week. The British forces which had been landed at Basra had secured that city and therefore the Abadan refinery, and were clearly too strong to be attacked yet by the Iraqis. Instead the Iraqi forces of Rashid Ali attacked the RAF base at Habanniya, where many of the British living in Baghdad had taken refuge, but they were having no success in pressing on with a fairly insipid siege. Aircraft from that airfield could fly over Baghdad, thus intimidating the population, and on 14 May the arrival of the German liaison officer with the Iraqi forces was spoiled when he was killed as he arrived at Baghdad. (He died from a rifle shot, fired either by a nervous Iraqi or by a British soldier: both used the same British weapons and ammunition.)

By that time a German command system had been set up at Mosul, and two squadrons of the Luftwaffe, one of fighters and one of bombers, were settled there (and oil once more flowed west to Tripoli, while the pipeline to Haifa had been closed). Soon German planes with Iraqi markings were overflying Baghdad; some of them attacked Habanniya, and others attacked the relief column ('Habforce') which was heading for that base from Trans-jordan, across the desert. In addition the first trainload of French arms had been sent from Damascus to Mosul along the old Baghdad Railway, which actually ran most of the way through Turkish territory. The Turks were told that the arms were needed to suppress internal dissent by the Kurds and so let them through without imposing the usual five-day delay. But the Iraqis never actually used these arms.

The German arrival had been swift, but it was too late, and it was in only limited force, mainly aircraft, which are noisy and dangerous but not capable of conquest. The British reaction to the attack on Habanniya air base was relatively slow, but it was quite sure. A few days after the German arrival in Mosul and Baghdad Habanniya was relieved by the armed column which had driven from Transjordan. This included troops who, only ten days before, had been facing the Germans and Italians on the Libyan frontier, and a contingent of Bedouin soldiers from the Transjordan Frontier Force. The crossing over the Euphrates at Falluja was secured, and so the road was opened to Baghdad. An Iraqi counter-attack at Falluja failed, and by 30 May Rashid Ali had given up. An armistice was signed and the previous govern-ment was restored.

The German arrival may thus have been swiftly arranged and accom-plished, but it was too late to have much effect, and was too small to be more than a nuisance. The Germans, in fact, had been caught in the same trap as the British had long suffered in the region. Both had too many projects on their hands at the same time. The British had forces fighting in Ethiopia, Iraq, Libya and Crete all at once, and had to watch the internal situation in Egypt and Palestine as well. The Germans were fighting in Iraq and Crete, consolidating their hold in Greece, and preparing for the invasion of Russia. The British, however, had stabilized the Libyan front by holding Tobruk, and were able to transfer some of their forces from the Libyan frontier to Iraq, using their control of interior lines. And, largely ignored in most accounts, which are fixated on the German aircraft and the romantic desert crossing by Habforce, the real power in Iraq (and soon elsewhere) lay with the 10th Indian Division arriving in sections at Basra.

The Germans, on the other hand, were preparing to use many of their aircraft and their airborne troops to attack Crete, at great cost, and could spare very little for Iraq – and most of their strength was about to be thrown against Russia. Plus the British had had a troop convoy at sea in the Indian Ocean which could be diverted to Basra. So the British won in Iraq, because they could concentrate the most forces at a crucial point by their use of interior lines and above all by their control of the sea; all the Germans had time to do was to bring in some aircraft and that was not going to win. The Egyptian citadel and British sea power had scored another victory.

For the French, however, the German adventure into Iraq turned into a disaster. The British had made it clear from the start, from July the year before that the Vichy regime in Syria would only be tolerated so long as the country was not used as a base from which German or Italian attacks could be launched against British territories. In return they had in effect protected the Vichy regime in Syria from attack by the Free French; it was an implicit bargain which the French in Syria understood, but those in the government at Vichy clearly did not. On 15 April, before the Iraqi crisis had developed into open warfare, before the British reinforcements landed at Basra, and weeks before any German involvement (other than rhetorical gestures), de Gaulle had proposed to use his Free French forces to gain control of Beirut and Damascus and the airfield at Rayak in the Bekaa Valley. But he needed transport support which, in the circumstances, the British could not supply – or so they said.[14] The effect of that refusal, or inability, to help was to prevent the Free French from making their attack. De Gaulle expected that his troops would be welcomed by the Vichy forces, a reaction which he had also, of course, claimed would happen at Dakar. The fact remained that it was a British decision to refrain from invading Syria, and that was a decision which could be reversed. The British-Syrian implicit bargain still held, therefore, in mid-April.

When the German forces in Greece were seen to be preparing for an attack, which turned out to be on Crete, the British suspected that other places – Cyprus, Suez, Syria – were possible targets as well, as was Iraq. Governor-General Dentz was warned about the German preparations, and was asked what preparations he was making to defend the country; further, he was also offered help if he needed it. The Free French were to be ignored in all this, and it was not being proposed to invade Syria with British forces: the idea was that a combined British and Vichy force would be quite enough to prevent a German takeover – the British would of course be present at such strategic points as the airfields and the ports.

Dentz explained he had enough strength to resist a German invasion, but he did ask his own government if he should resist if the Germans arrived. The reply was that he should not. This was soon amplified, and he was told that he should give the Germans every assistance on their way to Iraq. This is what he did when the first planes began to arrive, and on 12 May he told the British consul-general in Damascus that, if so ordered, he would certainly allow a German occupation of Syria.[15]

By then the British knew almost as much as Dentz. The substance of the Franco-German agreement was known in the Foreign Office, the arrival of German planes at Syrian airfields was known, and it was also known that the first trainload of French arms was on its way to Iraq. The sources of all this information were various, sometimes Enigma decrypts, or decrypts of Italian signals, interceptions of French signals traffic, and in all probability there was someone in the Vichy regime who was steadily feeding information to the British. The British and American consuls-general in Beirut and Damascus were also fertile sources of information.

In fact the agreement between Darlan and Hitler, effectively ratified by a meeting between the two at Berchtesgaden in 11 May (called the 'May Protocols'), had gone a good way beyond the use of Syrian airfields. It had included permission for the Germans to use the French port of Bizerta in Tunisia to send supplies to the Afrika Korps, the use of road and rail transportation in Tunisia, and the right to use French territorial waters along the Tunisian coast. All this would reduce drastically the length of the vulnerable part of the voyage for German supplies across the Mediterranean – the usual route was from Naples or Taranto to Tripoli in Libya – and would make it even more difficult for the Royal Navy and the RAF to interrupt that supply line. The agreement also included a clause by which the Germans would be able to set up a base at Dakar.[16] It was presumably intended that Dakar would become yet another French city from which U-boats could operate, like Bordeaux or Brest. The effect of the several concessions – Syria included – was in effect to open up all of the French Empire to German use. None of this could be defended in any way in terms of maintaining French neutrality.

This was all accepted by the ministers in Vichy, but they also needed, in effect, to get the agreement of the generals who had been put in power as governors in Syria, North Africa and West Africa – Dentz, Weygand and

Boisson. While Dentz, as he had said to the British consul-general, would do as he was told, neither Boisson nor Weygand was able to accept. Nor in fact was there full acceptance within the Vichy regime at home. The agreement was widely seen, both in Britain and among many of the Vichyites, and, vociferously, by the Free French, as a violation of the armistice agreement. The British Foreign Secretary Anthony Eden described it as such in the House of Commons on 15 May, only a couple of days after it was ratified.

The argument was vigorously pursued within the Vichy government, though the French population learned little about it – it was not done in Vichy to bother about informing the public – except in a broadcast by Pétain on 15 May, which gave little detail but made it clear that the Vichy government was convinced that the Germans would win the war and that a sensible foreign policy was to collaborate with the winners. With Boisson and Weygand opposed and entrenched in power in their regions, the implementation of the agreement therefore rested on events in Syria. If the result was the establishment of German power and influence in Iraq by way of Syria, that part of the agreement would be seen as successful, especially if the Germans carried out their part of it, and did release some of the prisoners of war and did reduce the occupation costs. At that point the other sections of the agreement might be worth implementing as well, even against the wishes of the Vichy proconsuls. But for the moment neither Weygand nor Boisson was prepared to accept them, which rather suggested that Vichy's control of its empire was less than firm. (Admiral Esteva in Tunisia, however, did permit the use of Bizerta – though Darlan soon withdrew that concession – and the Tunisian transport system helped supply the Axis armies in Libya.) If, on the other hand, the Germans failed in Iraq, it would not be worth their while holding on in Syria, and the other parts of the agreement could be forgotten. So all depended on Iraq.

The presence of German military aircraft on Syrian airfields was a sufficiently obvious threatening development for the British to begin hostilities. On 14 May the RAF in Palestine raided airfields at Palmyra, Rayak and Mezze, and more raids were made in the next days. Dentz plaintively explained that the German planes were in Syria as a result of forced landings, but no one believed him.[17] Then on 20 May the German airborne forces which had been gathered in Greece attacked Crete.

In the week between the beginning of the air raids on Syrian airfields and the German invasion of Crete (14–20 May) there was a furious argument between the British commanders in Egypt, the Prime Minister and the Chiefs of Staff in London, and the Free French chiefs in both places, over the plans to invade Syria. Churchill was keen to do something, almost anything. Wavell was insistent that he did not have the military resources for a large expedition, and that a small one would fail. He had to be on constant guard against a new attack by Rommel in North Africa, and much of his strength was wasting away in Crete. The Free French were present in the region in the strength of six battalions, organized as a small division of two brigades under the command of General Legentilhomme, late of Djibouti and the *Empress of Britain*; General Catroux was acting as de Gaulle's representative in Cairo. They were all just as convinced as de Gaulle that the Vichy forces would join them if they simply presented themselves at the Syrian frontier. Wavell was deeply sceptical of this. But the presence of German air power in Syria now made some sort of action to gain control of Syria an urgent matter. As was pointed out by more than one commander, this put German bombers even closer to the Suez Canal than they were in Libya.[18]

General Catroux received information that Dentz was moving his forces into Lebanon, which would mean that much of Syria would be open to attack, but it was also presumed that Germans would fill the space. This encouraged him to believe that the Free French could themselves move into the supposedly empty region with impunity.[19] This information also influenced those in London, and Wavell was ordered to submit a plan. Even as he worked on it, however, the invasion of Crete began, which meant that German forces were even nearer, though most were far too preoccupied to be available for use in Syria. It also meant that British forces and attention were fully occupied. Meanwhile fighting in Iraq continued.

Then on the night of 21/22 May a unit of Vichy troops crossed the border and announced they wanted to join the Free French. That leader was Colonel Collet, who had been involved in a plot aimed at kidnapping either Dentz or his army commander General de Verdilhac. Loose talk by NCOs in the mess and by the Free French on the radio betrayed the plot, and Collet brought over only part of his regiment into Palestine – he had to let those of his men who were loyal to Vichy go back (and those who were worried about their pay and their pensions). This alerted Dentz and de Verdilhac to the plot, and at once they brought their forces to the alert. Further, Collet's information about troop locations and the Vichy reaction demonstrated that Catroux's information about the withdrawal of Vichy forces towards the coast was completely false, and that Dentz was in fact reinforcing the Syrian positions between the Palestine border and the Syrian capital at Damascus.[20] Yet again, Free French over-optimism and lax security had discredited their aims and their methods. Wavell's scepticism was wholly justified.

Dentz, bombed by the RAF and threatened by a Free French *coup*, was now fully committed to outright resistance to any new attack by the British or the Free French. He had been told to allow Germans the use of the ports of Latakia, Tripoli and Beirut, as well as the airfields, and though he had balked at this at first, he now agreed to it, and hoped to receive reinforcements and supplies from France as well – a good deal of his reserves of arms and equipment had gone into Iraq. Another purge of suspected Gaullist officers was made, and those who were arrested were sent to France, sometimes in chains. All this finally convinced Churchill to accept Wavell's insistence that the Free French could not do the job alone, that more resources were needed, and that it would be necessary to wait until the battle for Crete was over before attempting an offensive either in Syria or in Libya.[21]

For the first time in their non-war with Vichy, therefore, the British intended to fight the French on land. This was a qualitatively different undertaking than the fighting at either Mers el-Kebir or Dakar. This time actual control of French territory was in question. For the British of course, the justification was that Vichy had allowed Syria to become a base for their active enemies, the Germans and the Italians; for the Free French the justification was their righteousness in continuing the fight for freedom for France and the overthrow of an illegitimate government in the homeland; for the Vichy French in Syria their case was that they were acting to oblige the legitimate government of France, which was acting in the best interests of France by collaborating with the victors in the European war, whose favour it was worth courting.

But there was also another aspect, which might well complicate this already complex situation. The population of French Syria was composed mainly of Sunni Arabs, but there was a large proportion who were members of other sects and religions. In the face of Sunni Arab opposition to French rule, which was based on the original Sunni acceptance of the Hashemite regime in 1919–1920, and on Sunni resistance to being ruled by foreigners and Christians, the French regime had favoured several of these minorities, and this was a decision and a preference which alienated the Sunnis even more decisively. So when the two states in Syria and Lebanon were organized by the French, the boundaries of Lebanon were deliberately drawn more widely than would be expected, so as to provide that state with a majority Christian population, and so dominate the Muslims. In Syria the Druze had fought a fierce rebellion in the 1920s, but other groups, especially the Alawites, were therefore favoured. The army in Syria – the Army of the Levant – was composed in large part of units recruited outside of Syria – Senegalese and North Africans especially, with a substantial part of the Foreign Legion stationed there as well – and this was yet another practice almost deliberately designed to alienate the Syrians. Colonel Collet's unit was recruited from

Circassians, people who had been settled in Syria in the latter years of the Ottoman Empire, originally from the Caucasus.[22]

This policy had not worked. In the end the French had succeeded in antagonizing the general population, both Sunni and Shi'ite, and some of the other minorities as well. They all generally supported the Arab nationalist cause, and also identified with the Palestinian Arabs in their disenchantment with British policy and Zionist pressure, and in 1941 they sympathized with the nationalist policies of Rashid Ali, insofar as they knew much about them. The British economic blockade, which had existed since July 1940, but was only enforceable by sea and along the southern boundary, had further exacerbated the nationalist feelings by imposing shortages and raising prices, and Dentz had been faced with considerable unrest – strikes, riots and so on – for, however much he might blame the British, those who were hungry and unemployed always blamed the French government.

For the British this alienation and unrest provided both a danger and an opportunity. The danger was that an invasion of Syria would set off a great Arab Syrian rebellion; the opportunity was that it should be possible, very simply, to harness that feeling. Accordingly, from the start the British intended to enlist that Arab nationalist sentiment on the side of the invaders, or at least neutralise it, by promising that Syria and Lebanon would become independent states as a result. General Catroux had approved this idea, but de Gaulle was dead against it. It was, however, something the British insisted on. They did agree not to be associated with Catroux's proclamation, which was watered down by de Gaulle, but they issued their own more explicit and precise version in parallel.[23]

As a result, when the invasion went in the Arab population in general remained quiet, content to let the two foreign armies fight it out between them, so it was only the Vichy forces of the Army on the Levant which the British had to deal with. It did store up trouble for later, of course, since General de Gaulle had no intention of being the man who was held responsible for the destruction of the French Empire. He could well have echoed Churchill's growl that he did not become the King's First Minister to oversee the destruction of the British Empire in a French version. (This was twenty years before de Gaulle did in fact dismantle the French Empire by granting Algerian independence and instant freedom to all the African colonies.) De Gaulle always regarded this aspect of British policy as being the product of the old enmity between the two countries over control of the whole of the Levant.[24]

In this de Gaulle was probably not wholly mistaken, but in public the British were clear that they knew quite enough about fighting Arab nationalists in Egypt, in Palestine, and in Iraq, and they had no wish to have to fight them also in Syria. It was, in fact, no more than the policy the British had pursued in Iraq, Transjordan and even Egypt in the last twenty years. They merely wanted Syria to remain quiet once the Vichy government had been removed, and trouble would have been a distraction from the essential fight, which was against Nazi Germany. One of the tools in the British locker in that fight was to appeal to nationalist sentiment in Europe – including France, personified by de Gaulle – and there was no obvious reason why this could not also be applied in the Middle East. Probably they envisaged a situation along the lines of those they had instituted in Egypt and Iraq and Transjordan, and if de Gaulle had been able to bring himself to understand that, he might have created less argument, but it would involve accepting the Syrian Arab nationalists into government under French supervision, and he probably understood that, given the unpleasant history of French rule in Syria, such a partnership would never work.

Chapter 8

Syria: The War

The Vichy Army which the British invaders would be fighting was a good deal weaker by June 1941 than it had been a year before. Considerable numbers of troops had been withdrawn to France in accordance with the provisions of the Armistice the year before, and some of the equipment had gone to Iraq (though a good deal of the army's equipment had been hidden in secret caches away from the eyes of the Armistice Commission). So the Germans had assisted the British invasion by their measures; nevertheless it was still a larger and better balanced and better trained force than that which the British were able to gather for the invasion.

Most of the Vichy forces were North African, six Algerian, one Moroccan and three Tunisian battalions. There were also four Foreign Legion battalions, which included Germans, Russians and Spaniards mainly, overwhelmingly loyal to their French officers – not to Vichy, not to their homelands, but to their commandants, who were all highly competent, tough, professional soldiers. The British fully understood this and they knew that these were the best troops of the Army of the Levant. There were also the Senegalese battalions, tough and well trained, but very unpopular in Syria, for the French tended to use them for crowd control and to suppress dissent; and there were three mixed Senegalese and French battalions. The vast majority of the soldiers were therefore not actually French. In addition there were three legionary artillery regiments and two armoured regiments with 120 guns and ninety tanks.[1]

The local Air Force was, as it proved, fully a match for the RAF. At sea, on the other hand, there were only a few French ships. There were some very nimble destroyers and a couple of submarines, and these were in contact with Admiral Godfroy, still in Alexandria harbour in his battleship. He maintained good and friendly relations with all the British chiefs – Cunningham, Wavell, and the British Ambassador Sir Miles Lampson – and gleaned a good deal of information from their talks and meals together. He was the source of a good deal of accurate information on British intentions, which was passed on to Dentz.[2]

The British had scraped together a variety of forces. The main unit was the 7th Australian Division, composed of nine infantry battalions, plus a machine-gun battalion, an anti-tank battalion, and divisional artillery – but this was a fairly new unit, not yet fully trained; there was also the Free French Division, which included a marine infantry battalion, a battalion of the Foreign Legion and four battalions recruited from Equatorial Africa. The British contributed the 5 Indian Brigade, composed of the two Indian battalions, the 6th Rajputana Rifles and the 1st Punjabis and one British battalion, the Royal Fusiliers. There was also a force of cavalry, partly horsed, partly in armoured cars, which had been culled from several British yeomanry regiments, and two Australian units in tanks. To these were added the Transjordan Frontier Force, commanded by Major John Glubb for the Emir Abdullah, the only men who knew anything of the ground.[3]

It is worth pointing out, as more than one writer on this subject has, that of the Army of the Levant's approximately 35,000 men, only about 7,000 or 8,000 – perhaps a fifth – were actually French. What is less commonly noted is that the British forces were even more imperial in origin, the largest proportion being Australian, some were Indian, others French; probably not more than a tenth were British (the Fusiliers and the cavalry). It was, as it had been from the beginning, an imperial war. Most of the commanding officers on both sides were metropolitan – though some of the British generals were Australians, but that was only because Australians would only be officered by other Australians. On the French side, General Dentz was an Alsatian, who had been born a German subject, and whose homeland had been re-annexed to Germany.

The shape of the country which these forces were to invade virtually dictated the plan of attack, and therefore also the defence. There were two main routes north out of Palestine and Transjordan, one along the coast towards Beirut, impeded along the way by towns and cities and river crossings, and hemmed in by the steep Lebanon Mountains on the right flank. The other main route headed for Damascus using roads out of Transjordan or out of Galilee, which converged south of the city. There was a third route, rarely used, which came out of the northern end of the valley of the Jordan and headed towards the Bekaa Valley, but this was impeded by narrow valleys and tracks and partly blocked by the flanks of Mount Hermon and Beaufort Castle; it was not a route normally used by invaders.

This was a land which had seen invasions in both directions for over 5,000 years. The latest invasion, by the British in 1918 had used these coastal and desert routes, just as had every other invader. There was thus little choice of routes to use, and even less choice of targets. The main first aims of the British were the cities of Beirut and Damascus, the capitals respectively of Lebanon and Syria, though a third target was also included, Rayak in the northern part of the Bekaa, where the Vichy Air Force headquarters had a major airfield.

The British invasion plan was thus wholly predictable. This fact has produced criticism, but it is difficult to see what alternative plans could be made when the fact that most of the British forces were only partly trained is taken into account. The plan had to be simple and blunt, for only the Indian brigade was professional enough to fight well. The British and Indian battalions were in good condition, but the Australians were not. Of the Free French Division some had seen a little fighting in Ethiopia, and the legionnaires had fought in Norway, but others were as partly trained as the Australians. Consequently it was perhaps just as well that no imaginative strategy was developed. The RAF was supposed to control the skies, but was preoccupied with bombing targets distant from the front line and it was the French Air Force which provided object lessons in providing support for their ground forces. The Mediterranean Fleet patrolled the coast enforcing the blockade and assisting the Australians on the coast road, but the French ships were able to sortie from Beirut more than once.[4]

On the other hand, one British unit was used in an attempt to exploit the British predominance at sea. A commando unit, the 11th Special Service Battalion, had been mouldering in Cyprus – until now no-one in the Middle East had imagination enough to use them, though if, as might have happened, the Germans had landed in Cyprus, the battalion would have been a very useful defence force. This unit was suddenly pulled out and given the task of landing behind the French lines to capture the northern side of the bridge over the Litani River, north of Tyre, while the Australians were to drive along the coast road to reach the southern side. But, fully in keeping with the amateurishness displayed at Dakar, the battalion was only briefed at the last minute, no rehearsals were possible, the conditions onshore were unknown, the first attempt to land was cancelled, and the second attempt was not only seen by the French, but some of the men were put ashore at the wrong place. The unit was destroyed in a serious series of fights against well-placed and well-motivated French units – helped materially by the Australians, who frequently mistook them for enemies.

The French defences were just as determined by the terrain as was the plan of attack. River crossings, strong points, towns and cities, hill forts and castles, were to be held. As a result, the French resistance proved to be much tougher and more vigorous than had been expected. After all, the suspicious

French had long expected the British to attack them, and had mapped the country and trained for defence for twenty years (whereas until this conflict, the British had never had any intention of invading, so had to cobble together a plan based on their 1918 conflict – Wavell had been a colonel in that campaign). The British commanders, from General Maitland Wilson down, were unable to escape from the notion that the obvious enemy was Germany, and so assumed that the French were really friends. They half expected the Vichy forces to make only a token fight and then surrender. The attackers were told to go into battle preceded by officers with white flags, who should try to persuade their opposing commanders to give in, or wearing berets rather than tin hats – shades of the white flag in Dakar harbour. These ploys never worked, but they did give the French defenders near the frontier time to organize either their defiance or their withdrawal. There can be no doubt at all, however, that all the British were very reluctant to undertake the campaign, while fully appreciating its necessity.

The British plan had been devised, if such a term may be used for something which was done with little conscious thought, by General Sir Henry Maitland Wilson, the Commander-in-Chief in Palestine. It was to be implemented by Major General J. D. Lavarack, in command of the 7th Australian Division, who was in command of the western and central attacks (along the coast and into the Bekaa); the attack along the roads towards Damascus were partly commanded by the Brigadier W. L. Lloyd of the 5 Indian Brigade, and partly by General Legentilhomme, commanding the Free French Division. In addition Colonel Collet with his Circassians was to operate in the territory between these two advances. On the Vichy side the overall command was with General de Verdilhac.

The invasions began on 8 June, and the first moves were generally, if deceptively, successful. On the right the town of Deraa was quickly taken by the Rajputs of the 5 Indian Brigade, and they were able to move on to Sheikh Miskine. From the north side of the Sea of Galilee the Royal Fusiliers moved forward to capture Kuneitra on the Golan Heights; Colonel Collet's Circassians linked these two forces. On the coast 21 Australian Brigade sent one battalion along the coast road, and a second battalion was sent with the Cheshire Yeomanry through the hills a little inland. Helped by an advance force which had seized the village of Iskenderun and distracted the local French, they headed for the Litani crossing, first capturing Tyre on the way. There was in fact little resistance, since the French had placed their first line of defence at the Litani. The commando force which had landed there therefore did so at exactly the wrong place.

The Mediterranean Fleet provided support for this coastal advance. Cunningham, whose forces had been grievously reduced by the Cretan campaign, allocated a cruiser squadron and a group of destroyers to assist, and they were to be covered by fighters based at Lydda in Palestine and Nicosia in Cyprus – this last was also to be on the watch for any German or Italian air interference from the Aegean. It was hoped to avoid any conflict with French warships, but the British ships were to be prepared 'to act as developments indicate'.

The Australians on the coast road were shelled by the French destroyers *Guepard* and *Valmy* on 9 June, and when the British ships came up they were also attacked. The destroyer *Janus* was disabled by accurate fire, and the cruiser *Phoebe* was attacked by the submarine *Caiman*, which missed with a torpedo. The destroyer *Jackal* was also damaged, and several aircraft were shot down. The arrival of more British ships finally persuaded the French to withdraw back to Beirut. Meanwhile Alexandria harbour was damaged by an air raid from German bases in Crete, and it was impossible to get local workers to work at night.[5]

On land the Litani River was crossed by the Australians on 9 June. They were shocked at the sight of all the dead commandos, but the French defenders largely retreated in good order. The invaders had suffered rather too many casualties for comfort, and there were more obstacles and river crossings not far ahead.

The central attack was made by three battalions of 25 Australian Brigade and some British cavalry (mainly in trucks). These were held up by strong positions, well defended, at Khiam and Merjayoun. The Australians had attacked with just three tanks, and quickly lost two of them. By the end of the first day they had made only a minimal advance.

These first moves made it clear that the Vichy forces were not going to simply surrender, not even after only token resistance. General Wilson thought that the first day was 'a good day's work', but if he or his troops thought they had won in any real sense they were displaying no military sense. Apart from at Merjayoun there had been no real resistance on the frontier, but then there had been no places worth defending. The Litani crossing had been contested, but the French had then retreated suspiciously readily. That is, the French were reserving their main defensive strength for properly prepared and manned positions well back from the frontier – again except for Merjayoun.

So for the next week there was hard fighting on all the axes of advance. Merjayoun was finally taken after four days when a full-scale attack by infantry went in preceded by a rolling artillery barrage, very much in the Great War style. Then a column was sent on a painful march through the night by way of an almost impassable track to Jezzine. The purpose was to bring assistance, by way of the road from Jezzine to the coast, to 21 Brigade on the coast road.

The coastal attack made slow and more painful progress. Once across the Litani the Australians were repeatedly held up by a skilful French defence manned by deliberately small numbers of well-placed and tough troops. The twenty miles from Tyre to Sidon took them most of a week. They were held up for a day by a Foreign Legion force firing from a complex of caves; they were repeatedly ambushed by well hidden tanks, who escaped as soon as real force was brought against them; they had to stop frequently to remove road-blocks or capture a hill or cross a stream where the bridge had been blown. They were assisted by fire from the ships of the Mediterranean fleet off the coast, though the original force had had to be reinforced by the Australian destroyer *Stuart* and the New Zealand cruiser *Leander*.

Air support was intermittent. There were not enough planes to provide cover for both the ships of 15 Cruiser Squadron and for the land forces. The Fleet Air Arm planes were now based in Cyprus and were watching the seas to the west to spot and stop any reinforcements, air or sea, coming from Europe. The result was that when the RAF in Palestine supported the land operations, the French ships in Beirut were able to come out.

The progress on the coast and in the Bekaa was equally slow. The road from Sidon up to Jezzine in the Bekaa was opened from inland when Jezzine was taken by men of the 25 Brigade coming from Merjayoun. But by that time the coastal column had taken Sidon, after a hard fight. And the French troops were then skilfully withdrawn during the night.

On the road to Damascus, the fighting became just as difficult, with the added ingredient of Frenchmen fighting each other. After the 5 Indian Brigade took Kuneitra and Sheikh Miskine on the first day, they let the Free French Division pass through to continue the advance. Documents which were captured revealed that two lines of defence had been prepared south of Damascus, one passing through Kiswe, and a second a couple of miles to the north, both making use of lines of hills of black basalt. They were well fortified and manned by men who were prepared to fight hard, especially, as it turned out, against the Free French troops. Between 9 and 13 June the first of the Vichy lines was attacked several times, but only part of the hill line was taken. In effect, little progress had been made.

General de Verdilhac, having thereby halted all the attacking forces at Sidon and Kiswe, and Jezzine, sent in carefully selected counter-attacks. The Australian force that had taken Merjayoun had then been dispersed over a wide area, despite having had to fight hard to take the place. Some went to Jezzine which put them a day's difficult journey away from their base, and some were then sent on a pointless patrol along difficult tracks on Mount Hermon. This all left the central position which controlled the Australians' communications back to Palestine held by a much reduced force, and a French attack aimed at this point therefore quickly succeeded in retaking Merjayoun and in pushing the Australians back almost to the original starting point. Attacks on the force at Jezzine compelled the Australians on the coast to send assistance into the hills – whereas it had been intended that the reverse would happen. As a result the coastal force was so weakened that no further attacks along the coast road were possible. Thus a single attack at Merjayoun stopped two of the Australian advances.

The main Vichy French counter attack, however, was directed at the main attacking force, in front of Damascus. A force of infantry and tanks slipped past the Free French in front of Kiswe and attacked the battalion of the Royal Fusiliers which was holding Kuneitra. A day-long fight produced a complete French victory. It was a well conducted and systematic assault on a battalion which had been left to hold too large an area – the same basic military fault which had operated at Merjayoun. At the end of the day the remnants of the battalion had been pushed back to the battalion head-quarters, and there they surrendered.

Again de Verdilhac had chosen a weakened section of the British position, for Colonel Collet's Circassians, who had protected the right flank of the Fusiliers on their original advance, had been moved to the eastern flank of the Free French in order to take part in the assault on the Kiswe line. The Fusiliers were therefore isolated and no-one knew what was happening until it was over. But more troops had arrived in Palestine by this time and were on the way north, so it was possible to send a scratch force to block the road to stop the Vichy forces if they pushed on. But they did not.

At the same time as the Fusiliers were attacked at Kuneitra by a force from the hills of the Jebel Druze, which lay on the right flank of the British and Free French advance, came another attack. These hills had been ignored by the British planners on the assumption that the Druze were so anti-French that the Vichy garrison would need to stay in position to deter any rising. But a weak French force of Tunisian infantry, with some tanks and ten armoured cars, came out of the hills and cut the road and railway at Ezraa, twenty miles behind the Free French headquarters, and thirty behind the front at Kiswe.

There was only a small force holding Ezraa, and there was little to prevent further advances by the Tunisians, who seem to have been hoping also to turn southwards to retake Sheikh Miskine. But there were enough troops there – a mixture of Indians, Free French and Transjordanians – to prevent any further conquests. From this force came that part of the scratch force which went to retake Kuneitra. That is, the attack on Ezraa was soon seen to be very weak. It seems that their vehicles had only a limited amount of fuel, which restricted their numbers and their range of action. (So this was in part a result of the British blockade, and the restriction of supplies along with Tripoli pipeline.)

Together these attacks at Kuneitra and Ezraa were clearly intended to force the Free French and the 5 Indian Brigade (what remained of it after the capture of the Fusiliers) to stop and turn round to safeguard their communications. This is certainly what happened at Merjayoun, where the Australians pulled in their detached forces in order to defend their positions south of the town – though the French had probably no intention of going further, just as they stopped at Kuneitra. The idea of these French attacks was good, and so was the execution. The counter attacks certainly stopped the Australian advance along the coast, and recovered some lost territory in the Bekaa.

De Verdilhac had chosen his targets well, and was clearly well informed of the British movements and strengths and positions. Partly this was clearly good fieldwork by his soldiers, and partly it was the result of long familiarity with the ground and equally long consideration of how the country was to be defended, but it was also a result of good reconnaissance by the Vichy Air Force. The Vichy planes were very active, and were scarcely obstructed by the RAF in that first week. The counter attacks were therefore neatly executed – the reconquest of Kuneitra was an especially professional piece of work – but they were only a means of delaying ultimate defeat.

The main problem which de Verdilhac faced was that the main enemy force, before Damascus, paid no attention to his counter attacks. Brigadier Lloyd had already put in the decisive attack towards Damascus even before his rearward communications were briefly cut. On the night of 15 June, the day before the loss of Kuneitra and Ezraa, Lloyd, having given the Free French – more than six battalions strong – several days to break through the Vichy lines, turned to his own troops. That night the Punjabis made a silent night attack, with no artillery preparation, on Kiswe, the centre of the Vichy line. The village was well fortified, notably by a wide and deep anti-tank ditch, which was quickly crossed by improvised ladders. By chance the soldiers arrived as there was a change of garrison forces going on, and so, at a moment of maximum confusion, they quickly captured the town. Behind them came the Rajputs who moved right through the town to assault the hill behind the town, Tell Kiswe, at dawn. This attack – with artillery support this time since surprise was no longer possible – took the hill, and then held it against three counter-attacks, the first two using tanks, and then a final despairing one by mounted cavalry, which was, in the face of machine guns, no more than a stupid suicide mission. Then in yet another night attack the two Indian battalions drove on to capture a line of hills to the west which had formed a major part of the Vichy first line, the Jebel Madani. While this was going on a brigade of the Free French finally took a part of the Jebel Kelb to the west of Kiswe. It was in the midst of all this that the capture of Ezraa and Kuneitra cut their communications.

The two commanders, Lloyd and Legentilhomme, having broken through the main Vichy line in front of Damascus at last, had no intention of turning away, particularly since, by the time these operations were over, it was clear that the Vichy counter-attacks were made by weak forces, and it was soon realized that the captors had no intention of moving further. The result was that most of the French forces in both Ezraa and Kuneitra quickly withdrew once they came under attack.

Damascus was now within reach. There were three positions close to the city which it was necessary to take for a clear victory. One was the airfield southwest of the city, at Mezze; to the west were a series of forts, presumably well manned and supplied; to the northwest was the gorge of the Barada River, through which the road and the railway passed and which was the route by which the French could withdraw, or be reinforced. The intention was that all three were to be taken by the two hard-worked Indian battalions in yet another night attack, on the night of the 18th.

This was an advance too far. The support elements of the Indian battalions fell into some confusion and became separated from the troops. The airfield was taken, but only by infantry, who were without any artillery or anti-tank guns. They were attacked there by a well-balanced Vichy force of infantry, tanks and artillery and gradually, as at Kuneitra, they were driven back into a single position, a house on the airfield. Three men went off on foot to get through to warn the brigade headquarters of their situation, and an Australian force set out to attempt relief. It was unsuccessful, and the surviving Indians were taken prisoner. This completed the destruction of the three battalions of the 5 Indian Brigade. They had clearly been by far the best forces on the British side, far more effective than either the Australians or the Free French, and, because they were the best, they had been used repeatedly. By the end, after three night attacks in four days, they were clearly worn out.

The strong resistance of the Vichy forces had by this time compelled the British to reinforce their army in Syria, and some of these had already been used at Kuneitra and Mezze. The attempt to push back the German–Italian forces in Libya had failed, so it was now possible to send some of those forces from Egypt into Syria. These were sufficient to form a new Corps (First Australian) under General Lavarack, to cover the whole front; in the Damascus area there were the remains of the Indian Brigade, consisting of survivors and sections no stronger now than a battalion; two newly arrived British battalions, the 2nd Queens and the 2nd Leicestershires, had been sent there in support. There were also two Australian battalions, one of which had already taken part in the unsuccessful attempt to relieve the Indians at Mezze. As a result of the attacks towards Damascus, however, the Vichy forces withdrew from the city the day after the Mezze fight, though they only did so to take up even stronger positions to the north and to the north-west. Meanwhile, since the fighting in Iraq had now more or less ended, General Wavell was able to order the troops who had originally been sent to raise the siege of Habanniya airfield ('Habforce'), to come back, by way of Syria.

The French defences had of course been concentrated along the southern border, for this was the direction from which any serious invasion would come. Some of the Vichy battalions had been left in the north in case the Turks decided they would like to join in, and a force of four battalions had also been placed centrally at Homs, a major route centre where the north-south road connecting Damascus and Aleppo crossed the east-west road from Palmyra and the Iraqi frontier to the Mediterranean coast. An invasion from Turkey was less expected by Vichy than one from Iraq, and the route of invasion would almost certainly be along the desert oil pipeline connect-ing the oilfields of Kirkuk and the port of Tripoli. Palmyra was more or less at the halfway point between Tripoli and the Iraqi border, but the crucial point along the route was Homs, so the French defence relied first of all on holding Palmyra in advance of that point.

On 13 June, the British forces in Iraq were ordered to gather for the invasion of Syria. The 10th Indian Division which had been landed at Basra would stay in Iraq for a time, while Habforce would invade Syria from the east. Despite the small size of Habforce, it took four days to collect the scattered units, and then three more days before they could begin to move. One unit, the Household Cavalry, came in along the road beside the Tripoli pipeline; the rest came from their mustering point at station H3 on the Haifa pipeline, which ran through Transjordanian territory into Palestine. The idea was that this movement would be a surprise. In fact, the French put up an air reconnaissance from Palmyra which located the southern force well before it reached Palmyra, and then sent bombers to attack the approach-ing British forces, which disconcerted them.

The small Vichy force in Palmyra was well prepared to meet this attack. Through a singular lack of initiative the whole British and Jordanian force became stuck at Palmyra, facing an entrenched and well-posted force only a quarter of its size. The French did, however, have a capable and daring squadron of bombers, recently flown in from Algeria, which were able to harass all the British forces with considerable effect.

This siege, if that is what this barely competent effort is to be called, went on for more than a week. Eventually the Transjordanian Frontier Force under Major John Glubb defeated a French relieving column coming from the north. This finally disheartened the garrison which was holding the fort at Palmyra. The garrison was composed half of locally recruited Arabs, and half of foreign legionnaires. When they were surrendered by their commanding officer, the Arabs simply went home, while the men of the Legion – all 165 of them – got drunk on the wine held in the stores. They had held up four British battalions for ten days.

Meanwhile the other fronts had become just as stuck as Palmyra. The Australians on the coast road had taken Sidon and had moved on another few miles towards the Damour River, but were blocked there by a skilled and determined defence by Legionnaires and Algerians. After the capture of Damascus on the day following the Indians' defeat at Mezze, the French forces had pulled out northwards towards Homs, and north-westwards up to the Barada gorge. They were followed in the direction of Homs by Legentilhomme's Free French; the Australians, the Queens and the Leicestershires went up the gorge. The Free French advanced about sixty miles, but then bumped up against the Vichy defences and outran their supplies. Until resupplied or assisted by the British forces from besieged Palmyra, they were as stuck as the Australians before the Damour. Similarly, in the Barada Gorge the French had taken up positions which compelled the British forces to attack uphill in the open, and defied all their attempts to break through.

Damascus had been taken, but every other route of invasion – Palmyra, Homs, Barada, Merjayoun – was blocked. Therefore the issue now came down to the capture of the political and military headquarters at Beirut and perhaps the Air Force headquarters at Rayak as well. The Australians were going to have to break the French defensive line at the Damour.

The fighting had been watched with considerable anxiety, even anger, by the French at home. Admiral Darlan had attempted in several ways to deliver reinforcements or supplies, and he was assisted by German planes from Crete. The destroyer *Isis* was damaged by these aircraft, and French planes damaged another destroyer, *Ilex*. As a result Cunningham ordered that, to avoid losing any more destroyers, the force off Syria must return to Haifa during the day. 'The army GOC must decide between naval support for his left flank and fighter protection for his troops.'[6] That is, the French defensive was as successful at sea as on land.

Some of the planes which were making life miserable for the besiegers of Palmyra had been flown in from Algeria, but Darlan's attempts to send ships with men and supplies almost all failed. One ship, the super-destroyer *Vauquelin*, conveying ammunition supplies, did get through to Beirut, but it was damaged by air attack almost at once. Darlan proposed to send out five cruisers from Toulon packed with reinforcements, but the Germans stopped him from using ships from the demobilized fleet. Supplies and men were sent by rail to Salonica and loaded on to hired ships, but one was sunk by British bombers from Cyprus, and the other took refuge in the Italian Dodecanese; a third ship was sunk off Antalya. And yet Dentz was ordered to fight on, being given the usual order to 'fight to the last man and bullet' produced by men in senior positions located in distant, safe and comfortable headquarters.

One question which was much debated between the Vichy government, the Germans, and Dentz was whether to ask for, or supply, German assistance, either by sending in supplies or by providing aircraft. The question resolved itself largely into whether Nazi Germany would supply Stuka dive-bombers to attack the British ships off the coast and the column of Australians on the coast road. In one attack the destroyer *Isis* had been damaged by a German air raid, but this was the only case of German involvement. (The German planes and personnel which had been in Iraq and Syria and had caused this war, had been withdrawn by air and by rail through Turkey even before the fighting began.)

The problem was, of course, that it was distasteful to all the French, at Vichy or in Syria, to bring in German help (just as the Free French were fundamentally unhappy at having to rely on British help). The Vichy rulers wished, as at Dakar, to show that they could defend their empire by themselves – even though it was becoming clearer by the day that they could not. The defensive tactics were working, but the fact remained that the invaders had fought their way deep into Syria. The reason they were being attacked in Syria was because they had already allowed Syria to be used by German forces, and if they accepted direct German help against British forces in the fight for Syria they might well find themselves at war – declared, open, and official war – with the British Empire, and hence necessarily allied with Germany. This was not a comfortable political position to contemplate, especially since 22 June, when Germany commenced its war with Soviet Russia. So, after considerable argument internally, and despite German offers, German help was refused. What help would have actually been given once the invasion of Russia began, of course, was unlikely to make much difference, though perhaps a few more Royal Navy ships would have been sunk. It does seem likely that one political result would have been very strong US animosity, and, apart from Germany, the US was the only friend Vichy France had left in the world.

Damascus had been occupied by the Free French, although as in 1918, some rude and noisy Australians got in first (having done little of the fighting to get there). General de Gaulle arrived on the 23rd to set up his administration, apparently believing that it was his forces which had won. But the Free

French had fought poorly, and it turned out that the British had been quite serious in their proclamation at the start of the fighting that they intended that Syria and Lebanon should become independent states.

By that time the Vichy forces in the central sector had begun to pull back. One after another, the positions they had retaken around Merjayoun several days before were evacuated. The Australians made one attack which largely failed, but then found that Merjayoun itself had been evacuated as well. Their attempts to move further north were blocked without much difficulty – the Australians were not very aggressive – and similarly no progress could be made in the Barada Gorge. But in none of these places would the conflict be decided. That had to be done in front of Beirut.

The front line was at the Damour River, and this had held for several days, but this was, for the French, no more than a gesture of despair. By the time it had come to this Damascus had been taken, and so had Palmyra. In the north some units of the 10th Indian Division, commanded by Major-General William Slim, had crossed the frontier from Iraq and were moving rapidly westwards along the line of the Euphrates and the Turkish frontier and were now approaching Aleppo. These Indian troops were in part looking for revenge for the death and imprisonment of their fellows at Mezze, and they were still the best soldiers in the whole region, with the possible exception only of the French Foreign Legionnaires. There was little hope that any of the French forces in the north could hold them up. The stand at Damour would only delay briefly the capture of Beirut. In the absence of any serious reinforcement from Europe, the Vichy forces could not win the conflict.

Both sides gathered their forces at the Damour, reinforcing the troops which had faced and fought each other along the coast road for over a month. The Vichy French held the north bank and the spurs of the hills inland. They had a considerable quantity of artillery, well sited, ranged in and hidden, though only a few tanks – there was now a crippling shortage of fuel, and in other areas French tanks had been captured because they had run out of oil. (The RAF had now successfully bombed some Vichy fuel tanks, but the main reason for the shortage was that the oil pipeline had been shut down for most of the past year.) They had placed and fortified many machine guns at possible crossing points and where it was possible to intersect the approaches. The French positions were hidden in the plantations of bananas and palms and oranges which covered the coastal plain, and a mile or so north of the crossing, the village of Damour had been converted into a series of strong points. In the hills other strong points had been made, and there were fortified hilltops directly overlooking and outflanking the Australian positions in the plain and along the river.

To balance, in a way, the Vichy control of the heights, the Royal Navy had brought up a strong bombarding force of four cruisers and eight destroyers (the 7th Cruiser Squadron of Rear-Admiral Rawlings). The French ships in Beirut had tried to break out on 23 June, when the super-destroyer *Guepard* came out. She fought the British squadron of two cruisers and three destroyers, who between them landed one hit, but she then got away by means of her superior speed. It was the French submarines which the British feared as much as anything; the submarine *Souffleur* was sunk by the British submarine *Parthian* on 25 June. Despite justifiable caution on the British side, their ships clearly controlled the local seas.[7]

Command of the air had been achieved by the allocation, at long last, of a force of fighters and a squadron of bombers, both of which were under the direction of the 7th Australian Division, so as to provide close air support for the ground forces. Lack of fuel had grounded what was left of the Vichy Air Force, and many of its planes had been destroyed on the ground. The ground forces on the British side were organized as three brigades, 17th, 21st, and 25th Australian. On the French side there were far fewer troops: a battalion and a half of Foreign Legionnaires, a battalion and a half of Algerians, one battalion of local infantry and some Tunisians and some Senegalese. The defence was outnumbered by perhaps three to one, not to mention the Royal Navy and the RAF.

The conditions and the forces involved made the battle very like one from the Great War, or, to be closer in time, like Alamein a year later, where, as Churchill pointed out, Montgomery reinstated artillery's role in battle. It was a battle of artillery bombardments against infantry positions, which were battered but were rarely broken. The actual attacks were infantry against infantry, with rifles, grenades and bayonets. In such a fight numbers generally prevailed, but the costs were always high. The Australian plan was, as usual in this constricted country, obvious. The 21 Brigade would attack in front to pin down the French; 25 Brigade would climb the hills to turn the French inland flank, fighting a series of small actions to capture hilltops and machine-gun posts, and winding their way through complex country. The third brigade, the 17, was held back to pass through the battlefield once the French had been broken by 21 Brigade, to exploit the victory and capture Beirut.

As always, the operation did not work out as planned. It took longer, and was harder and costlier than expected, but after three days the attack finally succeeded, as 25 Brigade's flank attack finally came down on the French line from the hills. The 21 Brigade had made virtually no progress down on the plain, and had been driven back from its only gains by an Algerian counter attack. The 17 Brigade had already been committed to the attack, so for two days the French defenders had held their positions against the attacks of all three brigades. It could not, of course, go on, and a final attack at midnight on 8/9 July cut right through the French positions. Next day, 9 July, General Dentz asked the American Consul-General in Beirut to arrange an armistice. Churchill, who had, of course, been much embarrassed by this war, announced this in the House of Commons, and the BBC broadcast it. The news reached the troops, who naturally found no further reasons to risk their lives in a final attack. (This did not apply at the Barada Gorge, nor at Merjayoun. General Evetts, in command at the Barada Gorge, insisted on putting in a final futile attack over open ground, thus losing still more lives. And in the Bekaa a Czech battalion attacked, took, and then lost a Vichy post, and so further casualties were incurred uselessly.)

It took two days during which these fights occurred to negotiate a cease-fire, which came into force at midnight on 11 July. Next day General de Verdilhac and a group of French officers met Generals Wilson, Lavarack and Catroux at Acre in Palestine to negotiate the armistice terms. This was not easy, but at least the forces were not still fighting each other – though Wilson had to threaten to restart the fighting at one point to force an agreement, and the Vichy negotiators refused to have anything to do with Catroux.

During these two days Dentz salvaged what he could. The surviving Vichy aircraft were flown out to France and North Africa. The ships in Beirut harbour were sailed to Turkey to be interned there. Three captured and interned British ships were scuttled in Beirut harbour. And, most invidious of all, Dentz ordered all the British officer prisoners to be flown out to be held as prisoners of war in France.

The Gaullist Free French were not a party to the armistice, though Catroux was present at the discussions, as was Legentilhomme. One of the clauses stated that the Vichy soldiers should have a free choice as to which French faction they should join. The British found themselves, as they should have expected, stuck between the two factions, intrigued against and vilified by both. The Vichy officers wanted to get back to France with the whole of their forces; the Gaullists wanted to recruit as many of the men to the Free French cause as possible, but de Gaulle also wanted to gain control of Syria and Lebanon.

The question of the troops was settled relatively quickly, with one nasty episode. When the British found that the British and Free French officer prisoners had been removed from Syria to be held in France, the armistice was deemed to have been broken. Most of the prisoners ended up at Toulon under the care of the French Navy. The British, who had become rather too friendly with the Vichy officers until that point, now became very angry. It was, of course, a violation of the armistice terms which had been agreed, for they had been moved during the cease-fire. And even if no direct violation had taken place it was deceitful and underhand. So thirty of the highest-ranking officers of the Army of the Levant, and then the four general commanders, were arrested, including Dentz. They were taken to Jerusalem and imprisoned in a Carmelite convent. This had all been done (except the arrest of the generals) with due notice and full publicity, and those in France knew in advance what was planned, though clearly they did not expect it to be done. When it did happen they quickly released the prisoners. Two, a Fusilier subaltern and a Rajput *subadar*, were still missing – they were in hospitals in German-controlled territory – when the rest had been returned, so two of the Vichy generals were held until these two were also released, despite their protestations that generals should not be held in exchange for mere subalterns, and still less for an Indian.

The great majority of the Army of the Levant's soldiers went back to France, only 2,600 of them joining the Free French; and a third of the civilian officials stayed on as well. Dentz was greeted as a hero and decorated when he returned, and 32,000 officers and men returned with him. De Gaulle was not pleased and, of course, tended to blame the British for not allowing his people to exercise direct persuasion – something which had been specifically forbidden by the armistice terms in which no recognition had been made of the existence of the Free French. But why anyone should have expected anything different, after the hard fight the Army of the Levant had put up, is hard to understand.

The British had hardly covered themselves with glory in this campaign. Their initial assumptions about the resistance of the Vichy army were hopelessly wrong, their plan of attack was obvious and displayed no imagination, and apart from the Punjabis and the Rajputs their fighting qualities had been shown to be poor. The reputation of Australians as fighting men took a serious knock, though their parallel reputation as thieves and vandals and drunkards was much enhanced. Similarly the Free French had proved to be generally uninspiring as fighters, and by no means as willing to fight as hard as their Vichy opponents. In fact most of the fighting, and all the successful fighting, was done by the British (which, of course, includes the Indians, Australians and even the Czechs). It was, in that sense, quite reasonable that the British should retain political control of Syria after the fighting ended.

De Gaulle nevertheless put up a fight to impose his authority on Syria, and to get the British administrators out, and so to ensure that the idea of independence was scotched. He failed in this too, though a long argument between the two went on until 1945, when the British finally lost patience. The constant disputation meant that the British had to keep a garrison in Syria, more to separate the French and the Syrians than to hold the country against the Axis enemy. The final result came as a consequence of anti-French riots in May 1945. The British locked the French in their barracks and arranged Syrian independence. It was hard to believe that the original idea for this had been accepted by the Free French.[8]

The fighting in Syria had therefore been mainly between the British and the Vichy French, just as it had been at Mers el-Kebir and Dakar, with the Free French proving themselves ineffectual, ludicrously arrogant and militarily both badly disciplined and ineffective. The Vichy French forces, even though they had fought hard and well, and had displayed a professional ability generally lacking in their opponents (except in the Indian battalions), had been beaten because they had fought a purely defensive war. At no point had the Vichy French forces penetrated into British-controlled territory. Such a war, against an opponent like the British who had surely demonstrated a determination to fight by 1941, could not possibly succeed. And, having brought the war on themselves by permitting the Germans to use Syria to reach Iraq, the Vichy regime compounded that mistake by refusing German assistance in the fighting which resulted. Truly Vichy policy was defeatist – that is, it seemed to invite defeat, and welcome it when it arrived. At least the Free French said they wanted to win.

Chapter 9

Islands and Raids

In the year since the Franco-German armistice the undeclared war between the former allies Britain and France had ranged over Africa, the Middle East, and the Pacific. It had necessarily been largely a naval war, though considerable military forces had been engaged in Syria. In the process the French overseas empire had begun to break up. The Pacific territories were under Free French rule in most cases, but it was Australian naval power which ensured that. In the Caribbean the United States Navy played the same role, though there it was to safeguard Vichy rule, not destroy it. The African territories were split between the two claimants. Syria and Lebanon had been handed to Free France after the British conquest, but it was clearly British policies which would prevail despite General de Gaulle's protests.

So far, however, the metropolitan territory had been largely unaffected by the quarrel with Britain. Certain Channel ports, from Dunkirk to Brest, had been subject to sporadic British attacks in their campaign of defence against a possible German invasion. Since the autumn of 1940, however, it was clear that such an invasion was highly unlikely, and after 22 June 1941 it was beyond Germany's capacity, so long as the German army was engaged in war with Russia. These ports, however, were still menaces to Britain, above all the great ports fronting the Atlantic, which had become major German naval bases. For it was, as ever, at sea that Britain was waging the greater war.

A month before the war in Syria began, while the argument about what to do about that country was still going on between London and Cairo, and between Vichy and Beirut, and while Rashid Ali in Iraq was feeling the pressure of a British force consolidating its landing at Basra, the German navy sent out its greatest ship, the battleship *Bismarck*, to raid the convoys crossing the Atlantic from the United States to Britain. For ten days the ship was searched for and hunted by every British warship which could be spared. The battle-cruiser *Hood* was sunk, but in the end, damaged and half crippled,

Bismarck was caught and battered and destroyed by the assembled aircraft carriers and battleships of the Home Fleet and Admiral Somerville's Force H. Sinking *Hood* was its only success, for it never found a single merchant ship. Nor did its companion, the cruiser *Prinz Eugen*, do any better, though it was at sea a good deal longer.[1] The convoys had been well protected.

When its course was plotted, it became clear that the ship was heading for the port of Brest, or perhaps St Nazaire. Had it reached one of those French ports it could have been repaired, and, along with its original partner, *Prinz Eugen* and the two battle-cruisers already at Brest, *Scharnhorst* and *Gneisenau*, it would have been a very potent threat to, once again, the Atlantic convoys – or even possibly a cover for a renewed attempt at invasion of the British Isles. It had taken the combined attentions of the Home Fleet, several ships taken from convoy protection duties, and Force H from Gibraltar, to corner and sink just one battleship. Three German battleships sailing together would, at the least, have been able to cut the Atlantic lifeline for a month, and at the most would have sunk far too many British ships.

This drew attention yet again to the Germans' use of the French ports. Cherbourg, Brest, La Pallice, La Rochelle, St Nazaire, Nantes, and Bordeaux were well used by U-boats and by auxiliary cruisers. Brest in particular was a major German naval base, where the big ships and the submarines were based. Lorient was the headquarters of the submarine command. Bordeaux was especially the port to which the ships used as blockade runners went. It was farther from hostile territory (that is, Britain) than almost any other French Atlantic port, and the Gironde estuary could be reached in part by using neutral Spanish territorial waters; and if a ship was caught in its voyage in the Bay or in the eastern Atlantic it may be able to take refuge in a Spanish port, even if a French port was out of reach.

So the Bay of Biscay was an intermittently active war zone. U-boats passing through were the objects of attack by British aircraft and submarines; minefields were laid outside many of the ports; French ships were sunk in these fields as often as German. Above all the German naval bases were the object of bombing raids, in particular when a major German warship was in port. For much of 1941 and into 1942 the presence of the battle-cruisers *Scharnhorst* and *Gneisenau* attracted RAF raids to Brest. Most bombs missed the ships, though it only took one hit to force a ship to stay longer in the port. For the French, who might well, in the occupied zone at least, be pleased to see a German warship damaged, the real problem was that the bombs which missed the ships tended to hit French property. And those which hit the dockyards created damage which reduced the chances of French workers having jobs the next day.

This situation made a mockery of the Vichy claim to neutrality. French territory, French ports and cities, were being used as bases for the attacks by German and Italian ships on the vital convoys bringing food and supplies to Britain. It was the same situation as had obtained in Syria at the same time that *Bismarck* was being hunted in the Atlantic – May was the month of both *Bismarck* and Rashid Ali. It might well be that the Vichy government could do nothing to prevent the use of French territory in this way, but there is no record of any of its ministers, nor its Head of State, making any protest. In the same way, these same men accepted with no protest the German demand to use their imperial territory as a basis for attacking British forces – in Syria and in Tunisia. The only areas the Germans had wanted to use and were denied them were West Africa, Morocco, and Algeria. It is no wonder that the British viewed Vichy with deep suspicion.

For the most part, the relations between Britain and Vichy in the second half of 1941, after the end of the Syrian fighting, were therefore as cold as ever. That is, the two countries reverted to the condition which had obtained before the Syrian war, in which Vichy could do nothing very much, and in which the British continued to harass Vichy in various ways. Bombing raids were one aspect of this, though none were yet being delivered into the unoccupied zone. German demands for industrial goods were bound to grow once the Russian war had begun, and that could lay the cities and factories even of that zone open to attack. Those in the occupied zone were already vulnerable to this, and the low-level conflict of convoy and threat essentially continued mainly at sea.

At Gibraltar Admiral Somerville, when warned that the invasion of Syria was about to take place, prudently took his ships out into the Atlantic the day before, just in case the French in North Africa sent more bombers in retaliation.[2] This does not seem to have happened, and the wary stand-off between the British in Gibraltar and at sea and the French in the Algerian and Moroccan ports continued. *Dunkerque* was still at Oran, but by April 1941 it was clear that the ship had been sufficiently repaired to sail. Regular flights checked on her condition and on her readiness to sail. If the ship did come out it was intended to torpedo her – again Somerville took Force H to sea to avoid the French retribution when it seemed that the ship was really going to sail.[3] But she did not.

At Alexandria Admiral Cunningham kept a wary eye on the interned French ships. He dreamed of being able to use the battleship *Lorraine* to supplement his fleet in blockade duties after the grievous losses to the Mediterranean Fleet in the Cretan campaign. He was worried that the news of the British attack on Syria would provoke a reaction among the French sailors, just as Somerville was. In fact Admiral Godfroy stopped shore leave for his men for a time, but then, even as the fighting was still going on in Syria, there was so little reaction that he reinstated it. But deserters welcomed by the British reported that scuttling charges on the French ships were still in place.[4] So the standoff continued, unaffected in any serious way by events in Syria.

The Vichy convoys between West Africa and the South of France also continued with few interruptions, though always liable to be detained and inspected and possibly confiscated by the British. Ships sailing independently were, however, always likely to be seized, especially if they were away from the recognized convoy routes, on the reasonable assumption that they were trying something clandestine. The steamship *Winnipeg*, operating under the Vichy flag, was captured off Martinique in May by a Dutch gunboat. In the same region, on 17 June, the auxiliary cruiser *Pretoria Castle*, one of the armed merchant ships used by the British to patrol distant waters, seized another Vichy ship, *Desirade*. The French islands in the Caribbean were, of course, subject to the British blockade, so any independent ships sailing in the West Indies were generally assumed to be blockade runners, perhaps carrying rubber from South America. A fortnight later, the *Ville de Tamatave* was taken by the cruiser *Dunedin* in the South Atlantic, and on 22 July the same ship captured *Ville de Rouen* off Natal. These were clearly moving goods from Madagascar to Europe.[5]

There is no sign of Vichy replies to these seizures, other than the usual expressions of annoyance, and where possible armed escorts to their convoys were provided, but in November a whole convoy from Madagascar on its way to Indo-China was captured off South Africa. The escorting vessel was permitted to go, but the four civilian ships in the convoy were taken into port.[6] Madagascar was one of the few sources of tropical products still under French control, and it had been blockaded successfully since June 1940. The result had been a drop by three-quarters in the quantity of its exports and a developing support for the Free French amongst the French population of the island.

The island lay athwart the British route from South Africa to India and the Middle East, which made the British particularly nervous about it as tension rose in the Pacific over Japan's ambitions. Japan had already acquired military control of French Indo-China, and had secured naval footholds there, using Camranh Bay and Saigon as naval bases. Should the Vichy governor of Madagascar succumb to the same pressures as the Governor-General of Indo-China, Madagascar might become not merely an unfriendly island, but an active naval base severing the British line of convoy and supply between the Atlantic and their Indian and Southeast Asian territories. The prospect of a pack of U-boats based at the modern fortified port of Diego Suarez at the north end of the island was distinctly unsettling; Italian ships escaping from Somaliland had already been given refuge there.

Vichy's essential problem was that its government was without military, and had little naval power; its situation is a perfect example of the need for armed backing for a government to be listened to. With two-fifths of France under German occupation, with large sections of the empire removed into Gaullist or British control, with a minimal army, and a fleet which was penned into harbour, with a population whose wealth was steadily declining, and with a rising tide of disobedience and resentment and resistance among its people, there was virtually nothing the government could do to delay, prevent, or avoid suffering anything which the British chose to inflict on them. In October the French coaster *Divana* was attacked inside French territorial waters off Tunisia by some British aircraft and driven ashore; nine men were killed. The only response that could be made was to order that such ships should in future be escorted, and attacking aircraft should be fired on.[7] There is no sign that this was ever implemented. The basic cause of the incident was that Italian ships were now permitted by Vichy to use Tunisian ports; these clearly became a legitimate naval target as a result. A fortnight later a dopey Italian submarine (*Dandolo*) sank the tanker *Tarn* outside Algiers harbour (and then went on to sink a Spanish ship – hence 'dopey').[8] There is no sign that the French government reacted. These were the sorts of mistakes which happen in war. The aggrieved party normally protests; the perpetrator either toughs it out or apologizes. But Vichy France could actually do nothing, not having the political clout.

December brought war in the Pacific. De Gaulle declared war on Japan on 8 December, the day after Pearl Harbour, on behalf of Free France. It was also the day after the Japanese invasion of Malaya was launched from Vichy territory in Indo-China. The Vichy government was by that time helpless to affect events within its own Far Eastern territories. The Japanese had extracted so many concessions from Governor-General Decoux, that the Japanese military had effective control of the whole territory by the end of 1941. In addition the Vietnamese nationalists broke out into rebellion in several areas – the Japanese, who had encouraged these revolts, then let the French suppress them – and then the Thais attacked. Despite being defeated, the Thais gained slices of territory because the Japanese insisted. In December 1941 Camranh Bay was the base from which part of the Malayan invasion force sailed, and Saigon was the source from which another section came. No member of the Vichy regime in Indo-China (or in Europe) protested at this misuse of their territory to attack a country with which both France and Japan were at peace.[9]

This permission, even if involuntary, to use French territory in such a way was clearly an unfriendly act – or perhaps non-act – which would normally fully justify a declaration of war by the victim (though it was no worse in essence than the German use of French ports and airfields to attack British ships and cities). No doubt, however, there were grim expressions of near-approval, particularly among French sailors with memories of Mers el-Kebir, but the image of Vichy in collaboration, even alliance, with Japan might have improved had there been at least an apology from a member of the government in France, perhaps pleading *force majeure*.

The British were, of course, unpopular among the French in Indo-China, not simply because of the memories of Mers el-Kebir and Dakar and Syria, but because they had imposed a naval blockade on Indo-China as on all other French overseas territories. The result, as in other regions, was a distinct reduction in the incomes of the planters, which was that part of the local population to which the Governor-General had to pay the most attention. A few ships did get through the blockade, perhaps three per month, a distinct reduction, though since it was a distant blockade, operating in the Indian Ocean and out of Singapore, it was not too difficult to breach it. Compared with other grievances, though, this was quite enough to harden local attitudes against the British and the Free French.

The enforcement of the blockade ended in February 1942 with the Japanese conquest of all the surrounding lands, particularly Singapore, though that scarcely helped the local economic situation, especially since the Japanese practice was simply to seize whatever resources they felt they needed. French Indo-China was thus being immiserated in much the same way as the French homeland, if rather more crudely.

Vichy's control of the French overseas empire thus continued to be whittled away gradually. The Japanese military were in effective control of Indo-China, the British had conquered Syria and now disputed its government with the Free French, the Free French losing the argument. The Free French controlled the Equatorial African colonies and the French outposts in India – Pondicherry and Chandernagore – and most of the islands of the French South Pacific. The entry of Japan into the war now triggered further losses, minor in themselves, but significant in respect of Vichy's general powerlessness. In the South Pacific two islands, Wallis and Futuna, north of Fiji and Samoa, had remained under their pre-war Resident, Vrignaud, who was a convinced Vichyite. The islands were so small and remote that it had not been worth dislodging him. At the same time the general confusion in the other South Pacific islands, notably Tahiti and New Caledonia, had been such that any man who actually was in charge was usually too busy holding on to his post to initiate expeditions. (The only French warship which had been in the region, the sloop *Dumont d'Urville*, had gone to Indo-China, when the Gaullists seized power in New Caledonia, and when the Australian cruiser *Adelaide* arrived.)

The rapid expansion of Japanese power in early 1942, however, put Wallis and Futuna in a particularly delicate position. The Japanese conquests reached to the Solomon Islands to the west and the Marshall Islands to the north. Distances were huge, of course, but so was the reach of carrier fleets, and these islands were separated from Japanese held islands only by the open ocean. Given the apparent co-habitation of the Vichy French in Indo-China with the Japanese military, it was inevitable that any Vichy French islands near to the Japanese conquests were regarded by Australians, New Zealanders, British, and Americans with profound suspicion – and quite possibly by the Japanese as easy targets.

The power in the South Pacific now lay with the United States, which had a strong tendency to ignore local sensibilities in the interest of the wider war, claiming the need to safeguard its own interests without allowing others the same self-interest. (This was much the same behaviour, if less physically brutal, as their Japanese enemies.) The new Gaullist High Commissioner in the South Pacific, Admiral Thierry d'Argenlieu (promoted from commander within the past year – he was an early adherent of de Gaulle), arrived in the region in November 1941 and soon became entangled in the local politics and disputes within the various colonies. Finally realizing just how strong US determination was to control the region he sent a Free French warship to Wallis, and displaced Vrignaud. This was in May 1942, the same month which saw the final conquest of the Philippine Islands, and the first major check to Japanese expansion in the Battle of the Coral Sea. The day after the Gaullist takeover of the two islands, an American force arrived, also intent on removing Vichy influence. Thus Vichy lost two more fragments of its empire, in its long slow death of a thousand cuts.[10]

Germany and Vichy could not agree on a peace treaty, but this was more due to German indifference and general satisfaction with the exploitative conditions produced by the armistice than to any French resistance. (The US aim of managing Vichy's independence could not work.) As with the Japanese in Indo-China German power meant that it was always possible for the Nazis to compel the French to give more. In the Protocols of May 1941 the use of Syrian airfields had been conceded – with disastrous results for Vichy's empire – and while German use of Bizerta and Dakar was contested at the time, by October and November Tunisia had become a regular supply route and base for the German and Italian forces fighting in Libya – with fatal results for the *Divana*.[11] This was, of course, as unfriendly and un-neutral an act as permitting Indo-China to be used as a base for the invasion of Malaya – but it was similarly something Vichy was incapable in the end of preventing. Had the British wished, they had received ample provocation which would justify their declaring war.

The relations of the United States with the Free French were curiously unpleasant. This was despite the gradual souring of US relations with Vichy, which should have brought the United States to appreciate the existence of Free France. The United States had deliberately maintained a diplomatic presence in Vichy, sending President Roosevelt's friend Admiral William Leahy there as ambassador in December 1940 with the explicit purpose of restraining Vichy from too ready an accommodation with Germany. The United States had also attempted to maintain its influence in Vichy by deliveries of food, which went to Morocco in Vichy ships direct from the United States. The British generally allowed these ships to pass their blockade.[12]

In late 1941 German pressure was exerted on Admiral Darlan's government to remove General Weygand from his position as Delegate-General in North Africa. The Germans recognized that Weygand was a major obstacle in the way of their penetration of the region. Already, they had had to struggle to get the use of Tunisian space, and to get German 'inspection teams' into Morocco – they had to wear civilian clothes, and, as the French had expected they would, they stirred up trouble amongst the Moroccans. Darlan certainly resisted these demands, but in the end had no choice but to do what the Germans wanted. In the end Weygand was removed and brought back to mainland France in November 1941. This was clearly yet another concession by Vichy to Germany, and was seen by the United States as a decisive change in German-Vichy relations, one which opened the Vichy empire to German exploitation.[13] The immediate result was that the British were told of the sailing of two Vichy food ships from New York for Casablanca, an item of information which indicated that they were to be seen as blockade runners rather than charitable donations by the United States.[14]

And yet the gradual US estrangement from Vichy did not produce a warming towards the Free French. This was in part because of de Gaulle's apparent arrogance, but also of President Roosevelt's instant dislike of him. It is, indeed, difficult to conceive of two more inevitably antagonistic personalities than Franklin Roosevelt and Charles de Gaulle. De Gaulle's prickliness and arrogance was, of course, the product of his lack of power. In no other way could he make himself heard, but by demanding, and at times obtaining, the respect due to France as a Great Power and himself as France's representative and embodiment. Yet that powerlessness also led to him, paradoxically, being regarded in the US as a British puppet.

Behind it all was the long-standing US aversion to the European empires, including Britain's, an aversion now extended to Japan's, and reconfirmed by the hideousness of the new German Empire. And de Gaulle was determined, as the British knew all too well, to maintain the French Empire – just as determined as Churchill was to maintain the British. (Just as determined as Roosevelt was to extend the US Empire.) Further, de Gaulle was also seen as being allied to unsavoury elements in France, such as the communists. (The French Communists had, of course, suddenly sprung into opposition to Germany on 22 June 1941.) This distancing of themselves from both French factions led to two results in the US administration: the eventual search for a third French alternative, for some Frenchman who was not Pétain or Darlan and was not de Gaulle, and it led the United States government to lay itself open to British strategic thinking.

There was one particular incident which decisively soured the United States' attitudes towards the Free French, and led to several years of almost overt hostility. The islands of St Pierre and Miquelon in the Gulf of St Lawrence had remained under their Vichy administrator Gilbert de Bournat since before 1940. He had considerable local support, though it was not unanimous, and the presence of the sloop *Ville d'Ys* gave him the decisive edge. He also had a short wave radio station with which he could contact Vichy, and through which weather reports (a crucial matter for the Atlantic war) were sent. It was also assumed that details of convoys, insofar as they could be known in these islands, would also be radioed, and that such information would go to the Germans, whose U-boat headquarters were, of course, at Lorient. Whether all these assumptions were correct or not, it was becoming necessary, just to be sure, to shut down that radio station. In December 1941 the Canadian government began careful negotiations with de Bournat to do so.[15]

De Bournat in fact was a subordinate, technically at least, of Admiral Georges Robert, the Vichy ruler of the French Caribbean islands. Robert's situation had been frozen by US intervention since 1940, and this was reinforced by a new agreement concluded between Robert and Admiral Horne of the United States Navy on 17 December 1941. (The United States now being in the war with both Germany and Japan, the exclusion of any German influence from the Caribbean was now not just preferable, but also necessary.) So by December both the United States and Canada were carefully moving towards a relatively gentle form of the suppression of Vichy influence anywhere in the Americas. There was also the Inter-American agreement of 1940 in which all the American states agreed not to permit any of the European colonial territories in the Americas to change hands. This was actually directed at Germany after the defeat of France, just in case a peace treaty included German acquisitions of French territories, but it was also used to block internal changes from Vichy to Free France within the French colonies as well. It was, of course, an item in the continuing US domination of both American continents, the old imperialist Monroe Doctrine being wheeled out in supposed justification.

Into this web of treaties and understandings and nods and winks, General de Gaulle drove a trio of warships. The Free French had been allocated three corvettes by the Canadian Navy, which they named *Aconit*, *Alysse* and *Mimose*, to be employed as escorts on the Atlantic convoy routes. It had been proposed that they be used by the Free French to seize St Pierre and Miquelon, one of the alternative policies which were being considered for dealing with the islands. The British had liked the idea, but, this being America, had raised it with the United States government. Roosevelt personally expressed opposition, so Churchill told the Free French, who agreed not to proceed.

Despite this the Free French naval commander, Vice-Admiral Emile Muselier, used the ships to take control of the two islands from de Bournat. It was done quietly, without casualties on Christmas Eve 1941. (It may also have been done on Muselier's own initiative, for he was an ambitious man, and did not at all agree with de Gaulle.) The *coup* was confirmed by a hastily organized referendum two days later, though many of the ballots were spoiled, presumably in protest at the Free French *coup*, and the questions were loaded.

In their reactions to the *coup* the publics and the governments of the Allies diverged. The public in Britain and the United States generally saw Muselier's deed as a stroke of liberation, for Vichy was by now popularly presumed to be aligned firmly with Germany and Japan and to be similarly oppressive to its subjects; the governments, however, were annoyed that their own schemes had been derailed. They claimed that there would be unpleasant consequences, pointing particularly to North Africa, which is just about the only place any new direct German reaction could happen. Actually nothing happened other than some annoyed rhetoric from Vichy. This soon died away, but the United States was confirmed in its dislike of both de Gaulle and the Free French.

The British, on the other hand, remained broadly supportive of Free France, despite de Gaulle's difficult temperament. At the same time, it was clear that no more armed expeditions would be conducted with Free French involvement. This St Pierre episode was minor, but its repercussions were unpleasant. The reason the Americans were annoyed more than anything else was that de Gaulle was perceived as having broken his word. For the British, who were more indulgent towards him, and more understanding of his difficult situation, and had invested much more in building him up, even all this was not enough to cancel out the uselessness of Free French at Dakar, the embarrassment and awkwardness of the Free French in Syria, and the lack of security awareness at both places. The clumsiness of Admiral Muselier at St Pierre imperilled British relations with the United States, which was always the overriding concern of Churchill, and if the United States was antagonistic to Free France, then Free France must be sidelined. On the other hand, it was evident, from information coming out of France by a variety of means, that de Gaulle and his Free French now did have a substantial body of popular support in the country. It was not organized, and it might well be utterly superficial and ephemeral. It might also be the result of the fact that there was no one else who was so active in his opposition to Nazi control of France and so he automatically attracted the support of Vichy's opponents. But it did mean that the vaunted support for Vichy – which the Americans still accepted well into 1943 – was actually hollow, and was based above all on nothing more than that the Pétainist regime was a government, and thereby exercised control over both the country and the sources of information.

The fact remained, however, that no matter what the attitudes of the French population, the people were very largely working to support the Vichy regime, and the Vichy regime was being exploited by the Germans to extract considerable resources for the use of the German forces. These included manufactures, food and labour. The factories which had produced armaments for the French Army and Air Force were now producing the same for the *Wehrmacht* and the *Luftwaffe*. The installations at the Atlantic ports, where the U-boats were serviced and provisioned and prepared and sheltered, were built by French companies, who employed French workers under contract from the German state. These companies, and what they made, were therefore quite legitimate military targets. The bombing of the Atlantic ports continued.

In March 1942 British programme of bombing industrial targets was extended to mainland France. The German military and naval targets had long been intermittently bombed – Brest, Cherbourg, and so on – but it was now clear that the industries of France were fully harnessed to German war production. On 3/4 March the giant Renault car and truck works at Boulogne-Billancourt in the suburbs of Paris was bombed by 236 aircraft. The factory was badly damaged, though by no means obliterated, and considerable numbers of French workers died. Production was disrupted, but not by any means stopped. The reaction amongst the Parisians was not the anger which the Germans and Vichy expected and hoped for; perhaps they had a right to expect it, after the reaction to Mers el-Kebir. Instead there was a general atmosphere of resignation and acceptance, which disconcerted Vichy thoroughly. It implied a deep dislike of the Vichy regime by the Parisian population – and, of course, it pushed the Vichy leaders even more into the embrace of Nazi Germany. A number of other French targets in the military area were also attacked in March, though these raids were much smaller in scale, involving a couple of dozen bombers escorted by a large number of fighters, the aim being as much to try and defeat German fighter attacks as to bomb specific targets.[16]

There was one particular installation which concerned the British above all others in early 1942. This was the great dock built at St Nazaire into which the grand French liner *Normandie* could go. It was the only dock of its size in Western Europe accessible to a German ship from the Atlantic, and it was there or Brest, that the *Bismarck* had been heading for when it was sunk. And now *Bismarck* had a sister, just as large, powerful, and threatening – *Tirpitz*.

The ship was employed in the Baltic for a time, but then came out to Norway in January 1942. Positioned at Trondheim *Tirpitz* was a standing threat to the convoys which were being organized to carry war materials supplied by Britain and the United States to Russia, and beyond these it was a threat to the Atlantic convoy routes as well, which were already under serious pressure from German submarines. If *Tirpitz* carried out the same sort of cruise as *Bismarck* had attempted, the obvious docking and repairing port for the end of the cruise was, again, either Brest or St Nazaire – and only St Nazaire had a dock big enough for the ship to be dry-docked for inspection and repair.

This was a construction of which the French were very proud – as was the ship it had served, even if *Normandie* was a burned-out wreck in New York by then. It also lay six miles inland on the north shore of the Loire, and was surrounded by the town of St Nazaire. The destruction of the dock was clearly a task for Combined Operations and the Commandos, and the task was made the more urgent by the first sortie by *Tirpitz* on 5 March against an Arctic convoy. The ship was clearly fully capable and operational, and attempts by bombers and submarines to damage or sink it had all failed.

The attack on the dock at St Nazaire went in on the night of 27 March. The old destroyer *Campbeltown* (the former USS *Buchanan*) had been converted into a giant ram, its bow heavily reinforced with a great concrete plug. Escorted by nineteen motor torpedo boats and motor launches, the ship reached and rammed the dock gates. Commandos landed, stormed the docks and set about destroying the gates and the winding houses. A German counter-attack, together with heavy fire from the coastal defences, killed or captured all the commandos and most of the sailors. Only four of the nineteen boats got away. A quarter of the assaulting forces were killed. Next day the ship exploded as it was being gloated over by many of the Germans, when a delayed action fuse operated. The dock was wrecked, as intended.[17]

The Germans were considerably shocked by the surprise and the violence of the assault. They suspected that many of the commandos and sailors had survived and were hidden in the town (though in fact the attacking forces were fewer than they imagined, and many of those not accounted for were in the river, either dead or trying to escape). They began to search the town. The great explosion shocked and unnerved them further, and two later explosions (delayed action torpedoes in the winding houses) made them even more nervous and angry. What else might happen if the missing British were not found?

In the meantime the reaction of the French inhabitants was similarly nervous, if somewhat less angry. Some thought that the liberating invasion had started and got out their hidden guns to join in. Some of the British really had got into the town and were hidden – several escaped from the town and five of them reached Spain. The Germans began firing at anyone and anything – including each other – and the more the firing went on the more frightened they became. In the morning they arrested over 1,200 French people in the old town of St Nazaire and put them into a camp as prisoners, threatening mass murders. (They had already begun the practice of shooting batches of hostages in revenge for the murder of German officers – one case had happened a few months earlier at Nantes nearby.)

St Nazaire was one of the places where forced labour contracted to French construction firms had been used to build U-boat pens. There were also important factories in the town, producing, for example, aircraft, which had been the scenes of strikes already against bad food, low pay, inflation – in short a series of complaints against the effects of the occupation. The reaction of the population had shown clearly enough that the people, in this town at least, were wholly unreconciled to the situation they were in.[18] The Vichy regime was as unpopular by its association with the oppressive Germans in St Nazaire as the Renault raid had demonstrated was the case in Paris.

It was perhaps only coincidence, or perhaps not, that it was just at this time that pressure was being exerted by the Germans on Marshal Pétain to replace Darlan as his Vice-Premier. This eventually succeeded, and he was replaced by Pierre Laval, who pursued the policy of collaboration with ever greater keenness. Darlan, however, remained as commander-in-chief of the armed forces, and Laval's policy was really only an intensification of that which Darlan had pursued. The new government had been opposed by the United States, who did not like the appointment of Laval in particular. His appointment led directly to the recall of Admiral Leahy from the United States embassy, leaving Vichy wholly entwined in Germany's grip.[19]

The reactions in France to the increasing pressure which came from both Germans and Allies were, as one would expect, various. Those convinced of the probability of victory for either side felt that either collaboration or resistance was the best attitude to adopt. These convictions applied to only a small part of the population, however. Most people simply endured. There were demonstrations against German demands, as in the strikes at St Nazaire, and there were demonstrations against Allied raids, as in a large one in Toulouse in early April. What was clear was that the pressure from both sides would certainly continue, and increase. For the French there was no end in sight.

This was confirmed later in the year by more raids by the British. In August a major part of the Canadian Division which had been in Britain since 1939, plus 1,000 commandos, attacked Dieppe. But their general purpose had become known, their approach was revealed by a preliminary encounter with a German convoy, and the landing went in against very strong opposition. On the continent many in Germany and France chose to believe that the defeat at Dieppe was the defeat of the campaign of liberation. In Dieppe itself the heavy German presence had inhibited any possible rising to assist the invaders – Hitler released the prisoners of war he still held from the town as a gesture of thanks, a double-edged compliment if ever there was one. At Vichy the reaction was one of relief that the apparent invasion had failed, and the Marshal tried to use it as a means of extracting concessions from the Germans. There was no reply to his letter, but the Vichy reaction demonstrated very clearly that the regime fully aligned itself, almost fawningly, with their Nazi conquerors.[20]

Of course, it soon became clear that this had not been the great invasion. A more ominous harbinger was the air raid two months later on the Schneider-Creuzot armaments plant at Le Creuzot, which was attacked by a large force of Lancaster bombers. As usual the aircrews believed that they had hit the target; as usual photographic reconnaissance showed that they had not.[21] But if a plant in eastern France could be attacked, no part of France was immune.

These two raids made it clear that in all likelihood France would be the land through which the Allies would attack Germany, and that this would be done by means of a landing somewhere along the English Channel coast. It was also clear that this would be very difficult. Meanwhile any major industrial plant was a target for the RAF, and the Vichy Empire was steadily being removed from Vichy's control.

By this time, a year after the loss of Syria to the British and the Free French, that empire had diminished still further. It could no longer be said that Vichy had any control over French Indo-China, the Caribbean islands were under even greater US control, and the two Canadian islands had gone to the Free French. Negotiations had also been going on between the Vichy authorities in Djibouti and the British commands in Egypt and East Africa, with a view to surrendering the colony, though the British saw no urgency, and let the colony linger on. And now Vichy could no longer defend its home territory, even under the protection of the German garrison. If the armistice had been intended to secure metropolitan France from further damage from warfare, the raids on St Nazaire and Dieppe and the air raids on Paris and Le Creuzot showed that it no longer did so. And by this time also, the last of the major overseas territories except North Africa, Madagascar, had also gone.

Chapter 10

Madagascar: Diego Suarez

The strategic importance of the great island of Madagascar in the Indian Ocean was only minor until the Japanese conquests in eastern Asia. Until the end of 1941 the only interest it had provoked was as the object of a successful British naval blockade and a few, rather tentative, Free French suggestions that, with lots of British air and naval support, a few French battalions landing at, say, Majungo, would no doubt induce a mass defection from Vichy to Free France among the population.[1]

After their earlier experiences, at Dakar and Syria, this idea was taken by the British with a pinch of salt. But the United States began to show an interest in buying the strategic materials produced on the island; mica, graphite, some metal ores and animal hides. The idea was to conclude an inter-governmental agreement between the United States and the Vichy authorities in Madagascar which would give exclusive rights of purchase in those materials to the United States. This would at least provide the island with an income in foreign currency, but it would also clearly breach the British blockade – not to mention pre-empting any British purchases. It was therefore put aside. It would also have blocked any attempt by the Free French to take over the island, for the political effect of such an agreement would have been to provide US protection to the Vichy regime there.[2]

It may have been in part this sort of US interest – or interference – in what the British tended to think of as 'their' Indian Ocean, which spurred on a British plan to seize the island. The justification later was that it might well form a base for Japanese forces, particularly for the fleet or for submarines. At the north end of the island, Diego Suarez was a very useful port, and one which had been fortified as recently as the 1930s. It was capacious enough to hold a large fleet, though the facilities were less useful. When the British plans were being made, however, at the beginning of 1942, the Japanese were still a long way off, and pre-empting both the United States and the Free

French must have looked to be a good idea in itself. As the Japanese came further west, however, the strategic justification grew more convincing.

The Japanese conquered Malaya in December 1941 and January 1942, and took Singapore in the first half of February 1942; a month later all the Dutch East Indies had fallen and the invasion of Burma was under way. From Timor to Rangoon, Japanese forces controlled all the eastern coasts and islands of the Indian Ocean. From Washington came word by way of Admiral Leahy at Vichy that if the Japanese forces menaced Madagascar, the Vichy government would ask for US help to keep them out. But in early 1942 this was scarcely a practical proposition given the current relative power of the two antagonists. The US Navy was fully occupied in the Pacific, and its army was as yet unequipped for any campaign.

Pétain and Darlan both insisted that any Japanese incursion would be resisted. These assurances were dismissed by the British, for it was not promises of possible resistance to potential attacks which were being looked for, but Vichy's track record. The Japanese had taken over Indo China without any noticeable resistance from the French, the Germans were exploiting France itself and steadily expanding their use of North Africa, and both of these were clearly happening with Vichy's acquiescence, even encouragement – and in Syria similar promises had been broken.

Early in March 1942 the War Cabinet in London decided that a possible Japanese acquisition of all or part of Madagascar was not something which could be allowed to happen, so the island would be taken over. This was the second most important military priority for the British, after the defence of Ceylon.[3] A landing was to be organized, and no Free French participation was to be allowed. The forces were found, including some which would stop off to invade the island on their way to India. Free French officers who might know or find out about all this were pinned down in Britain by refusing them transport facilities.

The advance of the Japanese into Burma meant that the Indian army was fully occupied, so the expedition had to come from Britain. Normally in the past any expedition in the Indian Ocean or the Pacific would have been mounted from India. Indian troops had recently fought in the Middle East – in Iraq and Iran and the Egyptian Western Desert. They had also fought in the past in East Africa, in China and in Malaya, and considerable numbers of Indian troops were captured in Singapore. But the arrival of the formidable Japanese meant that the defence of India now had the first call on the Indian army, so troops for Madagascar had to be found in Britain. This was not an easy task given the widespread calls on British manpower.

On 23 March a convoy set out from Britain carrying the 5th Infantry Division, which had originally been intended for India anyway, and was now to stop off at Madagascar to assist with the invasion of the island. The most important unit in the convoy, however, was the 29 Independent Brigade, which had been specially trained in making an opposed landing from the sea. To the brigade were added 5 Commando, a squadron of antiquated and light tanks, Valentines and Tetrarchs, an artillery battery and an anti-aircraft gun troop. It was intended that only one brigade of 5th Division would be used in Madagascar, and the other brigades were to go on to India without pausing. On the other hand, the commanders would know that these troops were nearby in case of need. The invasion force was thus to be seven battalions strong, with the tanks and artillery added.

The convoy reached Freetown in Sierra Leone on 6 April, where it was joined by Force H from Gibraltar which was to provide some of the naval escort and the covering force for the landing. Its presence did not in fact mean that the western Mediterranean now lacked a naval presence. This had been achieved by a complex set of moves rather like a line of naval dominoes. President Roosevelt had been persuaded that it would be a good idea to have some US ships operating with the Home Fleet out of Scapa Flow, whose task in 1942 was largely to cover the Arctic convoys to Russia, and to keep a weather eye open for any movement by *Tirpitz*. The commitment of the US to the German war was thereby to be made clear to everyone. The US Navy sent over to the great base at Scapa Flow the battleship *Washington*, the carrier *Wasp*, two cruisers, and eight destroyers. This was a major reinforcement for the Home Fleet.

The Admiralty was now able to send some of the Home Fleet to Gibraltar, and thus to dispatch part of Force H, under its new commander Rear-Admiral E.N. Syfret, to escort the Madagascar convoy. So the convoy was met at Freetown by the battleship *Malaya*, the carrier *Illustrious*, the cruiser *Hermione*, and attendant destroyers. It is a measure of how stretched the British forces were by this time that these moves had to be made, for there was no spare naval capacity available for this expedition, just as the only dedicated army unit which could be spared was a single brigade. It is worth noting that Britain had military and naval commitments throughout the world – India, Burma, the Pacific, the Middle East, the Atlantic, the Indian Ocean, and of course Britain, and that its military forces had been reduced by several tens of thousands of men as a result of the Japanese victories – no other power had such a wide spread of responsibility. It was, of course, the consequence of having an empire, and being the only remaining world power.

The prospect or possibility of a Japanese presence in Madagascar had not failed to interest others. The German naval Commander-in-Chief Erich Raeder had spotted the Japanese opportunity; the South African Prime

Minister Jan Christian Smuts had done so as well, particularly when prompted by the arrival of a Free French colonel, Zinovi Pechkoff, with sharp questions. Smuts in fact was useful, for he was a friend of Churchill's, and an *ex officio* member of the War Cabinet. He was wary of too great a US presence in his area, and he had, even before the arrival of de Gaulle's colonel, pointed to Madagascar as a problem in messages to Churchill. Further, he was skilled enough in political matters to string the colonel along without letting him know too much about the British intentions. It was regarded as essential that the Free French be kept in ignorance of what the British planned: there were to be no more security lapses; the lesson of Syria and Dakar had been that Vichy forces fought exceptionally fiercely when attacked by Gaullists.

The Japanese fleet of carriers and battleships which had raided Pearl Harbour, the 1 Carrier Fleet commanded by Vice-Admiral Chuichi Nagumo, had cruised with tremendous effect through the South Pacific and the Indonesian islands, raiding Rabaul in the Solomon Islands and Darwin in Australia, and encouraging and assisting in the conquest of the Dutch East Indies. As the British Madagascar convoy ('Operation Ironclad') was sailing through the central Atlantic towards Freetown, Nagumo's force came through the Indonesian islands into the Indian Ocean. He had five carriers and four fast battleships with attendant cruisers and destroyers and submarines, and this force spent 5 to 9 April in raiding Ceylon, while a subsidiary cruiser force carried out commerce-raiding in the Bay of Bengal, and a transport convoy moved an army to land at Rangoon in Burma. When the Japanese soon afterwards occupied the Andaman and Nicobar Islands in the Bay of Bengal they were halfway along the sea route from Singapore to Ceylon.[4]

The British Eastern Fleet, now under the command of Admiral Somerville, formerly of Force H, was substantially out-numbered, and it was kept well away from Nagumo's fleet. Several ships, including the small carrier *Hermes*, were sunk, and Colombo in Ceylon suffered a nasty air raid, but after 9 April Nagumo withdrew eastwards through the Strait of Malacca to, ironically, Singapore.[5] This brief but destructive sortie frightened the British very badly. For a time it looked as though Ceylon would be invaded, and if Ceylon was lost, the Japanese would control the waters on both the east and west of India – and Madagascar would be, if strategic thinking was well conducted in Japan, the next target for Nagumo's fleet.

Madagascar's importance partly consisted in its geographical position, but this was enhanced because it contained the capacious natural deep water port of Diego Suarez at its northern end, a harbour big enough to hold Admiral Nagumo's whole fleet and have room to spare. If he was based there and at Ceylon, the British hold on India and the Middle East would be badly threatened since both relied to some extent on supplies sent from Britain by the Indian Ocean route. India, already the scene of substantial unrest, could well be lost, or at least become a large battleground. The Japanese could well attack the Suez Canal by sea from the Indian Ocean side, and this was the very time when General Rommel was pushing hard at the Eighth Army, which would soon be driven back to within 200 miles of Alexandria. It was perhaps fortunate that neither Germany nor Japan ever showed much interest in co-operating with each other.

But the great Japanese force withdrew. One of the reasons was presumably because Nagumo had been unable to locate Admiral Somerville's British Eastern Fleet. No doubt it withdrew also because the Japanese forces were so spread out by now that further operations had become virtually impossible, and re-supply and maintenance were needed. Conquests had to be consolidated, ships serviced and maintained, and celebrations conducted. The Japanese, in fact, no more than six months into the war, were already facing the problem of overstretch, and were soon to be fighting in Burma, the Solomons, and the Pacific, as well as China.

So when the Ironclad convoy and the Force H warships met at Freetown on 9 April – the day that Nagumo's fleet began withdrawing eastwards – and the commanders, Rear-Admiral Neville Syfret, a South African, and Major-General Robert Sturges, set about discussing plans and timings, they would have learned that the great carrier force had turned away. Having dissembled some misinformation about their destination, the joint force sailed on to South Africa, where *Malaya* turned back, and on 4 May the convoy and its escort arrived off Diego Suarez in the north of Madagascar.

One of the conclusions reached in the discussions at Freetown had been that, to be on the safe side, another brigade out of 5th Division was needed for the Madagascar force, and at Durban agreement to use this arrived, so 13 Brigade was detailed for the landing, as well as 17 Brigade. 13 Brigade's shipping had therefore to be rearranged to make its contents for landing useful, a lesson of Norway and Dakar. The two brigades from the division now allocated were also given some instruction in landing techniques, though it was intended that 29 Independent Brigade would lead the way at the initial landings. In the back of the minds of everyone involved were the problems thrown up in Norway and at Dakar – Dakar in particular was recalled, for the landing at Diego Suarez was also to be at a fortified port held by Vichy forces.

One thing which did not differ from the Dakar preparations was that the Vichy forces in Madagascar were underestimated. The number of troops on the island – 8,000 – was correctly estimated (the Special Operations Executive had agents on the island) but, since they were three quarters recruited from the Malagasy population, it was assumed that they would not fight well. One would have thought that one of the lessons of Dakar and Syria was that France's 'native' troops fought fully as well and skilfully and staunchly as did those recruited by the British. The British, after all, were enormously proud of their Indian regiments.

In a conference at Cape Town between Prime Minister Smuts and the commanders of the invasion force, Admiral Syfret and General Sturges, the point had been made by Smuts that Diego Suarez was only one of several places on the Madagascar coastline which were useful as naval bases – Majunga and Tamatave were mentioned in particular. Smuts, of course, was especially worried that Japanese forces might arrive on South Africa's own doorstep, and South Africa's racial environment was tailor-made for Japanese propaganda to be effective. Smuts suggested that it would be sensible to seize these places as well. He undertook to ask the War Cabinet to add them to the list, but in the end the decision was left to the commanders, who sensibly decided to take on only one place at a time – though it was a sign that the single harbour of Diego Suarez, no matter how useful and distinctive, was only part of the island, and that, if the whole island was to be refused to the Japanese, the whole island would have to be occupied.

In the back of the commanders' minds, of course, was the same hope which had animated every commander involved in every one of the incidents of this Franco-British war: that the Vichy French supporters were clearly deluded, or were really closet Gaullists to a man, that it would not take much to bring them to see the light, and that once the British got ashore the whole edifice of Vichy control would cave in. It was a version of the Free French creed, but the British had learned the hard way (Dakar, Syria) that it was well to separate the military and political elements of an operation such as this, and to be fully prepared for strong resistance. So, although the British commanders hoped that the Vichy people would come over without making difficulties, they were not prepared to take a chance on it. Consequently the military operation would go in no matter what political hopes there might be – that is, as though entering enemy country. Once firmly ashore, victorious, and in control of the essential place, Diego Suarez, then the political negotiations could begin and surrenders would be welcome.

Besides the detachment of the Vichy army which were in the island, there were a number of naval vessels in Diego Suarez when the British forces arrived. In another echo of Dakar, the submarine *Bévéziers* was one of them, and there were four more submarines with her, which had arrived from France by way of Dakar months before. There were also two sloops, *D'Entrecasteaux* and *D'Iberville*, and two auxiliary cruisers. These ships, especially the submarines, were not to be underestimated, as Dakar had also shown. The British Eastern Fleet, having evaded any contact with the Japanese carriers, provided further secure cover for the landings, in the form of the carrier *Indomitable* and two destroyers; the cruiser *Devonshire*, three destroyers, a minesweeping flotilla, and an escort group had also been added in South Africa. The naval force now comprised one battleship, two carriers, two cruisers, eleven destroyers, eight corvettes, and four minesweepers. Clearly another lesson had been learned from previous expeditions: that no landing force can be too large, no matter how easy the conquest looks, and no covering force should be less than overwhelming. Apart from the opposing ships and troops, the Vichy forces included a number of aircraft, both fighters and bombers, and there were several airfields they could use, including one close to Diego Suarez – hence the two carriers.

Another lesson from Dakar was that there needed to be specialized landing craft, especially for vehicles. Churchill had pointed this out on seeing the report of the Dakar misadventures. Landings from the sea were invariably made on to the beach, not at docks, for places with docks were defended, and a successful landing is one in which no casualties are taken. It was, of course, not intended to land actually at Diego Suarez, but some distance away, and to get the vehicles to shore would need a properly designed ship.

One of these was with the expedition. The need had been for a ship with a wide hold, unroofed, which would hold the vehicles, and having a very shallow draught to allow it to get close to the shore, and so be able to put its vehicles directly on to the shore. It had not been necessary to actually design a new ship, only to find one which was already built with the basic capabilities which were required. Tankers had the required design, if one took off the deck, and one particular type, which needed a shallow draught to get it over the bar at Maracaibo in Venezuela, was clearly adaptable. There was one with the Madagascar expedition, SS *Bachaquero*, but she carried trucks not tanks. The weight of the tanks would be far too much for the ship's construction to support, so this ship's participation was in the nature of an experiment. A properly adapted design, with a stronger keel, and so able to carry tanks, would come later.

The target of the invasion, Diego Suarez, was at the northern tip of the island. A northward pointing peninsula formed bays to east and west. Courrier Bay and Ambararata Bay lay to the west; to the east a larger area was much divided by peninsulas and narrow passages into several bays, which were connected to the ocean through the Orangea Strait, a little more than a mile wide. This was overlooked from the south by five artillery batteries ranged around Orangea Headland. The entrance to Diego Suarez Bay itself, one of those leading off Orangea Strait, was another narrow passage, flanked by the town of Antsirane on the south and the village of Diego Suarez on the north, and both sides were fortified by other batteries facing out into the bay.

Antsirane, a town which essentially served the military and naval base, was also fortified on the south side, towards the mainland, by two forts and a linking line of well-made trenches. Altogether it was a formidable obstacle, intended to be defended from the land and the sea, though it is clear that most attention was given to the possibility of the seaborne attack.

The answer to such fortifications is, of course, to evade them. This time there was to be no preliminary warning, no flags of truce, no assumptions that because the enemy was French the troops and officials were really friendly and would give in easily – though during the fighting this attitude did tend to resurface at times. Instead of the sort of frontal assault under-taken at Dakar and in Syria, the landing of the British forces took place at Courrier Bay, which was overlooked, it was thought, by only two batteries and an observation post, and was several miles from the town and its troops. The reason for the neglect of providing for a serious defence here was that the Bay was protected by a number of awkward islands which made entrance from the open sea difficult, and these had been supplemented by floating mines, which did in fact cause difficulties. But the Royal Navy was adept at such problems, and it is the essence of a successful strategy to do the un-expected. Military history is littered with examples of attacks at neglected places providing a means to victory for the enemy.

The night of 5 May was a full moon, which allowed the landing forces to approach during the dark hours in relative safety and with adequate visibility. The minesweepers went in first, detonating and removing the mines, and the landing vessels followed, navigated carefully with skill and persistence. The landing beaches had been designated, from north to south, as Red, Blue, White in Courrier Bay, and Green in Ambararata Bay. 5 Commando landed first at the three Red beaches, which were supposedly covered by a French battery sited a little way inland. Despite the explosions of the mines and the noise the ships must have made, the landing was not noticed, and the battery was captured while the troops were still asleep, and it turned out that the other expected battery did not exist.

The other landings were almost as smoothly performed. At Blue beach the 2 East Lancashires were briefly opposed by a group of Senegalese riflemen, who were awake this time, but at White and Green beaches the 2 Royal Welch Fusiliers and the 1 Royal Scots Fusiliers landed with no opponents within sight or sound. By dawn, therefore, all the initial landings had been successful.

The second stage at the landing sites was to bring the heavy equipment, tanks, trucks, guns and so on, ashore. The original plan had been to wait until this was completed before moving against the town, but General Sturges demanded that exploitation of the initial landing should begin as soon as possible, and that the mobile equipment should follow the advancing infantry once it was ashore. So the infantry advance went ahead while the vehicles were still arriving, and the soldiers pushed on as quickly as possible towards Diego Suarez and Antsirane.

This stage also included activity at sea and in the air. At sea to the east of Diego Suarez the cruiser *Hermione* put on a display of deception, including setting out smoke floats to simulate a large number of ships, and shelling the batteries on Orangea Headland, all intended to distract Vichy attention from events at Courrier Bay. In the air, as soon as it was light, leaflet raids were made on Antsirane enjoining no resistance, but these were accompanied by a rather more convincing display – an air raid on Antsirane airfield which left the hangars and their sheltering planes on fire and other planes on the ground damaged. There was no French air activity at all in the next days, and hardly any during the rest of the campaign on the island. This raid was accompanied also by another deception, a parachute drop of dummies carried out in plain sight, which convinced many that the town was now cut off by land.

The leaflet raid on the town produced another avowal from the commander of the Vichy forces in the town to fight to the very end. By this time this sort of announcement was generally understood to mean that the man issuing it was facing imminent defeat and was unsure of the loyalty and the abilities of his troops. French commanders were especially prone to such statements – several more will be noted in his campaign. (And they usually insisted on being awarded the honours of war when they surrendered, and if this was refused they tended to fight on uselessly; most British commanders were sufficiently pragmatic to agree, so long as the fighting stopped.) The Governor-General of Madagascar, Paul Annet, was similarly defiant, though he was far off in the island's capital Tananarive, several hundred miles away, and his only contribution was words expressing outrage and enjoining resistance 'to the end'.

The aircraft from *Indomitable* carried out the raids on the airfield, and those from *Illustrious* concentrated on the ships in the harbour, dropping a mixture of bombs, depth charges, and torpedoes. The result was that the submarine *Bévéziers* was sunk, and the sloop *D'Entrecasteaux* was set on fire; the latter was run ashore north of the Diego Suarez and the fire was extinguished. The auxiliary cruiser *Bougainville* was sunk. This did not finish off the naval ships based in the harbour, but it certainly had a powerful effect onshore. In Courrier Bay the British corvette *Auricula* hit a mine which had been missed by the minesweeping flotilla and was sunk.

So, within the first few hours the Vichy air wing had been effectively destroyed and its naval strength was badly damaged. Meanwhile, 5 Commando had marched across the base of the peninsula, a distance of ten miles or so, and had captured the village of Diego Suarez by 4.30 pm. They had met only sporadic and weak resistance, capturing twenty-three French and 200 Malagasy soldiers at the barracks of the battery, and on the way. These surrenders, usually by small groups, were not surprising in the face of the locally over-whelming strength of the commandos.

The larger force which had been put ashore, the East Lancashires, the Royal Welch Fusiliers, and the Royal Scots Fusiliers, were joined during the day by the 2 South Lancashire battalion and the tanks. This force, which was much larger, of course, than the Commando, had a longer and more difficult journey to attack Antsirane. It turned out that there was another line of fortification before the main line in front of the town, pillboxes and machine guns on a line of hills called the Col de Bonne Nouvelle. This held the attackers up for much of the day and was eventually cut through by the tanks and taken in the flank by the Welch Fusiliers. The tanks – a mixture of Valentines and Tetrarchs, neither type of any great weight – then moved forward towards the main defence line, which consisted of Forts Caimans and Bellevue connected by a well-made trench line. It was also supported by well-served field guns, which succeeded in destroying or crippling most of the tanks during the next couple of hours. The tanks had been sent forward unsupported, very much in the same way as was being done in the western desert, and with much the same disastrous results.

The attack on the main fortification line was thus necessarily left to the infantry, though it was supported, when they moved forward, by the guns which had been brought along from the landing place. An initial attack in the late afternoon failed. A night attack was then organized, by which the South Lancashires were to pass round Fort Bellevue along the eastern shore, where there was a gap between the fortifications and the sea, and then attack the flank of the French trench line at the same time as another frontal attack upon the main line would be made by the rest of the infantry.

This did not actually work. The South Lancashires succeeded in getting behind the French line, but they became disorganized in the process, so that smaller sections operated independently behind the lines. This succeeded in creating much confusion among the French, but they did not do so at the time intended, and did not manage to communicate what they were doing to the brigade headquarters, since all their radio sets failed to work. So the frontal attack by the rest of the infantry failed again. Another part of the grand plan, whereby 5 Commando would cross the strait from Diego Suarez to land in Antsirane from the sea, also failed, because the commandos could find no boats. It seemed like a stalemate – though the activities of the South Lancashires' 'guerrilla groups', as they called themselves, would have a powerful effect soon. 5 Commando was also being shelled by the gunners of the sloop *D'Entrecasteaux*, which was still grounded on the north side of the peninsula the Commando had occupied. The ship was bombed again, by aircraft from *Indomitable*, and when that did not silence her, shelled to destruction by the destroyer *Laforey*.

General Sturges persuaded Admiral Syfret to send in a destroyer, *Anthony*, carrying a party of fifty Marines out of the battleship *Ramillies* who were to land in Antsirane instead of the commandos. This was widely seen in the fleet as a suicide mission, at least for the ship. But *Anthony* reached Orangea Strait soon after dark and her approach was not seen until she was through the strait, at which point the batteries fired, but wildly and without effect. The ship was then backed up to a jetty and the marines leapt ashore. *Anthony* then left at high speed, wholly undamaged, and firing a rude reply at the batteries as she left. She received a heartfelt welcome from the fleet on her return.

The marines had landed in Antsirane near the artillery and naval depots, which were separated off from the town itself by a high wall. They were apparently unperceived by the French, despite the noise from the batteries, and were able to gain control of both of the depots by their stealthy approach, and then got into the town to create more confusion. The result was a complete collapse of the French positions in the town and the rapid surrender of any soldiers there. 17 Brigade (2 Northamptonshires, 6 Seaforth Highlanders, and some of the Welch Fusiliers) attacked the main positions once more at the same time as the marines were landed, and found that the French defences had virtually collapsed – no doubt in part as a result of the activities of the South Lancashire men during the previous day as well as those of the marines in the town. By 3.00 am the town was captured and most of the French forces had given themselves up.

In daylight the forts were still under French control and were still fighting, though they were all now isolated. Otherwise the only area remaining in French hands was the Orangea peninsula with its ring of six batteries, and, of course, the remaining ships of the Vichy squadron. One of the submarines, *Héros*, which had been away from the base escorting a convoy, returned and attempted an attack on the British ships but was sunk by aircraft from *Illustrious* and by depth charges from the corvette *Genista*. The batteries on the peninsula could now be attacked from the south by land and bombarded from the sea. They began to negotiate a surrender, but when there were delays and no agreement had been reached by 10.30 in the morning of 7 May, the fleet began a bombardment. White flags appeared at once and surrender of all the batteries took place twenty minutes later. The two forts, Caimans and Bellevue, finally gave up the fight a few hours later.

The surrender of the town had not stopped the forts and the batteries fighting on for a time, nor did it prevent the submarine *Héros* from making its attack on the British ships. Later on 7 May the British minesweepers swept the mines in Diego Suarez Bay and the fleet came in, the last of the land forces then going ashore. Next day, however, the submarine *Monge*, which had also been away from the base, attempted an attack on *Indomitable* and was sunk by the destroyers *Active* and *Panther*. The last two Vichy warships, the submarine *Glorieux* and the gunboat *D'Iberville*, escaped and went to ports in the south of the island before eventually returning to Toulon.

This had been a neat operation. In less than three days the whole well-fortified Vichy position in the north of Madagascar had been seized. Casualties were relatively light – about 500 between the two forces – and only one British ship had been lost. There were some errors. The use of the tanks had been inept, and they had suffered accordingly, but the infantry had shown a heartening initiative and a willingness to improvise. In particular the South Lancashires overcame their disorganized situation to get on with the necessary work without waiting to be told what to do. This was an interesting change from the woodenness of tactics employed in earlier expeditions.

On the French side there was little to cheer about. The troops in the forts and the trenches had fought well when under the protection of the concrete, but everyone had been surprised at almost every stage – at the landing, at the airfield, by the landing of the marines, by the fleet's final bombardment. It was perhaps excusable to be surprised by the landing in an unexpected place (but why were the sentries at Courrier Bay fast asleep?) but to be surprised by the landing of marines in the middle of the battle in the town showed a lack of military sense which brought on the deserved defeat.

Chapter 11

Madagascar: The Long Island

The control of Diego Suarez was the crucial part of the operation against Madagascar. It was the most important place from the strategic point of view, since holding it denied the port to the Japanese fleet, and to its possible use by German or Italian submarines. It was also the first step in the campaign to suppress the Vichy administration of Madagascar. Some may well have seen it as all that was necessary, given the relative naval unimportance of the rest of the island by comparison. It was also, of course, hoped that Governor-General Paul Annet might crumble and change sides. Certainly there was no danger of the British in Diego Suarez being dislodged by the local Vichy forces, though a distant threat from the Japanese fleet might still exist – but without eliminating Somerville's Eastern Fleet first, the stretch right across the Indian Ocean was too much, even for Nagumo's ships.[1]

The 5th Division was now urgently required in India, for Burma had been almost completely conquered by the Japanese army and an invasion of India looked probable. Thirteen Brigade, with sickness beginning in the troops, sailed on 20 May. Five days later Madagascar was transferred to the East Africa Command, under Lieutenant-General Sir William Platt, who had very competently commanded the liberation of Ethiopia the year before. His first task was to get 17 Brigade also on its way to India; he sent two battalions of the King's African Rifles across to the island from Mombasa, and 17 Brigade left on 20 June. In the meantime the area under British control in northern Madagascar was expanded, partly for security reasons, in case the Vichy forces in the rest of the island tried a counter-attack, unlikely though this was, and partly to control the area from which Antsirane could be fed.

The overall purpose of the operation had been to pre-empt any Japanese seizure of Diego Suarez. While it was going on the Vichy Premier, Pierre Laval, had asked the Japanese to occupy the island in order to exclude the British, a neat reversal of the former Vichy idea of asking the US for help to exclude Japan, but even before that it had been made clear to Governor-General Annet that he should allow Japanese submarines to use Diego Suarez.[2] This was in late April 1942, before the French anywhere knew of the British expedition: it was, that is, a gratuitous offer clearly founded on hostility to Britain, and presumably to the United States as well. (This offer was made in the aftermath of the raids on Boulogne-Billancourt and St Nazaire, when Laval believed he had some popular support for his collaborationist policies – certainly there were some anti-British demonstrations in the wake of the landings.)

The British capture of Diego Suarez harbour was thus fully justified since it was about to become a hostile base. On 29 May the Japanese submarine *I-10* sent her aircraft to fly over Diego Suarez to locate the British naval force; the next night two midget submarines from *I-16* and *I-20* went into the bay and attacked the battleship *Ramillies* and the tanker *British Loyalty*. *Ramillies* was badly damaged and the tanker was sunk. (Two Japanese sailors were captured a couple of days later, and papers on them confirmed their mode of attack.) The submarine sent its aircraft over the harbour again the next day to check the results. None of these air reconnaissances seem to have been noticed, still less intercepted, by the British aircraft.

The Japanese attacks were not a response to the appeal by Laval, but their presence may well have been to investigate the possibility of French hospitality at the port. The submarines involved had been touring the Indian Ocean looking for the British Eastern Fleet, though they never did find it. They had investigated the entire East African coast from Djibouti to Durban and even Simonstown in South Africa. Five submarines were involved in the search, and between them they sank twenty-two ships.[3] For the British, however, the attack on the *Ramillies* was confirmation that Madagascar would have been vulnerable to a Japanese landing.

At the same time it was obvious that such an event as the Japanese occupation of Diego Suarez would hardly take place out of the blue. Madagascar was scarcely the first Indian Ocean target for Japanese forces, and the patrols by hostile submarines or even by German auxiliary cruisers were by no means new or unexpected in the Indian Ocean. If an expedition aimed at Madagascar set out it would in all probability be noticed, and to reach its target it would need to sink the Eastern Fleet first, by which time it would itself be damaged. On the other hand, if it did get through, now that there was a British military presence on the island, and a British naval presence at Diego Suarez, it would probably be welcomed by the Vichy authorities at some other port on the island, especially given the earlier instruction for Vichy to be hospitable.

So, while there was no particular urgency about further conquests on the island, it would clearly be helpful to the war effort for the British to have control of the whole island in a fairly short time. This also raised the issue of who should control the island once the Vichy authorities had succumbed. The British had no real wish to keep it, but to hand it over to the Gaullist Free French was only marginally more acceptable than to leave the Vichy government in charge, and might well stimulate a stronger Vichy resistance; not that either of the French groups believed British protestations of a lack of interest in the island in the long term; de Gaulle was, or claimed to be, convinced that part of Britain's war aims was to take over the French Empire; Vichy said the same thing, but with more fervour in that it was Vichy's Empire which was being demolished. If Annet and his officials could be brought to agree to accept some sort of detailed British supervision, that would be acceptable. Free France was not going to be given the island on a plate, considering the long difficulties and arguments which had resulted from the similar situation in Syria and Lebanon over the past year. So the British wanted Gaullist concessions on Syria before handing over Madagascar – that is, Madagascar was dangled as a carrot before the Free French: accept the British terms on Syria and they would get the great island; the stick was that without concessions they would gain neither Madagascar nor Syria.

But there was still another consideration. Free France had been kept out of the planning and execution of the Madagascar expedition because of its bad security. This had in fact proved to be a sensible decision, and the arrival of British forces and their landings at Diego Suarez had come as a complete surprise to the Vichy regimes in both France and Madagascar. (At Vichy the government learned of the British landing in a message from President Roosevelt.) And now an even greater and more important expedition and landing in a different Vichy territory was in its final planning stages. This was Operation Torch, the Anglo-American landings in French North Africa. It was of infinitely greater importance to have this expedition kept secret and made successful than that of Madagascar.

This consideration had its effect also on the situation in Madagascar. If the Vichy French regime in France thought that their administration in Madagascar would be maintained, in however subordinate a position to the British conquerors, they might be induced not to oppose the North African landings very strongly. If they saw, on the other hand, that the British quickly handed over the island to the Free French and its traitor leader de Gaulle, and dismissing or even interning Vichy's faithful officials, they might be so incensed that their opposition to the North African landings could be intensified. So until the issue in North Africa was determined, Free French control of Madagascar would need to be delayed. At the same time the Free

French could not be told any of this, because of their past security lapses. So the Syria-Madagascar linkage proved very useful, not just in hopefully promoting a deal over Syria, but in distracting the Free French away from North Africa. It also meant that there was no urgency in Madagascar, for so long as fighting was going on the British had a good excuse to delay any political decisions.

In Madagascar the linkage with Syria was not visible, any more than was the prospect of landings in North Africa. Contacts between the Vichy administration in Tananarive and the British commanders in Diego Suarez began soon after the landing had succeeded. The intermediaries were Captain Fauché, Governor-General Annet's aide and military intelligence officer, and Leslie Barnett, the representative of the Vacuum Oil Company of South Africa in Tananarive, who was presumably in the city at the time of the invasion. Annet was intent on preserving as much of the island under his control as possible, and on maintaining his control over its administration, and so he appeared to be offering a quasi-acceptance of the British position; the British commanders did not really wish to embark on a conquest with the relatively weak force they had on hand after 5th Division and the big ships had left. So both sides thought they were playing for time, and stringing the other along, while blaming the other for doing so. The War Cabinet in London was quite content with the stalemated situation, though eventually it was the British intention to deliver the island, all of it, to the Free French, once its usefulness as a bargaining chip and distraction was ended. Meanwhile no Free French representatives could get anywhere near the island because the British controlled their transportation.[4]

The changeover of the British forces at Diego Suarez took place over a period of two months, for the British were really in no hurry, and partly because of the shortage of shipping. The campaign now became a largely African affair. Apart from the British 29 Independent Brigade, the specialists in opposed landings, and 5 Commando, the rest of the British forces present were the 27 Brigade of the King's African Rifles, with battalions from Kenya, Tanganyika, and Nyasaland, the 7 South African Brigade, recruited mainly from the Transvaal, and assorted artillery, engineering, and other units. On 11 August the overall commander, General Sir William Platt, was given permission from London to begin a campaign to conquer the rest of the island. Again speed was hardly of the essence, but thorough planning was. Late in August 29 Brigade was taken to Kenya for further training. The 1 City Regiment of the 7 South African Brigade (the 'city' was Pretoria) was also given rudimentary training in landing from the sea at the island of Nosi Mitsio off the north-west coast, beginning on 4 September. They had to use dhows, not the most convenient vehicles for the purpose, but all that was available.

The night of 9 September was designated for the next forward movement. A new brigade, 27 Northern Rhodesian, had arrived in a convoy at Diego Suarez late in August. That same convoy was now to be used to collect the East African Brigade and bring it to the landing place, with the hope that the enemy, whom it was reasonably assumed had good sources of information in Diego Suarez, would think that this was a process of routinely exchanging brigades. The Eastern Fleet once more provided a substantial covering force, including the carrier *Illustrious*, the cruisers *Birmingham* and *Gambia*, and the Dutch cruiser *Jacob van Heemskerck*, plus three British, one Australian, and two Dutch destroyers.

No less than five separate operations were to begin at the same time on 9 September. In the north the 1 City Regiment began its march southwards on a rough road from Diego Suarez along the west coast, while one company of the regiment made the landing they had practiced for at Antanambao in advance of the main body. Eight armoured cars of the Pretoria Highlander Regiment, a field battery, and part of the 88 Field Company (engineers), were with it. This set of forces – armoured cars, some guns, infantry, and some engineers, was to be the norm for any force which set out to campaign in Madagascar. It took the force two days to move along the road and join the landing force at Antanambao. The road was basically of sand, and went through mangrove swamps at times. Physical progress was therefore slow and laborious. There was only occasional opposition from Vichy forces, but those forces did carefully destroy every bridge along the road, and planted roadblocks as well. The movement of the northern force therefore depended mainly on the speed with which 88 Field Company could lay its one box-girder bridge over a waterway where the original bridge had been broken, get everyone across, then pick up the bridge and move it on to overcome the next obstacle the infantry had encountered. Occasional snipers were the other real obstacle – apart, of course, from the active and numerous mosquitoes and the high sickness rates these produced among the white soldiers.

At the same time a company of the regiment moved by land across to the east coast, where there was a road of sorts, rather better than that on the west coast, connecting the coastal towns and villages. Progress was reasonably good for the first two days during which a hundred miles was covered as far as the village of Vohemar. But the road deteriorated, and from then on culverts and bridges were regularly broken. It took another nine days to go the next hundred miles to Sahambava. After that just one more village was to be reached, but this campaign was not going to win the war.

The island of Nosi Bé, off the north coast, was attacked before dawn on 9 September, preceded by a bombardment by the minelayer *Manxman*. Then the landing by part of the Pretoria Highlanders and some Royal Marines captured the local town of Hellville. The island was in British control by noon, with the few uncaptured Malagasy soldiers coming in to surrender voluntarily.

This was the first of five landings at different places which took place on 9 and 10 September. The main landing was to take place at Majunga, 200 miles south of the operations at Nosi Bé and Antanambao. This was an important port at the mouth of the island's main river, the Betsiboka, and from the town a relatively good road ran through to the capital Tananarive. Majunga also had an airfield, and when this was taken there would be no Vichy air capability north of the capital. The force to be used in the landing was, of course, 29 Brigade, coming directly from its training in Kenya, together with 5 Commando.

Landings were made at three places, one of them some miles north of Majunga and one in Majunga itself. The third was to take place south of the harbour, where it was thought there was a coastal battery; 5 Commando carried out this part of the operation, but there was no battery. The commandos went on inland to secure a bridge thirty miles along the road to block the arrival of any force which might come from inland to interfere. None did.

The main landing was the northern one, a few miles from the town, undertaken by the East Lancashires and the Welch Fusiliers. There was little resistance and by daylight on 10 September they had moved inland and had reached the road which led to the town. The landing in the town itself was by the South Lancashires and again they met some resistance which ceased when the local garrison commander was captured and immediately ordered his men to cease fire; he then toured the town with a British officer to ensure that various separated groups of his men stopped fighting. The East Lancashires captured the airfield, and had been about to attack a Vichy position north of the town when the potential defenders were alerted that the fighting had ended.

The fifth landing was by a single troop of 5 Commando, who landed by boat from the destroyer *Napier* at the small port of Morondava almost 400 miles south of Majunga. This was also the terminus of another road from the capital to a port, but the object of the landing – which was by only a few men, after all – was to cause a distraction, like *Hermione*'s antics at the battle of Diego Suarez. They landed in daylight, met no opposition, occupied the town, and sent a party inland supposedly to mark out the billets for a larger force, meanwhile carefully being careless to 'reveal' that a larger force was due to arrive. The absence of opposition seems to have been accompanied by an absence of local alarm at the attack, so they themselves had to telephone the capital to report the landing of a large British force. Hoping to have distracted the government in the capital and to have caused the dispatch of a force which might have gone to Majunga down the road to Morondava, they then withdrew. It seems unlikely that anything was achieved, for the official in Tananarive who answered the phone had said that they could do nothing to help.

The 29 Brigade was used just for the initial landings at Majunga, and not even all the men had been landed by the time the fighting in and around the town ended. In the rest of the convoy was the East African Brigade, who were landed over the next few days while 29 Brigade was withdrawn. The change having been completed, a curiously constituted army began to advance along the road from Majunga to the capital, over 250 miles away. A squadron of South African armoured cars manned by Afrikaners from the Pretoria region of the Transvaal was accompanied by successive battalions of the infantry of the King's African Rifles, recruited from various parts of East Africa. The infantry was intended to be moved in trucks where possible, but this turned out to be very optimistic. The first objectives were two bridges, over the Kamoro and the Betsiboka Rivers. The first, ninety miles along the road, was reached and crossed by 4.00pm, but on the succeeding part of the route they met delays in the form of plenty of roadblocks, so the Betsiboka Bridge was not actually reached that day. When the advance resumed on the morning of 11 September they found that the bridge cables had been cut and the bridge itself had been tumbled into the river, though it proved to be relatively easy to get across the next day.

The same tactics had thus been employed as in the north: breaking down the bridges, occasional snipers opposing the advance, and frequent road-blocks, which were clearly rapidly improvised. They could also be fairly quickly cleared by recruiting local Malagasies, who were often actually the same people who had blocked the road in the first place on French orders, but it always meant that the soldiers had to disembark and deploy. Often they had to drive out the snipers, and sometimes had to cross the rivers under fire, before the bridges could be restored. This was all somewhat annoying and had held up the advance considerably, as it was intended to. At the same time it was not clear whether this was all a process of drawing the British forces ever deeper into the interior as a prelude to mounting a more determined resistance, perhaps by a series of ambushes at the broken bridges or at particularly large roadblocks when the British had outrun their supplies and support. It was therefore necessary to advance with some care. It was slow and laborious, as in the north, but progress was maintained.

In the north the advance along the western coast road by the Pretoria Regiment was as slow as any other movement in this island of bad roads. There was the usual lack of large-scale opposition, but this ended on 14 September

when a force of some size in an apparently strong position south of Jangoa
was at last encountered. It seemed to be strong enough to be able to hold up
the advance and cause some casualties, so a landing was organized in the rear
of the position, by the force of Pretoria Highlanders which had held Nosi Bé
for the past few days. They were landed at Sahamalaza Bay on the 15th, and
marched inland to cut the road behind the Jangoa position. Whether it was
the prospect of being attacked from the rear, or the ominous deployment
of the rest of the Pretoria Highlanders in their front, or the bombardment of
their position by the 16 Field Battery, or more likely a combination of all
these factors as well as being outnumbered, the defenders of the Jangoa
position surrendered on the 16th, a day after the landing, and they included
in their surrender all the forces in the region. The fighting in the north
was thus effectively over. But it took four more days for the force moving
south to meet up with the men coming northwards from the bridgehead at
Majunga. Even without opposition, travel was tediously slow.

The main force advancing along the road towards Tananarive, the
armoured cars and the askaris of the KAR, faced the same problems as all
the other columns, but since they were aimed at the capital, the problems
were greater. The Betsiboka crossing had to be taken under fire by a platoon
of Nyasaland infantry, who drove off the defendants – Malagasies – and
captured most of them. The crossing then took a day, but the next village,
Maevatanana, was defended, again imposing a slowing down of the advance.
On 16 September a fight at the next crossing place took place, Nyasalanders
against Senegalese this time. Then the bridge had to be replaced.

That was also the day when the defenders of the Jangoa strongpoint
surrendered. The defeat of the Senegalese took place near the town of
Andriba, which meant that the main force was by then halfway along the
road from Majunga to Tananarive. But with his northern force defeated and
the road to his capital clearly fully available to the invaders despite all the
delaying tactics being employed, Governor-General Annet now asked for
terms. He sent envoys to discuss them with General Platt at Majunga, but
it appears that surrender and the acceptance of British authority was not
an option for them – so it was probably just another tactic designed to delay
the British advance. The envoys returned to Tananarive, and two days later
Annet moved out of the capital southwards, apparently fully intent on
continuing the fight to the end, as he had proclaimed in May.

His going may have been hastened by another landing by 29 Brigade.
The troops had been re-embarked at Majunga, once the askaris had arrived
then were ferried round the island to Tamatave on the east coast. This was
another port, but more importantly it was also the terminus of the railway
which connected Tananarive with the coast. It was clearly a place which

needed to be controlled, both because it was a port and because it was a possible escape point for the Governor-General and his remaining forces.

The troops, in the transports and in the landing craft, were covered by the presence once more of *Illustrious* and her aircraft, and by the battleship *Warspite* with the cruisers *Birmingham* and *Jacob van Heemskerck*, together with some destroyers. The implied threat of the bombardment of the town was made explicit when the envoys that went in to discuss the surrender of the town were fired on. At this, the ships opened fire, though *Warspite* restrained herself. After only three minutes' shelling a white flag indicated the town's surrender; the charade – 'honour' – had cost the lives of several men. When the troops did land, half an hour later, they were welcomed, but it soon became clear that the Vichy forces which had been in the town had used the delay over the surrender to withdraw inland – and they left the usual roadblocks and broken bridges behind them as they moved.

So the same painful advance along roads broken at bridging points and blocked here and there by obstacles appeared likely. However, a train arrived at the station unexpectedly – no doubt the driver had not been told what had happened – and was quickly commandeered, so the advance went partly by rail, though a couple of the railway crossings had been blown up as well as those on the parallel road. This advance was not going as quickly as had been hoped – but then none of the moves in this island went quickly.

On the main advance from Majunga the last village before the capital, Mahitsi, was the scene of the nearest thing to a battle since the fight at Diego Suarez. A ridge overlooking the road was occupied by Vichy troops, and their guns were ranged in on the obstacles of trees and stones blocking the road, which could not therefore be removed. It took all day on the 21st to bring up guns to counter those on the ridge, and an infantry attack by askaris on the right flank was resisted with some determination. The fighting set the bush afire, which did not help. The ridge itself and some of the infantry positions were taken before nightfall, and the next day the Vichy gun positions were located and their guns were bombarded into silence. Attacks on both flanks finally drove the defenders out.

Another position just outside Tananarive had to be threatened and bombarded, but it was held by only about 250 men, who were thus very badly outnumbered, and hardly capable of much resistance. Once these troops had given up a flag of truce appeared and the city was surrendered. This took place on 23 September; the force coming up the railway from Tamatave was still only halfway there, and a little annoyed to come in second in the race to the capital.

Governor-General Annet had moved south, to the town of Fianarantsoa, another 200 miles away. On 25 September the main column of South African armoured cars and East African infantry left Tananarive once more in pursuit, meeting with the same obstacles as before. Occasional brief fights took place, bridges had to be repaired, and roadblocks were removed. Again, speed was eschewed (even had it been possible), and more than one pause for rest was made. An attempt by a small mobile Vichy force to cut the column's communications never came to much. Just in case the Governor-General was still considering escaping by sea the last port under his control, Tulear, at the southern end of the road along which the advance was taking place, was occupied by part of the Pretoria Regiment, which was carried from the north in the cruiser *Birmingham*. Two French transport ships were also captured and sunk near the southern end of the island by the destroyer *Nizam*, the first on the 24th, the day after Tananarive was captured, and the second on the 30th, the day after the occupation of Tulear. Annet now had neither a port nor a ship available for his escape.

Nevertheless it took another month and more and another battle to complete the conquest of the island. The only hope for Annet and his people now was that the British would become exhausted and simply stop, since any help which might come from elsewhere could no longer reach the island. But, after all the effort, the road clearances, the landings, the small fights, it was hardly likely that the invaders would give up. Sickness among many of the soldiers was common, and they were undoubtedly weary of clearing roadblocks and rebuilding bridges. After a fairly short advance south from Tananarive, at Antsirabe, the column halted for several days' rest. Perhaps the Vichy forces were encouraged; they certainly were thereby given time to organize further resistance.

South of Antsirabe the land was higher, less wooded and a lot more open and rocky, but the climate was wetter and often misty. The column ran into a series of small ambushes, and had to fight a battle at Ambositra. Then, soon after that fight, they reached a well-held and well-chosen position which had to be elaborately outflanked and subjected to a formal bombardment. The resistance by the Malagasies was strong against the first frontal attack by the Kenya Battalion, until the Tanganyika Battalion opened fire on them from their rear. Eight hundred prisoners were taken at the end, so, assuming that some men escaped and some died, Annet clearly had kept a substantial force with him until that time.

But the fact that most of the enemy had given up, together with the surrender of a steady stream of deserters from the Vichy forces, were clear signs that the end was near. The column of South African armoured cars, British artillery, and African infantry reached Annet's headquarters at Fianarantsoa on 29 October – but of course he had gone again, further south, to Ihosy. So yet another chase went on, but the capture of a weakly-held position on 4 November at Ambalavao ended his last hope. The Pretoria men at Tulear had begun to advance up the road towards the Ihosy on 2 November, so the area of Annet's authority was reduced to perhaps no more than a couple of hundred miles of road, blocked at both ends by his enemies, and steadily shrinking. Next day, 5 November, he asked for an armistice, was presented with the same terms as six weeks before, and this time accepted them.

Annet's resistance had been long and stubborn – though he had not, as he had exhorted his troops, fought to the end – and he had managed to hold the loyalty of many of his troops, even if they did tend to surrender rather too readily when faced with a serious fight. His methods had evoked a certain admiration from the British higher command, though the foot soldiers were less complimentary. He had, however, been only feebly supported by the French settlers and by his officials. The former had generally welcomed the arrival of the British troops, for British conquest implied access to British markets and money – this was the same reaction as had been seen in Equatorial Africa. The officials had almost entirely settled down once more as soon as the occupation began and had continued their administrative duties with only a passive show of enmity, which did not last. The troops Annet could rely on were largely Malagasy, who were not prepared to do much more than fight briefly, no doubt mainly because they knew they were outnumbered and that Annet's strategy was to retreat. Inevitably they were demoralized. He had not received any material assistance from Vichy, and he was not really helped by a radio message from Admiral Darlan on 6 November, the day after the armistice had been signed and implemented, urging him to fight on. He did his best to obstruct the new administration, but this only lasted until he was removed to South Africa to be interned. He deserved to be commended by his Vichy superiors for the long fight he had made – but this was also a tactic which had played into British hands, though he and they cannot have realized it.

The conquest had taken long enough to allow the British to delay any promised handover to the Free French with the plea that the fighting was still going on. Investigations on the island made it clear that de Gaulle had almost no support among the French settlers and officials, other than from a small number of individuals who had been jailed for expressing themselves too publicly. If further trouble on the island was to be avoided a period of time was clearly needed to accustom the French there to the idea that they were no longer subject to Vichy regime, and that they would soon be part of Free France. The success of the Torch landings (which began two days after the armistice in Madagascar), and the consequent German conquest of the unoccupied zone of France, no doubt helped the French in Madagascar to realize Vichy's failure, and its likely extinction. The officials of the administration proved to be very adaptable, first to Vichy, then to the British, and then, perhaps with some relief, to their fellow Frenchmen – so their salaries and pensions were safe. By the time the Free French were ceded control of the island, it was clear to those who could see what was going on that they were now on the winning side. When General Legentilhomme finally arrived to take up the island's governorship in January 1943 there were not even any murmurs of annoyance.

Meanwhile the Free French had been capitalizing on the British victory by snapping up yet another little island. Three hundred miles east of Madagascar was the French island of Réunion. On 30 November the Free French destroyer *Léopard* (one of those seized at Portsmouth two years before) landed a force on the island, having first bombarded and silenced a defensive battery. As usual this independent Free French activity annoyed both its allies and Vichy, but it was *Léopard* which eventually brought Legentilhomme to take up his post at Madagascar.[5] Of course, Free France's allies eventually realized and accepted that the removal of Vichy authority from Réunion was a worthwhile action.

Chapter 12

Operation 'Torch'

The Torch plan had emerged from the politics of the 'Grand Alliance', as Churchill grandly termed the uneasy and bickering relationship between Britain, the United States, and Soviet Russia. This was combined with the internal pressures on, above all, President Roosevelt for some action by US forces in Europe to balance the fighting in the Pacific and justify the policy of 'Germany first'. There was now a substantial naval force at Scapa Flow, and a strong US participation in guarding the Atlantic convoys, but it was land activity – the conquest of Nazi and Fascist lands – which was necessary. In addition the German attack on Russia was renewed in the summer of 1942, and as the German armies drove deeper into Russia, so the demands from Stalin that the western powers do something to help became steadily shriller. The Communists in Britain capitalized on the general good feelings towards Russia in its predicament to agitate for a 'second front', which gained plenty of publicity, though the British military decision-makers were generally immune to such agitations.

In the United States, however, where similar wishes to help Russia were perhaps less insistent, Roosevelt was under a different sort of pressure. The anger against Japan ran deeply through the political nation, but at the same time a general dislike of the British Empire was felt. In fact a consistent element in United States foreign policy was aimed at dismantling that empire, and this policy was pursued even while the two countries were allied against Germany, Italy, and Japan. Roosevelt, however, was convinced that Germany was the real enemy, at least for this war. He was, as ever, well ahead of – or perhaps in this case, at a tangent to – United States public opinion which had been outraged by the surprise of Pearl Harbour and hungered for revenge.

Further, the United States had entered the war only partially ready. The attack in the Pacific had seriously damaged its naval strength, except in the weapon which turned out to be crucial in the Pacific war, aircraft carriers. During 1942 these carriers fought and won two crucial battles, Coral Sea and Midway, and meanwhile the British in the one region where they were fighting the Germans, North Africa, were beaten again. It began to look to Americans as though the war in the Pacific was winnable, but that in the Mediterranean and Europe would be burdened by an incompetent ally. The temptation to concentrate on the Pacific war was necessarily strong.

In order to deflect the US public, the press, and the politicians from their obsession with the Pacific war, Roosevelt decided it was necessary to get US troops into action in the European war.[1] During July 1942 the US Chiefs of Staff met with their British counterparts in London, and argued over what the next step in that war should be. The Americans were keen on landing on the continent; the British were wholly opposed to this in 1942, and not too happy about it for 1943. The British argument was convincing. Calculations of the numbers of trained troops available, and the numbers of landing craft, plus intelligence of the size of the German army in France which was capable of reaching Normandy, the suggested places of invasion, within two or three days, made it clear that any landing was out of the question. The inability to land sufficient forces in northern France in 1942 to withstand the German counterattack would mean that any troops sent would likely be lost. An alternative proposal, code-named Gymnast, was put forward, originating it seems in the brain of Winston Churchill. This was to be a landing in Morocco, where it was assumed that the Vichy French forces would put up little resistance.

The President and the Prime Minister were both convinced that a cross-Channel invasion was too dangerous. Churchill had been an advocate of Gymnast from the start, and was horrified at the potential cost of a cross-Channel expedition, especially as it was clear that all the British calculations indicated early failure, and if the attack failed it would be difficult to mount another for years. But the US chiefs of staff, especially General Marshall, were keen still to make the attempt. So in the end it was President Roosevelt who made the actual decision for Gymnast, directing the chiefs to work accordingly. But it was also to be boosted to a more formidable undertaking and was given a new codename: Torch.[2]

The basis for the belief that the French in North Africa would not resist was the assumption that French hearts were really with the Allies and were really anti-German. The British should, of course, have known better after their experiences during the last two years. The United States still had diplomatic relations with the Vichy regime, which was technically neutral in the wider war. Also the US had for a year had an important consular presence in French North Africa, notably in the person of the Consul-General in

Algiers, Robert Murphy. He was optimistic that the whole Vichy establishment in North Africa could be persuaded to support an Allied intervention.
But this was something the British had heard all too often, in Dakar and
Syria and Madagascar. In all those places the Vichy forces had fought
well against invasion, though they had been beaten, and the Vichy French
officials had been conspicuously loyal to the Vichy regime. And in Syria
their greatest animosity had been reserved for their domestic enemies, the
Free French. The optimism of the Free French had apparently transferred
itself to the Americans, even though each detested the other.

At the same time it was recognized that the forces for whom Vichy
felt most animosity after the Free French were the British. For some time
Roosevelt wanted Gymnast/Torch to be a purely US matter, which would
of course also resonate very well in the United States. They would think of
themselves as the Americans crossing the Atlantic yet again (the first time
was 1917–1918) to sort out those squabbling Europeans. But Roosevelt
could not actually do the job without the British, especially given their navy
and their hard-learned planning expertise. But he drew the line at de Gaulle.

This therefore dictated the same decision as over the invasion of Madagascar,
which was to keep de Gaulle and the Free French in ignorance of the plans
for North Africa until the last minute, and not to employ any Free French
troops. The reasons varied with the ally, of course, the British above all
concerned with keeping the plans secret, the Americans simply not liking
de Gaulle. On the other hand, the United States, where the President and
many others were very suspicious of de Gaulle, did feel that a French figure-
head was needed, someone who could be put forward as, at least, a military
leader, and possibly as a political one as well, and who could therefore appear
as an alternative to the tainted men of Vichy and the awkward de Gaulle,
who was tainted with the brush of independence. Surveying the field, they
came up with another French general, one who outranked de Gaulle in the
French army establishment, who had a popular reputation based on defiance
of Germans, from whose prison camp he had escaped, and who had a substantial military reputation, General Henri Giraud. He had the advantage of
believing, even in mid 1942, that Germany would lose the war.

The expansion of the original Gymnast idea took time to sort out. At first
a landing in Morocco alone was intended, then it was altered to landings in
Algeria, and then landing along the whole coast from Morocco to Tunisia
was recommended. A calculation of the available troops and shipping finally
brought it down to landings in Morocco, and at Oran and Algiers, followed
by a drive to take Tunisia, by land and by marine landings. Command was
given to General Dwight D. Eisenhower, who had been in charge of the
planning, and also because the largest contingent of troops would be from

the United States. It was also a diplomatic gesture, for the only alternative would be a British commander, which would put French backs up at once.[3]

The participation of British troops was a problem, given the general animosity felt by the Vichy regime and its forces towards Britain – and that one of the places at which landings would be made was Oran, next to Mers el-Kebir. But it was to be an *Allied* expedition, and Britain was still the member of the western Allies with the greatest number of troops in the field against the enemy, and had the forces available, both soldiers in Britain who had been in training since 1940, and the Royal Navy, which would provide much of the shipping.

It was not until 15 September that the targets for the landings were finally agreed, and the date for the landings was set for 8 November. There was time enough for the plans to be made for the organization of the convoys by Admiral Bertram Ramsey, who had run the Dunkirk evacuation, and was to plan the D-Day Normandy landings. There was also a good deal of political and diplomatic intrigue, but not enough time for the collection of sufficient accurate information about the landing places and about the situation in French North Africa. For example, when they landed in Morocco the US commanders did not know who was in command of the French forces; and they landed at beaches which were less than suitable, and failed to land at the most obvious place, a beach near Rabat, the capital, which was unguarded. (The only reconnaissance of the beaches had been by submarines.) The quantity and quality of French troops was not known, nor was their political allegiance understood. The reaction of the German and Italian forces was hardly even guessed at, though a good deal of apprehension was felt about Spanish reactions.[4] The geography of the landing places chosen was only poorly known. In retrospect, it all has the appearance of the making of a super-Dakar fiasco – except that it was eventually successful.

The motivations of the British and US leaders were, if not quite contra-dictory, then not in total harmony. Probably Roosevelt did not particularly care where the landing to attack Germany took place – Norway, Normandy, North Africa, the South of France, were all suggested at one time – but he did care that US troops should be fully involved. For a time he wanted the Torch landings to be an exclusively US affair, until it became clear that the naval forces would need to be at least half British. But none of the Americans, from the President down, were ever fully convinced that the Mediterranean was the best place to be fighting. For Churchill, on the other hand, the removal of Vichy, Italian, and German military power from all North Africa from Egypt to Morocco was a vital preliminary to the eventual fall of Nazi power in Europe. It would open the Mediterranean to Allied shipping, it would relieve the pressure on Malta and Egypt, it would open up much more of Europe to Allied attacks by land and air and would stretch Axis forces even further, it would reduce the demands for shipping going through to the east – it would, in short, rebind the ties of the British Empire, and help to lead the way to the recovery of lost imperial territories in the east – Burma, Malaya, Borneo, Hong Kong. This was not an ambition which resonated well with the President of the United States.

Churchill was also much concerned with what would be the condition of Europe when Germany had been defeated. He never seems to have had any serious doubts, even in 1940 that Germany would eventually lose the war, though he knew full well from the start that it would be necessary to gain US help if Germany was to be beaten. If Europe was to become safe for Britain to be a part of, or a neighbour to, a restored and powerful France was absolutely necessary. In Eastern Europe the alternative to a strong Germany was a strong Russia which, under its greedy Communist dictator, would be as great a threat as Nazi Germany. It was not clear just how far the United States could ever become part of the European political system; it may well be that the country would pull out again, as in 1919.

In almost any imaginable post-war situation a strong France would be a political necessity to help balance a strong Russia. For Britain a strong France would be a shield and a partner in such a circumstance, as it had been since 1904, and that had ceased to be in 1940. Hence Churchill's support for de Gaulle and Free France, since it was only around a strong and independent leader such as de Gaulle that a strong and independent, and friendly, France could be built. It bothered him that Roosevelt did not see this. He was willing to go along with the US sponsorship of Giraud, or even with the US fondness towards Vichy, but this did not stop him continuing to support de Gaulle.

In other words, there were quite enough omissions, complications, and uncertainties in the political areas to make it quite certain that things would go wrong with Operation Torch at some point, quite apart from the military difficulties inevitable in an operation organized without adequate reconnaissance, using deficient intelligence, and with less than sufficient time for training.

Murphy in Algiers had made contact with some Free French sympathizers, and also with some officers who were by now anti-Vichy. These two groups scarcely intersected. The leader of the latter group was General Charles Mast, and he had gathered four other officers to make the 'Group of Five'. Another sympathizer was General Bethouart, the commander of the army in Morocco. But neither of these men was in overall command, and neither was willing to work with de Gaulle – indeed Mast's group had a strong royalist tinge to it. This was where Giraud proved valuable, for he was acceptable to both of these North African generals and to the Americans.[5]

Within France Giraud had been attempting to organize a sort of resistance movement in opposition to, or perhaps rather in competition with, the Vichy regime, though it was not at all clear exactly what he intended. He was contacted by the British SOE at his home in Lyons, and persuaded to leave France. His inflated sense of his own importance and his naïve ambition made him lay down conditions, including that he should be in command of any operations in French territory, which he believed included North Africa, and that he could be extracted from France by an American ship. He was first disconcerted by the fact that the submarine which picked him up was actually British, though with a temporary American captain and carrying an American flag.[6] He was further amazed and angered to discover that Eisenhower was actually in command of the invasion, and knew nothing about any promises made to Giraud by the President. Roosevelt had been practicing his normal peacetime political methods on these generals; he was testing that Eisenhower was tough enough and diplomatic enough to face down Giraud. Eisenhower had to argue with Giraud for seven hours at Gibraltar, just at the time when the invasion was beginning. Giraud in fact had wanted not just to command the whole force, but to divert part of it to a landing in the South of France.[7]

Meanwhile Eisenhower's deputy, General Mark Clark, had been landed near Algiers (using the same British submarine, *Seraph*, as was used to collect Giraud) to meet Murphy and Mast. The French handed over a great deal of useful information concerning the organization and the locations and numbers of the Vichy troops in North Africa, though it was too late for it to be of much use in the planning, and Clark in return gave vague information about the forthcoming invasion, but without detail and without revealing the date. He was quite reasonably uncertain about how secure Mast and his group were, but this vagueness made it difficult to coordinate the invasion and the activities of the anti-Vichyites. All that could be done was to get Mast's people to organize themselves and wait for a signal to go into action. Their main purpose was to seize control of important people and positions in the cities, but they also intended to bring over the Vichy air force, and seize control of coastal batteries – but without knowing the date of the invasion they could not co-ordinate these actions.[8]

So, even as the planning went ahead, and the clandestine contacts and intrigues were undertaken in France and Algiers, and the convoys sailed from Britain and Virginia, the complications were piling up. Into the midst of it all came Admiral Darlan, who went on an inspection tour through North and West Africa. He was still the commander-in-chief for all the

Vichy French forces, and still Pétain's designated successor, despite Laval's supplanting him as Premier. In addition his son Alain was in hospital in Algiers suffering from polio, so an inspection tour would also let him visit the hospital. Darlan had made some tentative moves to contact the Americans during the autumn. The messages had been so vague, and Darlan's record of collaboration with Germany had been so detailed and lengthy, that no direct response was made. However, as it turned out, Darlan was actually in Algiers when the invasion forces arrived. Several messages reached him describing the movements of the convoys through the Mediterranean, but he dismissed them all, partly because he was preoccupied with his son's illness – he was at one point making funeral arrangements – and also because he believed he had received assurances from Murphy that no invasion was intended until next year. So, his son's illness having taken a turn for the better, he went off to dine; and he was fast asleep when the landings began.[9]

The French forces in North Africa were heavily concentrated in the west, in Morocco. There were six divisions of ground troops stationed there, perhaps 55,000 men under the command of General Bethouart, but the Commander-in-Chief in the sultanate was the Naval Commander, Admiral Michelier, who was also subject to the authority of General Noguès, the Resident-General. Bethouart was in the anti-Vichy conspiracy along with Mast in Algiers, but he was unable to bring in many of his officers, and those he did bring in were not prepared to simply lie down and allow the invaders to walk in. They all tended to be anti-Vichy rather than pro-Allied, and certainly not pro-de Gaulle. It was the same reaction as at Madagascar, Dakar, Syria, Alexandria and Mers el-Kebir.

The naval forces were also largely concentrated in the west, specifically at Casablanca. There was the still-unfinished battleship *Jean Bart*, removed from France in 1940. It had only one battery operational and was encased in a concrete dock, as its engines were being installed. It was therefore immovable; on the other hand, its battery was operational. There were also a large number of smaller vessels, including the cruiser *Primauguet*, which had been at Casablanca ever since it had been turned back from attempting to reach Libreville in 1940. There were also two super-destroyers, *Albatros* and *Milan*, seven destroyers, eight sloops and eleven submarines. At Oran there were three destroyers and four submarines and one super-destroyer, *Epervier*, which had just been renovated. At Algiers there were only one sloop, a submarine chaser, and two submarines.[10]

The naval force at Casablanca and the sizeable army in Morocco were clearly the main problem in North Africa, while those at Oran and Algiers might be no more than nuisances. But the wider problems were how the main French fleet at Toulon would react, whether the Italian fleet would intervene, and what would be the German reaction. At Toulon were battle-cruisers and battleships and smaller vessels galore – though they were disarmed – and the Italians had also several battleships; then there was the Luftwaffe. Also the Italians had, unlike the French, much recent battle experience, especially in their smaller ships. A nightmare scenario would be that these two fleets would join and, covered by the Luftwaffe, the Regia Aeronautica and French planes from North Africa, would be able to get among the transports carrying the troops. A sortie by even one of these fleets would be highly dangerous. The re-armament of the French fleet would need German permission, but this might not be too difficult to get if the French command was really determined to defend North Africa. Admiral Cunningham, in command of the Mediterranean Fleet, and naval commander for the expedition, actually relished the prospect of a fight, but perhaps it was just as well that he didn't get one. In other words, the naval situation in the Mediterranean had not basically changed, despite a great deal of fighting, since the escape of the battle-cruiser *Strasbourg* from Mers el-Kebir over two years before.

The gathering of forces at Gibraltar could scarcely be hidden from the eyes of the several agents of Spain, France, Italy, and Germany who watched the events from the Spanish side of Algeciras Bay.[11] But the conclusions they drew as to the ships' destinations could certainly be affected, by spreading misleading rumours and by careful leaks of information, or misinformation, in one notable case by floating a dead body carrying revealing documents ashore in Spain.[12] The result was that only Mussolini and Field Marshal Kesselring came to the right conclusion, whereas the German naval command believed that the ships were headed for Malta and/or Crete, and others suggested Dakar or the south of France or Sicily – which is what the Allies wanted them to think.

Amid all the welter of possibilities the North African targets were usually mentioned but were lost in the general noise; in effect the Axis were paralysed by these possibilities. The departure of a British aircraft carrier eastwards, which was always the prelude for running a convoy into Malta, was taken as a clear demonstration that Malta or the eastern Mediterranean or even Tripoli were intended.

The convoy bringing the British forces arrived at Gibraltar, and it could be hinted that they were for Malta; meanwhile the US invasion forces heading to Morocco came directly from Norfolk, Virginia, and remained wholly unknown to, and unanticipated by, anyone on the Axis side. The deception about Malta was maintained even as the convoys reached their Algerian targets, for the ships, which were being carefully monitored from North Africa by the French, as well as the Germans and Italians, sailed on past Oran and Algiers during daylight and then turned back to reach the landing places in darkness. In the event surprise was more or less complete at all the landing sites, though that was not enough to ensure immediate victory.[13]

The landings were to be made at some distance from the real targets, which were the cities. They were to be as simultaneous as possible, and of course in the middle of the night, at 1.00 or 2.00 am, though inevitably those timings were not usually met. There would be eight landings in the darkness, designed to take the cities by pincer attacks, all at roughly the same time along a thousand miles of coastline. Hopefully there would either be *coups* in each of the cities, or in the several French army headquarters, which would mean that there would be no opposition and no fighting, or at least confusion and a delay in French reactions. But it would certainly be best not to rely on that.

At Casablanca landings were made at three places, while a very powerful naval covering force hovered offshore. The landings were to be at Mehdia, north of Rabat, from which the airfield at Port Lyautey, the only one in Morocco with a firm concrete runway was the main target. Once it was captured, it was to receive planes being brought in by the American aircraft carriers, of which the US Navy deployed no less than six.

The southern landing was to be at Safi, a smallish port 140 miles south of Casablanca. It was at the end of a railway line, but the main purpose of landing there was to protect the southern flank of the attack on Casablanca, in case French forces from the south and the interior moved to defend the city. Both of the landings were more or less successful, that at Safi being particularly well conducted, a model of how such an operation should be carried out. Two destroyers sailed into the harbour, and landed 200 marines each, thereby quickly seizing control of the docks. The marines defeated a rather weak counter-attack, then the transports were able to land the other forces, including fifty Sherman tanks, and the main force set off north for Casablanca. The northern force at Mehdia got ashore with some difficulty, and found even more problems in actually locating and reaching the airfield; in the end they succeeded in capturing it on 10 November, after two days.

The central attack was to be at Fedala, a small port fifteen miles northeast of Casablanca. The US Army commander, General George S. Patton, was present at this landing, and though he was vociferously unimpressed by the zeal of his troops (as was General Truscott at Mehdia), he had got them ashore during the day. Of course, none of his forces were anywhere near Casablanca, and the city and its forces had now received ample warning of the forthcoming attack. And, even with 35,000 troops on shore, Patton was actually considerably outnumbered, if the French could get all their troops to the vital point.[14]

On shore General Bethouart's plans to provide support for the invaders largely failed because he was not a good conspirator, and because, despite his rank, he was not high enough in the Vichy hierarchy to carry others with him. His officers did detain Admiral Michelier, but they failed to ensure that he could not communicate with Resident-General Noguès, and Noguès, who was also arrested, was able to call on loyal troops to free him. Both men reacted cautiously to the news of the landings when they were told of this about 5.00 am, but then they decided that they were probably no more than commando raids and they both decided to resist. So it was eventually Bethouart who ended up under arrest. But the whole situation was, from the Allied point of view, a most helpful confusion. However, this confusion on the French side was matched by inexperience and confusion at the landing sites.

The US forces did actually get ashore at their three landing places, though movement away from the sites towards the city was always slow. They were largely unopposed at first, having taken the majority of the French by surprise, and the confusion among the French commanders meant their forces did not react for a time. At 7.00 am, several hours after the landings had begun from the huge American armada, five of the submarines sailed out of Casablanca on a normal patrol, not apparently apprehending that there was a major US armed force close by.

Safi was covered by the old battleship *New York*, vintage 1914, with a more modern cruiser (*Philadelphia*) and the escort carrier *Santee*, all these being screened by ten destroyers – two of which went into the harbour with the marines. The fighting on shore was over quickly enough that the covering forces were not needed. Off the northern landing site, Mehdia, was the battleship *Texas*, the cruiser *Savannah*, the escort carriers *Sangamon* and *Chenango*, and nine destroyers, with assorted other craft. Again the landing was unopposed, if messy, and the covering ships were not required to do anything.

The central landing, at Fedala and aimed at capturing Casablanca, was aimed directly at a place which the Vichy submarines were to transit on their way to their patrol areas. Out at sea were the battleship *Massachusetts*, two heavy cruisers, *Wichita* and *Tuscaloosa*, and five destroyers under the direct command of the naval commander, Rear-Admiral Hewitt; the actual landing forces were covered by the carrier *Ranger*, the escort carrier *Suwanee*, three cruisers, *Augusta* (carrying General Patton), *Brooklyn*, and *Cleveland*, all being covered and supported by no less than fourteen destroyers.

The French naval force in Casablanca was no match for all this. This did not stop the ships from trying. It became clear just before 8.00 am that the American forces would be seriously opposed when French planes challenged the approach of US aircraft from *Ranger*. Five American planes were shot down and the surviving crewmen captured; seven French planes were also shot down. Soon afterwards anti-aircraft guns in Casablanca fired at a naval spotting plane, though ineffectively. The gunners had not had any serious practice at anti-aircraft work.

This finally brought the realisation to Casablanca that war had arrived, and to Admiral Michelier that something more than a commando raid was involved. The two most powerful guns at the city, the usable battery on *Jean Bart* and the coastal battery at el-Hank just to the west of the city, began firing on the US ships offshore, and the ships in the harbour were almost ready to get to sea. *Jean Bart*'s battery was quickly silenced when lumps of concrete from the surrounding buildings fell on it and masked and damaged it, but the guns on the headland went on firing for some time.

The *Massachusetts*, firing 16-inch shells from twenty miles away, aimed partly at the battery on el-Hank, but also at the harbour. Three submarines were sunk at their moorings, and a super-destroyer and two destroyers were badly damaged. In the commercial harbour ten ships were sunk. Meanwhile the ships which were capable of sailing did so. They were organized as the 2 Light Squadron, commanded by Rear-Admiral Gervase de Laford, who had been in command in a similar, if less unpleasant, situation in Beirut the year before. He took to sea his super-destroyer *Milan*, with six destroyers. The cruiser *Primauguet*, its machinery under repair, came out later.

The squadron's aim was to interfere with the landing at Fedala, so the ships kept close inshore, hoping that the rising sun would blind the US gunners, and they also made much use of smoke to hide their movements. It was no good, for the US ships were equipped with range-finding radar. Also the Vichy ships came under attack from fighters launched from *Ranger*, who carried out machine-gun attacks which caused heavy casualties among the officers on the bridges of several of the ships. They did get close enough to the Fedala forces to damage the destroyer *Ludlow* and some landing craft, but then they came under fire from *Massachusetts* and from three of the US cruisers. The destroyer *Fougeux* was sunk, *Milan* was so damaged she had to be beached, *Albatros*, *Frondeur*, and *Brestois* were all badly damaged; *Primauguet* joined the squadron just in time to be hit and set on fire. Only one destroyer survived, *Alcyon*.

The three remaining submarines in Casablanca harbour were sunk during the later bombardment. Those which had got to sea at 7.00 am were gradually picked off one by one. *Sidi Ferruch* submerged when it was attacked on the surface, but was then sunk by aircraft from *Suwanee*. *Meduse* had to be beached. *Conquerant*, unarmed, got away towards Dakar but was sunk on the way.

Tonnant survived during two days of attacks, but was damaged and then was scuttled. The other two boats got away to Dakar.

Next day, the US land forces advanced on Casablanca from Fedala, and more were coming north from Safi. Two sloops which had survived the shelling of the harbour came out to harass the advancing forces. The battery on *Jean Bart* had now been cleared of its concrete encumbrances and repaired, and suddenly began shooting again. Also the battery on el-Hank was still in action. *Jean Bart* received the full attention of *Massachusetts* and of the dive bombers from *Ranger*. The ship more or less survived, and by drawing such attention on itself, it helped save the two sloops, but the battleship's battery was silenced again.[15]

The overwhelming US naval forces covering the landings had therefore so far been decisive in ensuring that the troops were safely ashore, and Casablanca was clearly under imminent threat. Its defence now depended on the French army, which had not yet taken much part in the fighting. If it did the US forces might find themselves pinned to the coast while the French dominated the interior. And Casablanca was ringed by substantial forces in good defendable positions. As it happened, though, the decision as to whether to go on fighting was made a thousand miles away.

At Oran the attacking force was British, which inevitably produced a vigorous French reaction, and at Algiers it was both British and American. The surprise landings were paralysing for a time, with the addition of a more successful set of plots among the French officers. At Oran, two landings, to the east and west of the city, were made. In the territory around the city there was an infantry division, a motorized cavalry brigade (which had been hidden from the German armistice commission), and three military airfields – all in addition to the naval forces in the harbour. General Mast's preparatory intrigues had made no progress among these forces, so when the landings were detected there was only minor confusion and the alarm was raised at once. In fact the navy learned of trouble approaching even earlier, when a small French convoy found itself mixed up with the Allied ships; the vessels in the harbour had been ordered out to investigate what was going on.

The landings in fact went well, with opposition from only the small groups of French soldiers who were on guard duty. The early objectives were the airfields, both to prevent French air attacks, and to have them as bases for the invaders' own aircraft. All three were captured on the first day. A third landing, however, was a disaster. This was an attempt (as at Safi) by two ships, former US Coast Guard cutters which had become HMS *Walney* and HMS *Hartland*, to put ashore 400 Royal Marines in the harbour area. But this attack went in two hours after the first landing, into a port now fully alert (whereas at Safi this had been the first move). Both ships were shelled to destruction, and of the 600 or so soldiers and sailors involved only 200 survived.

Offshore the covering force included three British battleships (*Duke of York*, *Nelson*, and *Rodney*), the battle-cruiser *Renown*, three carriers (*Victorious*, *Formidable*, and *Furious*), three cruisers and sixteen destroyers. This was, like the *Massachusetts* taskforce off Casablanca, mainly intended to deal with any unexpected opposition onshore, but also for protection in case the French or Italian fleets came out. In fact it was scarcely needed, but is a good example of the sensible use of overwhelming force at the crucial point (as at Diego Suarez and other places in Madagascar – and in sharp contrast to Dakar, or even Mers el-Kebir).

The inshore covering force had two escort carriers, *Biter* and *Dasher*, two light cruisers, *Aurora* and *Jamaica*, two anti-aircraft ships, and numerous smaller ships, all co-ordinated, as were the landing forces, from the head-quarters ship *Largs* (which had been a French merchant ship captured in the central Atlantic in 1940). The idea of a specifically designated and equipped headquarters ship had originated after the Dakar failure, one of whose causes was perceived as being a lack of co-ordination between the several commanding officers. One result of these Torch landings was that the US came to appreciate the usefulness of such a ship.

This was the force which the ships which came out of the harbour faced, and they were destroyed one by one as they emerged. The super-destroyer *Epervier*, only just overhauled, three destroyers, four submarines, and a mine-sweeper were sunk, mainly by fire from the cruiser *Aurora*. Two submarines tried to counter-attack, but were also sunk.

The land attack on the city was resisted with some effect, and in a counter-attack one airfield already being used by US planes came under fire. The coastal batteries proved to be as willing to fight it out as the ships from the port, and as those at Casablanca, and had to be shelled to destruction, though a premature report that the city was about to be captured led the admiral in command to order all the ships in the harbour to be scuttled. This continued resistance at Oran was fierce enough to bring the Allied commanders to threaten a full-scale air, artillery, land and sea assault, which would surely destroy the city. Of the ships in the harbour only one escaped, the submarine *Fresnel*, which made an unsuccessful attack on *Jamaica*, and then got away to Toulon (shades of *Strasbourg* in 1940).

The attack at Algiers went rather differently. The covering force this time consisted of the carrier *Argus* and an escort carrier, a monitor, three cruisers, and over twenty destroyers, co-ordinated by the headquarters ship *Bulolo*. There were three initial landings. Two American Regimental Combat Teams, each about 5,000 strong, landed at Sidi Ferruch west of the city and at Cape

Malifré to the east; the British 11 and 36 Brigades landed near Castiglioni, also west of the city. They were met at the beaches by French officers, who prevented any immediate retaliation by French forces, though the navy personnel manning the coastal batteries did fight back. As at Safi and Oran, two ships, the British destroyers *Broke* and *Malcolm*, attempted to land forces in the harbour; as at Oran, however, the port had been alerted and both of the ships were severely damaged before they could do very much. Some American rangers got on shore and into the city but were soon captured.

Algiers was the scene of the most effective attempt to seize power by the Free French partisans. They cut telephone wires, seized inimical officers, and generally controlled much of the city for a time. But the fighting in the harbour alerted everyone to the emergency. General Juin and Admiral Darlan were seized briefly, but were then released; so was Consul-General Murphy, who claimed to the others that half a million Allied troops were landing.[16]

Had the Vichy command been really determined to fight on, it seems likely that the battles in Algiers and Oran could have been maintained for quite some time. Their soldiers and above all their sailors, were generally loyal and obeyed orders. It soon developed that the number of the plotters was fairly few, and those who could be found were quickly arrested by the Vichy authorities. And had Vichy been really sympathetic to the Axis there were German and Italian air reinforcements to call on. Hitler offered to send part of his air power to assist as soon as he heard of the landings, and when both Pétain and Laval temporized on this – it was very like the old request to send planes via Syria into Iraq – he became insistent. Indeed German aircraft and troops were at Tunis airfield by the day after the landings, 9 November, though not in large numbers.

At Algiers the French naval forces were few. The submarines *Caiman* and *Marsouin* got away out of the harbour, and went to Toulon. The concentration of Allied ships was also an excellent target for German planes, even if the French resisted their intervention. In the week after the landing five transports, a sloop, the carrier *Argus*, and the monitor were all sunk or damaged, but these attacks came too late to affect the outcome in Algeria, for the landings were all successful right away. More importantly the resistance among the Vichy commanders was no more than half-hearted.

The problem for Vichy was that the high officials were perplexed as to what they should do. German pressure and demands had grown in the past year and had fuelled both Vichy resentment at Nazi Germany and popular resentment at the Vichy regime; Allied power had also visibly grown, while German forces had been less than successful of late. In Russia the Germans were stuck at Stalingrad and would soon be besieged there. In the eastern

Mediterranean Rommel's army had been beaten at Alamein and was now in steady and unstoppable retreat before a British army which had at last learned how to campaign with success in the desert. The landings in North Africa had displayed Allied fighting power at sea and in the air for everyone to see. The size of the convoys, the size of the covering forces, and their general immunity to attack by air or by sea or by U-boat, was a signal of things to come.

Then again the political signals coming from the Allies along with events in North Africa were not by any means as unpleasant to Vichy as they might have been. For a start de Gaulle and his traitors were nowhere to be seen. It was noticed that the British conquest of Madagascar was not a total disaster for the men of Vichy, for the former officials there continued in office, with the exception of the Governor-General. This could be seen as a model for North Africa. Secondly, the puppet that had been put forward by the Allies, Giraud, was widely seen as a nonentity and his claims to any sort of authority were generally disregarded. When he arrived in Algiers on 9 November, still disgruntled, he was ignored. Furthermore, the presence of Darlan in Algiers seemed to provide a useful means by which the Vichy regime could negotiate peace and then continue.

Darlan had been brought into play by General Juin, the Vichy army commander in Algeria. General Mark Clark, who also arrived in the city on 9 November, and had earlier intrigued with Mast and the Circle of Five, had welcomed his presence as a useful means to bring an early end to the fighting. The main purpose of the Allies, once on shore and in command of the main ports, was to push on to the east in the hope of being able to gain control of Bizerta, the port through which the Axis supplies for Rommel's forces were being channelled, and Tunis, whose airfields were equally useful for dominating the central Mediterranean. So the sooner the French in North Africa gave up the fight, the sooner the march on Tunis by the British and Americans could begin; indeed if the French co-operated, it might be possible to get there even quicker than hoped.

Darlan chopped and changed, at times agreeing to an end to the fighting, at other times referring everything to Pétain, and later changing his mind over ordering the French forces in Tunisia to cease fire. It took until 10 November to convince him, eventually under threat of being jailed on an Allied ship in Algiers harbour, to agree to a cease-fire, and even then Noguès in Casablanca seemed likely to disobey.

Darlan in fact was able to get a cease-fire accepted at Oran and Algiers in part due to his own authority as commander-in-chief and as Pétain's publicly designated successor, and to permission which he claimed to have from Pétain, but also because it was clear that the Allies were quite determined to conquer the cities if necessary and that they were capable of doing so. At Casablanca, on the other hand, the fighting went on. The message from Darlan ordering a cease-fire was sent by radio, but was distrusted, and it seemed to be contradicted by a 'fight-on' broadcast from Marshal Pétain. Time was spent getting clarification from the Admiralty in Vichy, during which the *Jean Bart* was pounded once again by dive bombers. The clarification added the phrase to Pétain's words that resistance should continue 'as long as possible'. This gave Michelier and Noguès an exit, and they agreed to a cease-fire a day after Darlan's order, on 11 November.

Darlan had thereby succeeded in fully establishing his own control over the French forces in all North Africa, and at the same time he had his political control recognized by the Allies. It had been a very clever political performance. Giraud was inserted into the system, but remained a cypher. Admiral Auphan describes Darlan's reaction on being informed of the arrival of the invading forces. He 'seemed about to explode', Auphan wrote. 'Then he gave it a second thought, his eyes inscrutable behind his blue-tinted glasses. He must have foreseen the opportunity that now presented itself.' (Auphan was not actually present, but he knew Darlan well; this is clearly how he believed Darlan had reacted; and it rings true when one considers how he persuaded the Allies to accept him.)[17]

The Allies' march on Tunis went ahead, but only in relatively small steps. There were more landings, first by the British 36 Brigade at Bougie, 100 miles to the east of Algiers, and then on 12 November, Bône was captured. But the Germans in Tunisia, despite being few in number, reacted with much greater vigour, imagination, and decision. The French forces in the area were as unwilling to face German fire as they had been willing to fight against the British and Americans to the west. The result was that most of Tunisia was held by German forces by the end of the month.[18]

The 'deal with Darlan' made by the Allied commanders was ratified by both Churchill and Roosevelt in the cause of preventing further bloodshed. Neither liked the idea of fighting the French, and Roosevelt was still three-quarters convinced that the Vichy regime was secretly friendly, though neither man had a good word to say for Darlan himself. This was in part because it suited both of them to both accept and vilify him. Admiral Cunningham, who had referred to him in his private correspondence as a 'snake' and a 'skunk' repeatedly, changed his tune when he finally met him and found that he was charming and intelligent.[19] His assassination on Christmas Eve was therefore a considerable relief to all on the Allied side, since Darlan's ability and authenticity was clearly what held up the Vichy regime in North Africa.[20] Only when he was removed were there any openings for the Free French.

The Vichy regime was, of course, secretly neither friendly nor hostile to anyone, but was concerned above all with its own survival under the massive threats from all the antagonists. Its policy of coping with German power by a submissive armistice had, however, clearly failed, though in a way this was the same policy which was tried again in the face of the Allied invasion of North Africa. The empire had been gradually removed from its control, by the Allies, by its friends, and by its enemies. The loss of North Africa proved to be its death blow, though there was one more blow to come in the homeland.

Chapter 13

Scuttle

The conflict between Britain and France between 1940 and 1942 was a naval war in the sense of most of the action taking place at sea or close to it, and in the parallel sense that it was the fate and use of the French fleet which was the matter at issue. The various engagements in the fighting had been between ships and fleets – Mers el-Kebir, interceptions of convoys – or between ships and shore installations – Dakar, St Nazaire – or by landings from the sea – Madagascar, North Africa. In the process the British had managed to enlist on their side of the conflict the might of the United States, as well as being able to use its own imperial might, with African soldiers in Madagascar, Indians and Australians in Syria, and using the Free French as well. The same type of events, the same puzzled procrastination, the same exasperations, had come to characterize US relations with Vichy as had, in a more violent way, those between Britain and Vichy. And just as the British, as early as July 1940, reached the conclusion that the only way to impress Vichy was by sinking some of its ships, so the United States had arrived at more or less the same conclusion at Casablanca. Despite two years of diplomatic conversations with the Marshal and Laval and Darlan and the rest, it had proved to be impossible to divert Vichy from its course of collaboration with Nazi Germany.

Of course, Vichy's only recourse, given its powerlessness and disarmed condition, was procrastination, delay, and intrigue. In this it was Admiral Darlan who proved to be the master, exploiting the old Marshal's suggestibility and his curious concept of national honour. In North Africa Darlan was able similarly to harness the Allies' haste and their wish to avoid fighting and killing Frenchmen to their own need to hold on to power. By the end of November Darlan had established himself as the indispensable man in North Africa, at least to all appearances, receiving the gratitude of the French for maintaining the Vichy regime, and the gratitude of the Allies for stopping the fighting and switching his forces through 180 political degrees so that they were now fighting on the Allied side. Of course, his indispensability proved to be only apparent, but his murder did ultimately open the way for de Gaulle to edge out first Giraud, and then the Vichy men, so that Churchill's support for him was eventually vindicated. De Gaulle had proved to be the most cunning of the lot.

Allied control of Algeria and Morocco largely freed the Mediterranean for Allied ship movements, which permitted major savings in ship capacity and time, since the Cape route was no longer necessary. In addition the Torch campaign had taught the Allies a great deal about war making on a large scale, about cooperation, and about command. This was necessary because whenever an attack was to be launched against Germany, it would need to be by sea, and it would need to be on a vastly grander scale than Torch.

The quarrel between Britain and Vichy France had always been, at its root, concerned with the potential of the French fleet. The imperial campaigns Dakar, Syria, Madagascar, the Pacific, and North Africa – had been aimed at removing possible hostile bases which might be used, or which were being used, by Britain's active enemies. But it was the French fleet's potential which was the most worrying. Despite that fleet's gradual degradation in number and condition since 1940, most of it still existed, and in the past two years the major units of that fleet had been steadily gathered together at Toulon.

The Casablanca forces had now been destroyed, but several of the ships at Oran and Algiers had escaped and had also moved to Toulon. Outside Toulon there were still considerable numbers of ships in several places, but most of them were effectively interned or detained. There were a few old and decommissioned ships at Bizerta under Admiral Derrien and at Dakar Admiral Collinet commanded the only substantial French naval force outside Toulon which was, so to say, tree. Admiral Godfroy's ships in Alexandria harbour were still stuck there, effectively interned, though the news of the Allied invasion of North Africa had stimulated renewed mutters about breaking out. The few ships in Indo-China were effectively lost to the Japanese, and the aircraft carrier *Béarn* and other ships in the West Indies had been compelled to be demilitarized by United States pressure.

At Toulon, however, there was still a major fleet. The three battleships *Strasbourg*, *Dunquerque*, and *Provence* were there, as were seven cruisers, no less than eighteen super-destroyers, seven destroyers, and twenty submarines. Some of the ships were under repair, such as *Dunquerque*, or were in the process of being overhauled; others, about a third of the whole, had been decommissioned, and all were effectively disarmed – but this was still a fleet of power. Whenever brought to action the sailors of the fleet had fought their ships hard – at Dakar and Beirut and Diego Suarez and Casablanca, and, just a few days before, at Oran and Algiers. This was a fleet still to be wary of.

One of the main arguments for accepting Darlan as a pseudo-Ally in North Africa had been that it seemed as though he would be able to bring the Toulon fleet (and the ships at Dakar) over to the Allied side – and possibly those in the Caribbean. In the event Admiral de Laborde at Toulon, who hated Darlan, replied to Darlan's instruction to hand his fleet to the Allies with the one word '*Merde*'.[1] Godfroy at Alexandria was similarly, if less rudely, unwilling, and Robert in the Caribbean did not obey either. Boisson at Dakar thought about it for some time before agreeing. But Laborde was the main target. His reply expressed his contempt for Darlan, but it was also impossible for him to obey.

The German reaction to the Allied seizure of French North Africa was to carry out a parallel seizure of the Unoccupied Zone of France, which had suddenly become a very vulnerable hole in their continental defences. They had already in effect done the same in Tunisia, so the Allies had been unable to seize it themselves. On 11 November, the day fighting finally ended in Morocco, the German contingency plan for the occupation of the Unoccupied Zone, ominously originally code-named 'Attila', but renamed 'Anton', was ordered into effect. Hitler excused it to Pétain as merely a temporary measure, and Pétain's weak protest was, of course, ineffectual.

The operation involved simultaneous invasions along the valleys of the Garonne, the Rhône, and the Allier. There was actually nothing to stop them, of course, and Marshal Pétain collaborated, despite his protests, by ordering that there should be no resistance, and that his troops, such as they were, should stay in their barracks. As a campaign it was a walkover, completed within twenty-four hours. The only exception was at Toulon. In addition, Italian forces crossed their demarcation line into Provence and Savoy, and a scratch collection of ships brought an Italian force from the naval base at Livorno to occupy Corsica.[2]

Two places of importance were, however, not occupied by the German forces, at least at first. The city of Vichy was carefully bypassed by the German force motoring along the Allier Valley, which was headed for Nîmes and the Spanish border at Perpignan. The Vichy regime was supposed to continue, exercising whatever authority it had left, as the legal government of France, and the German occupation of the centre of the French government would send very much the wrong signal – as if it made much difference, for this authority, such as it was, had become less than convincing even before 11 November 1942; afterwards it was no more than a transparent fiction. Darlan, in fact, claimed that the Marshal was effectively imprisoned and operating under duress and this became the basis for his further claim to have the real authority over the Vichy Empire as the Marshal's designated successor.

There was just one small group of soldiers, a few hundred strong led by General de Lattre de Tassigny, which resisted the new occupation openly, and they were quickly rounded up and jailed. Toulon was the second place which was not occupied by the Germans on that first day of invasion. The situation there was different, neither occupation nor resistance, but a stand-off. The senior admiral at the base, Admiral de Laborde, faced the same dilemmas as every Vichy loyalist eventually faced: whether to obey the Marshal, obey the Germans, or break for the Allies, and like almost everyone in France the several and contradictory dilemmas he faced made it impossible for him to act. The one thing he refused to do was obey the orders of his commander-in-chief.[3]

The men at Toulon had now been subjected to a series of severe shocks in a very short period of time. Within only three days they had heard first of the invasion of North Africa by the Allies, including the killing of a large number of their mariner comrades at allied hands at Oran and Casablanca and to this the arrival of the refugee submarines gave direct testimony. Then on 11 November came the invasion of the last free part of the homeland by Germans and Italians. Not surprisingly, there were a variety of reactions, including anti-German demonstrations on some of the ships, but the overall reaction was a sort of hypnotic paralysis, like a rabbit caught in the headlights of an approaching car. To those with a larger perspective than the immediate effects, all this was the inevitable consequence of the collaborationist policy of the Vichy regime, and of the effective demilitarization of France.

Refugees, in minor replay of 1940, escaped from the German advance and ended at Toulon, the only remaining part of France not under German control – apart from Vichy itself. Some Vichy army units also arrived to assist in the defence of Toulon, if that should be needed. The base was walled off from the town, and the gates were manned and shut. Inside it, Laborde decided that he must do two things: prepare to defend the base against anyone and everyone, Germans, Italians, or Allies, and second, try to get clear instructions from Vichy.

The fate of the fleet was now of immediate concern to everyone involved. It was clear that the Germans hoped and intended to gain control of the ships, though Hitler was pessimistic over the prospects of success; he promised the ships to Mussolini anyway. He, and everyone else, had his memories of the reaction of the German High Seas Fleet at Scapa Flow in 1919, which had been scuttled when it seemed to be threatened with seizure by the British.

The French in Toulon were thus presented with a variety of possibilities and of possible actions they could take, and a seductive example from the enemy.

The most obvious prospect was that the Germans would seize, or at least attempt to seize, the ships as they were, in many cases fully operational, though disarmed. It was to prevent this that the gates of the base were shut and the wall was manned. A second possibility was a repetition of Mers el-Kebir, an Allied attack on a much more massive scale. This would presumably involve a major air raid, perhaps several air raids, but also the presence of a large Allied fleet offshore aimed at intercepting any escaping ships. There was a third possibility: that the ships could sail out of the harbour and join the Allies.

This last was not really a possibility, for a good third of the ships were decommissioned, and the rest were all short of fuel. (This was, of course, the basis of Laborde's refusal to obey Darlan's order. But Darlan clearly knew this; any promises he made to the Allies to bring over the fleet were obviously fraudulent.) In addition the Exit Channel from the harbour was narrow and could be easily blocked by closing the revolving bridge which crossed the channel. Nor is there any sign that the Allies contemplated attempting the destruction of the ships. Toulon, especially now that the Germans had occupied the hinterland, was far too close to German and Italian air power to be attacked, and the Allies' fleets were too valuable to be risked on such an uncertain venture. (On the other hand, had it been known that the ships were likely to become part of the Italian fleet, which already had six active battleships, the British in particular would have been strongly tempted to mount an attack at some point – just as, when the surrendered Italian fleet was being transferred to British custody in Malta in September 1943, the Germans attacked it.)

So the only real possibilities facing the Toulon admirals, above all Laborde, were that they might retain the ships in their present state, or that the Germans would seize them. Admiral Laborde visited Vichy on 15 November but got little help in resolving his problem, and ended up broadcasting vague exhortations to do their duty to the sailors, without saying what their duty was. Soon after he left Vichy to return to Toulon, the minister of the Navy, Admiral Paul Auphan, resigned so any instructions or advice he had provided were likely to be modified, or at least changed. In effect, the result of Laborde's visit was that it was clear that the fleet at Toulon was on its own; the decision on what to do was his.

The terms of the armistice, despite their clear abolition by the German invasion, combined with Darlan's promise to Churchill in 1940, became the guidelines to action, or inaction, at Toulon. The promise to Churchill had been that the fleet would not be allowed to fall into German hands, and in the armistice terms the Germans had agreed that the fleet should remain under French control; certain units were permitted to be used to defend the empire, and others could be employed in escorting convoys. In the absence of clear guidelines for action from his government Admiral Laborde fell back on these two undertakings to give him the effective limits to his actions. And there was one further order he had in mind all the time: Darlan's 1940 instruction that if the Germans (or the Allies) appeared to be about to gain control of the ships, those ships should be scuttled. He might disobey Darlan's order to surrender, no doubt arguing that he was in enemy hands and so his orders were invalid, but that scuttling order was still in his safe.

These were the parameters which marked out the response by Admiral Laborde to the events of the next couple of weeks. This was despite the fact that none of the original conditions of those agreements and promises and orders applied any more. The promise to the British had clearly not been enough to satisfy Churchill or the British Admiralty, and it was surely cancelled by the attack at Mers el-Kebir, not to mention all the other fights the two nations had had in the past two years. To consider such a promise still binding on one side when the other had manifestly decided it was irrelevant suggested a blindness to the facts which could only be wilful. Yet it seemed clear that Laborde did so consider it.

The same may be said about the armistice with Germany. The terms had been repeatedly broken by the Germans over that same two years, culminating in the invasion of the Unoccupied Zone. (Not that the French had been unwilling to ignore the terms when they could get away with it.) The changes had often been done by a process of pseudo-consultation and pretend-negotiation between the two sides in the context of the Armistice Commissions, but the end result had been a comprehensive shredding of the terms, and a progressive insinuation of German power into France and its institutions. The latest and perhaps most unpleasant of these violations had been the 'temporary' occupation of the Unoccupied Zone. Even the Marshal had been moved to make a token protest at this. But he did so as if the rest of the terms he had signed had not already been bent and broken and twisted by such events as the shooting of French hostages, the continuing imprison-ment of French prisoners of war, the forcible transportation of French forced labour, the repeated demands for Italian and German access to the empire and its resources, the 'offer' of planes to 'help' in the defence of North Africa, the use of French Syrian airfields to attack the British in Iraq, the use of Tunisian ports to supply the German and Italian armies in Libya, and now the occupation of Tunisian bases for attacking the Allies. Again to imagine that the armistice terms still held was to exercise wilful blindness to the changes of the last two years – but Admiral Laborde clearly did that.

Nor could it really be claimed that Darlan's order of 1940 that the fleet should be scuttled was still valid. Darlan himself was now in Allied hands in Algiers and had been repudiated by the Marshal, though the usual Vichyite ambiguity attached itself confusingly to the repudiation. But Darlan's order had been produced as a consequence of his promise to Churchill, and that promise had effectively evaporated in the fires of Mers el-Kebir. If the order still sat in Laborde's safe it did so only as a result of bureaucratic inertia, or because no one had cancelled it. Again, the ambiguity was a useful cover, but only a rigidly bureaucratic mind such as Laborde's, without the imagination to keep track of events and their implications, could take refuge in an out-of-date and discredited order to cover his indecision.

In the face of all this it could hardly be maintained that the armistice terms were still being observed by the German side (or the French, for that matter), though this was the basis for the Marshal's complaint. Yet this was the one remaining political foundation for the Pétainist regime, whose rationale had always been that it brought peace to France in dire circumstances, and that to maintain peace it pursued a policy of collaboration with Germany. This, of course, given the nature of Nazi Germany, and the requirements of the German war machine, inevitably meant repeated increases in German demands, for money, for goods, for manpower, so that what had been merely collaboration in 1940 had become all-too obviously heavy and detailed German exploitation by 1942.

There had also been two bases of political power which had given Vichy some clout in dealing with Germany: the empire, with which a certain amount of trade had continued, and the fleet, which remained under French command and control. Between 5 and 23 November the first of these, control of the empire, finally disappeared, though it had been dwindling ever since 1940, as colonies were stolen by several of Vichy's and Germany's enemies.

Between the 8th and 11th North Africa was either conquered or defected, on the 5th Annet had finally surrendered in Madagascar, and on the 23rd Boisson changed sides at Dakar, taking all French West Africa with him. All that remained was Djibouti. From then only the fleet was left, and Vichy clung to this last fragment of the French armistice terms, that which concerned the fleet, because the fleet was its last remaining element of real power. To delay the German seizure of the fleet was therefore to maintain the last item of credibility for the Vichy regime.

To the admirals at Toulon it must have seemed possible to defy the Germans over the fleet. They knew that the Germans knew that any overt attempt to seize the fleet was likely to end in a scuttle, so it must have appeared to the French that the Germans would not risk the prize. (This was certainly the German Navy's view.) The problem was that the Germans did not just make a sudden attempt to seize the ships. Instead they sliced away at Laborde's position until he was the literally left standing virtually alone on his ship facing one of their tanks and arguing with German officers about the armistice. It is a process uncannily similar on a much smaller and more intimate scale to that which had happened to the country and to the empire. It was, of course, all the result of France's defeats, whereby the surrounding political vultures seized on and carried off choice pieces of the body.

So, having gained control of all France, except for Toulon, the Germans took their time over this last item. First, they required that the French soldiers who had come into the base to help the Navy defend it should be removed; this was, of course, fully in agreement with the marshal's non-resistance order. Then they required the French air force units still in the area around Toulon to remove themselves. A requisition order was issued that all the French merchant marine vessels still in French hands should be handed over to German control. Laval had negotiated this, and had managed to reserve eighteen ships for French use, so the Germans gained control, at least in theory, of 158 ships, totaling over 600,000 tons. (They later insisted that the French government should pay the ships' running costs as well, even when they were technically chartered to German use.)

Laborde and his base and ships were being gradually hemmed in and their possible supports removed. Without the soldiers or any air support in a fight with German tanks and infantry the French sailors would have no chance – unless perhaps they could fight with the ships. But there was no support anywhere. When Admiral Jean Abrial, Auphan's replacement as Navy Minister, came to visit Toulon on 23 November the only advice he could give was that the ships, if they had to be scuttled, should settle to the bottom upright, so they could be refloated relatively easily. This presupposed that the Germans would have gained control of the base and that they would be doing the raising. He ended by approving plans for defending the base against an attack from the sea, not, therefore, against the German takeover, but against a possible Allied attack. Furthermore, this was a defence which would be made in co-operation with the German forces. Collaboration was alive and well in Vichy.

Abrial had intended to go on from Toulon to Marseilles to smooth over any problems concerning the German acquisition of the French merchant ships. However, news arrived that the Governor-General of West Africa, the defender of Dakar, General Pierre Boisson, had declared for Darlan, carrying with him, rather reluctantly perhaps, the naval commander in Dakar, Admiral Collinet. Therefore the battleship *Richelieu* and the assorted ships and submarines which were stationed there, including the two submarines which had escaped from Casablanca, now joined the Allies – without, note, being scuttled.

This was another blow to the French navy. The Dakar ships were the last French ships in the empire which were still outside Allied, Free French or Japanese control, apart from the fleet at Toulon, which was now finally alone. The handing over of Dakar ships without scuttling them was, in fact, a clear signal to the Toulon fleet that this was what Darlan wanted, though the situations were, of course, very different. The feeling that the two enemy forces, Allied and Axis, were closing in on them must have been over-whelming, and this perhaps explains the failure of Laborde to take any action to affect the situation. The day after Abrial's visit, 24 November, several French merchant ships was seized by German troops at Sete and Port-Vendres, and the naval air base at Hyérès, close to Toulon and within the base area, was occupied by German troops. German liaison officers dismissed this as overzealousness by subordinates, without revealing that they were simply carrying out their orders earlier than intended. But it was more pressure.

The Admiralty at Vichy had received some German 'requests' which, in the spirit of collaboration, they might normally have acceded to. But this time the French decided to stand firm on their interpretation of the armistice terms. They rejected the Germans' proposal to put back into service some demilitarized coastal batteries along the Mediterranean coast, and refused to undertake any sea operations. Such manoeuvres could only have been directed against Allied shipping, and presumably the German aim was to provoke a full-scale war between France and the Allies. (A really Machiavellian French Admiralty would have agreed to all this, accepted the ammunition and the fuel, and even accepted German commissars on the ships, and then sailed their ships to join the Allies – but this would have breached the armistice terms, of course.) Admiral Laborde in his beleaguered base was not the only Frenchman who clung to the very end to the tattered remnants of the armistice terms in justifying his actions.

All the preliminaries for the seizure of Toulon were much better organized and executed by the Germans than the actual seizure of the base. The army was given the task, because the German Navy knew full well that attempting to seize the ships was pointless, and that all that would happen was that they would reach the quays to see seventy or eighty ships slowly sinking into the mud before their eyes. So the German Navy wanted nothing to do with this attempt. This abstinence made it even more certain that the outcome would be disastrous, because the army units which had been given the task tended to get lost in the complications of the naval yard, an environment with which they were completely unfamiliar.

The first alert that the Germans were moving in reached Admiral Laborde long before the Germans found him, on board his flagship *Strasbourg*. Even after the events of the last fortnight he still did not believe the Germans would so blatantly break the armistice terms. He had, however, made all the preparations to scuttle, a process which involved more than simply letting the ship sink. A good deal of destruction of guns, engines, and so on, had to be accomplished as well as opening the sea cocks. It could also take some time for the ships to go down so considerable advance preparations were required.

It took the German soldiers almost three hours to get into the yard and another hour to find Laborde. By that time the order to scuttle had gone out, by radio and by signal lamp. As the first German tank pointed its gun at Laborde on *Strasbourg* he gave the order to execute the scuttling of the ship. Explosions throughout the ship destroyed sensitive equipment, the sea cocks were opened, and the great ship sank slowly and elegantly into the mud.

It was, in the event, a close race, even closer in some cases than with *Strasbourg*. On more than one ship the Germans were trying to board even as the French sailors were abandoning their foundering vessels; in some cases the Germans were actually on the ships as the scuttling charges were fired. In the midst of it all an enigmatic order came from Laval in Vichy. He had been told that this operation would begin by being woken at 4.30 am, and his message insisted that 'all incidents are to be avoided'. No-one knew what this meant, and trying to find out tended to delay the scuttling, which was perhaps Laval's intention, though in all likelihood he was merely covering himself to avoid German anger. Not that it mattered, for the sailors knew what they were doing and the German soldiers did not. Even had they been on board the ships in strength they could scarcely have prevented the sailors from scuttling.

The two battleships in commission, *Strasbourg* and *Provence*, were both disabled. They sank, in both cases even as the commanding admirals argued with the German officers who had come to seize them. All the super-destroyers were sunk (though four were raised and taken to Italy later). The *Dunkerque*, in dry dock undergoing repairs for damage received at Mers el-Kebir, was sabotaged and her guns were blown up. All the cruisers and destroyers, and most of the submarines, were sunk, though two cruisers and seven of the destroyers were later raised and in some cases put back in commission.

Only five ships, all submarines, escaped. They were bombed by the Luftwaffe, had to dodge mines which had been laid in the Exit Channel, and had to wait for nets and revolving bridges to open. One of them, *Venus*, was too badly damaged to get away, and was eventually scuttled; another, *Iris*, escaped to internment in Spain. *Marsouin* and *Casabianca* reached Algiers – *Marsouin* being one of those which had escaped from Algiers only a couple of weeks before. *Glorieux* got to Oran, and *Calypso* and *Nautilus* went to Tunis. Of those ships which were raised and refloated, the French eventually recovered just two; the rest were either sunk in later fighting or were scuttled again by their new owners.

The whole French fleet was thus destroyed. By a combination of British and American action, and by its own inaction, the fleet had ceased to exist. Very few of the ships were sunk by the action of France's enemies, Germany and Italy. For some extraordinary reason, the suicide of the fleet was regarded as a meritorious action. 'An act of sublime patriotism', the clandestine Communist newspaper *L'Humanité* called it. Certainly the scuttle deprived Germany, or rather Italy, of most of the ships. It also deprived the Allies of them, who could have made better use of them. It was thus a properly neutral action. But it also deprived France of something which had been built with French tax money over a long period of time and which had scarcely ever been used for its proper purpose, which was to fight France's enemies. A much more convincing display of patriotism would have been for the ships to make a fight of it – still better would it have been to see them breaking out of Toulon harbour. Scuttling the ships was precisely in tune with the melancholy defeatism which pervaded the whole Vichy regime. It is fully in accord with this defeatism that Admiral Laborde, as the ship sank under him, argued with the German officers, who were pointing their tank guns at him, that they were breaking the armistice terms. It is also fully in accord with the ethos of Vichy that it required an order from Marshal Pétain personally to get him off the ship as it went down.

This action marked the end of the war between Britain and France, which had been fought intermittently since July 1940. During November 1942 the Vichy regime in Madagascar, in Morocco, and Algeria came to an end, and the Unoccupied Zone was seized by Germany. The precise subject of the argument of the last two years, the intentions of the French fleet, was now finally settled. Now all concerned could concentrate on the real issue, defeating Italy and then Germany.

Conclusion

The inter-dependence of empire and navy in the period of European empires was never as clearly demonstrated as in the destruction of the French Empire between 1940 and 1942. (The last of Vichy's colonies, Djibouti, surrendered to the British blockade before the end of 1942.) The French navy was not able to move in any strength out of the Mediterranean area after July 1940, partly by the terms of the German armistice, but mainly because of British hostility. As a result it was easy for a whole variety of enemies (or friends who acted as enemies) to pick off bits of the empire in various ways. Australia in the Pacific, the USA in the Caribbean, Japan in Indo-China, Britain in Syria and Madagascar, and the Free French in other places. Had the French fleet been able to reach these places, or even merely been free to do so, this destruction would not have been so easy, and might not have happened at all.

The motor behind all this was Britain. Fuelled by fear that the French fleet would fall into its enemies' control, Britain supervised or permitted the destruction of that empire. It was a straw in the wind, also, when Syria was conquered in order that it should be made independent. Thanks, however, to the actions and intrigues of General de Gaulle, one French faction succeeded in emerging from the war on the winning side and so France was able to retain or recover most of its former empire. The various aggressors had to return their spoils, though the very fact of French defeat and civil war had decisively encouraged the aspirations to independence among the subject peoples. Even so, France still has a mini-empire in the Caribbean and Pacific, and very powerful influence in the former African colonies.

Britain was already glutted with colonies before the war began, and was not interested in seizing France's imperial possessions, at least not permanently. Both Vichy and Free France were always ready to make that accusation, but this was to ignore the individual cases. Any British moves against the French colonies were designed against the regime in Vichy and its German sponsors, and not against France itself. All those lands which the British conquered were eventually handed over to the Free French. To Vichy, of course, de Gaulle was merely a British puppet, though any Frenchman who knew the man also knew that such a characterization hardly made much sense. The only alternative to Free French rule was independence, and only Syria and Lebanon were promised that, for these lands were League of Nations mandates, on a different legal and social footing from the other colonies.

So, if Britain was not interested in seizing French colonies for itself, why did it attack them? The answer is, of course, to prevent them from being used by Germany or Japan or Italy as bases for attacks on British lands or positions. The use of Indo-China by the Japanese to invade Malaya and the British parts of Borneo was a clear example of what could happen, as was the use of French ports and airfields to attack Britain itself and its ships.

So Syria was attacked and conquered because it had become a German base from which Iraq was attacked. This was despite the fact that all the German personnel had been withdrawn by the time the British invasion started – for they could still return, and all the more easily since they had used the place once. One would have thought that it would have been irresistible to the Germans to send forces to Syria in the summer of 1942, when Rommel was as close to Alexandria and the Nile Valley as Alamein. Similarly with Madagascar, a potential Japanese naval base, and even with the Pacific Islands – the sloop *Dumont d'Urville* which had so effectively intervened in New Caledonia and Tahiti was based in Indo-China, which was even then falling under Japanese control. Had the Vichy regime controlled the New Hebrides and New Caledonia when the Japanese seized the neighbouring Solomon Islands, Australia might have found itself menaced by Japanese aircraft as well as submarines, and the Battle of the Coral Sea could scarcely have been fought where and when it was – for Vichy had shown that it was wholly unable to stand up to Japanese pressure.

All this is a clear demonstration that empires exist only so long as the rulers deploy overwhelming armed might. The disarmament of metropolitan France by Germany in 1940 gave Britain the opportunity to seize control of Syria and Madagascar, and the inability of the Vichy regime to support its viceroys in North Africa made it relatively easy for the Allies to seize Morocco and Algeria. Their inability to do the same in Tunisia makes the point, for it was virtually annexed in November 1942 to the Nazi empire, and was then defended by German and Italian forces.

The paradox is, of course, that it was the German-dictated armistice terms which so reduced Vichy power that the empire was opened up to theft by other imperialists. The Army of the Levant was reduced from 160,000 to

40,000 men by German order; had it remained at 160,000, the British would never have attacked Syria. Indo-China's garrison was much reduced, and so the country lay open to Japanese infiltration. Only the forces in West Africa and North Africa remained strong, even being reinforced, and these areas held to Vichy the longest. Germany and Britain were co-operating in the dismantling of the French Empire.

The lesson was that powerful armed forces were needed to hold an empire, and this was reinforced by the results of the war in the British Empire. Britain's armed forces in 1945 took over other European colonies – part of Indo-China, the Dutch East Indies, and Libya – as well as reoccupying their own lost colonies in the east, and providing an occupation force for part of Germany. Over-extension, already evident before 1939, took its immediate toll, combined with the demobilization of much of the army at home. In the next four years half the empire, and all the additions, had gone – India, Pakistan, Burma, Ceylon, the Dutch East Indies – and essentially for the same reason that Vichy lost its empire – lack of armed strength. The result geopolitically was that the two states willing to maintain large armies and/or navies – the USA and the Soviet Union – were the only imperial powers left, and in the next decades their power flowed into the many empty spaces left by the evaporation of the European empires.

Notes

Chapter 1

1. The decision was Churchill's, despite vacillation and delay at lower levels: Churchill, *The Second World War*, vol. 2, London 1949, 92–93; cf. Gates, *End*, 109–113 – this is perhaps the best account of these events.
2. J. Lukacs, *The Last European War, September 1939–December 1941*, London 1976, 49–50.
3. Gates, *End*, 65.
4. Gates, *End*, 41–42.
5. Among many accounts, that of Gilbert, *Finest Hour*, 288–318, from Churchill's viewpoint, is as good as any.
6. Gates, *End*, 166–168, 173–174, 378–380.
7. Gates, *End*, 170.
8. Sir Edward Spears, *Assignment to Catastrophe*, vol. 2, London 1954, 46–47.
9. Ibid, 92.
10. Michael Glover, *The Fight for the Channel Ports*, London 1985, 140–183.
11. Gilbert, *Finest Hour*, 500–520; Gates, *End*, 172–176.
12. Andrew Roberts, *The Holy Fox, a Life of Lord Halifax*, London 1991, 210–250; John Lukacs, *Five Days in London, May 1940*, New Haven RI, 1999.
13. Gilbert, *Finest Hour*, 505; Gates, *End*, 173.
14. Churchill, *Second World War*, vol. 2, 137; Gilbert, *Finest Hour*, 520; Gates, *End*, 176.
15. Gates, *End*, 181–186.
16. Gilbert, *Finest Hour*, 528–535; Gates, *End*, 187–200.
17. Arthur Bryant, *The Turn of the Tide*, London 1965, 141–145.
18. L. F. Ellis, *The War in France and Flanders, 1939–1940*, London 1953, 301 and 305.

19. Gates, *End*, 182 and note 2 on p. 499.
20. Gates, *End*, 211.
21. Gates, *End*, 211–213.
22. Gates, *End*, 215–216 and Appendix F.
23. Gilbert, *Finest Hour*, 556; Gates, *End*, 216–217.
24. Gilbert, *Finest Hour*, 557; Gates, *End*, 223, quoting the Foreign Office record of the telephone conversation between Churchill and Reynaud.
25. Gates, *End*, 225–226.
26. Gates, *End*, 227–233; Gilbert, *Finest Hour*, 558–560.
27. Gates, *End*, 234–241.

Chapter 2

1. Rohwer, *Chronology*, 28 and 29.
2. Cordell Hull, *Memoirs*, New York, 1948, vol. 1, 792; William L. Langer, *Our Vichy Gamble*, New York 1947, 45; Gates, *End*, 256 and note 1 on p. 525.
3. Quoted in Gates, *End*, 259–260; cf. Robert Dallek, *Franklin D. Roosevelt and American Foreign Policy, 1932–1945*, New York 1979, 231.
4. TNA ADM 205/4, Record of a Conversation held at Bordeaux, 18 June 1940; Paul Auphan, *Les Grimaces de l'Histoire*, Paris 1951, 256 – Auphan was present at the meeting as Darlan's aide.
5. Rohwer, *Chronology*, 28–29.
6. Charles de Gaulle, *Mémoires de Guerre, L'Appel, 1940–1942*, Paris 1954, 78–80.
7. Rohwer, *Chronology*, 29.
8. Gates, *End*, 264.
9. Paul Baudouin, *Neuf Mois au Gouvernement*, Paris 1948; Camille Chautemps, *Cahiers sécrète de l'Armistice*, Paris 1963; Albert Lebrun, *Témoignage*, Paris 1945; Gates, *End*, 262–266.
10. An English version of the terms is in Walter C. Langsam, *Historic Documents of World War II*, Princeton NJ 1958, 37–44, reprinted from the *New York Times* of 26 June 1940.
11. Gates, *End*, 274–291; Thomas, *Britain and Vichy*.
12. Philip Bell, *A Certain Eventuality, Britain and the Fall of France*, Farnborough 1974, 102–103.
13. Gilbert, *Finest Hour*, 589–590.
14. *Hansard*, 25 June 1940, cols 301–307.
15. Rohwer, *Chronology*, 31.
16. Rohwer, *Chronology*, 31.
17. Gates, *End*, 310–311.
18. *Somerville Papers*, no. 21.

Chapter 3

1. The documentation on the action at Mers el-Kebir is in *Somerville Papers*, nos 21–43; see also Gates, *End*, 352–368; Arthur Marder, *From the Dardanelles to Oran*, Oxford 1974, 198–206; Stephen Roskill, *The War at Sea*, vol. 1, London 1956, 240–241; Smith, *England's Last War*, 68–88.
2. For details of the situation and negotiations at Alexandria see *Cunningham Papers*, vol. 1, nos 35–63, and Rene Godfroy, L'aventure de la Force X a Alexandrie, 1940–1943, Paris 1953.
3. TNA ADM 199/822, for official reports and the capture of *Surcouf*; for events at Portsmouth see William James, *The Portsmouth Letters*, London 1945; also Smith, *England's Last War*, 47–56 (only on *Surcouf*).
4. *Cunningham Papers*, no. 48.
5. *Somerville Papers*, no. 23.
6. *Somerville Papers*, no. 34.
7. *Somerville Papers*, no. 31; Roskill, *War at Sea*, 242–244; Gates, *End*, 252–260; Marder, *Dardanelles*, 253–256; Smith, *England's Last War*, 75–84.
8. *Cunningham Papers*, no. 61.
9. *Somerville Papers*, no. 31; Smith, *England's Last War*, 84–85.
10. *Somerville Papers*, no. 31; Smith, *England's Last War*, 84–85.
11. Ibid.
12. TNA ADM 199/826.
13. Georges Robert, *La France aux Antilles, 1939 a 1943*, Paris 1950.
14. *Somerville Papers*, no. 41.
15. Gates, *End*, 369–371.
16. Gates, *End*, 371; George E. Melton, *Darlan, Admiral and Statesman of France 1881–1942*, Westport, CN, 1998.
17. Gilbert, *Finest Hour*, 641–643.

Chapter 4

1. Alexander Werth, *De Gaulle*, Harmondsworth 1965, 106–107.
2. Thomas, *French Empire*, 39–40.
3. See, amongst many studies, Jean-Pierre Azema, *From Munich to the Liberation, 1938–1944*, Cambridge 1984, Maurice Larkin, *France since the Popular Front, 1936–1996*, Oxford 1997; Robert O. Paxton, *Parades and Politics at Vichy*, Princeton NJ 1966, and *Vichy France, Old Guard and New Order, 1940–44*, London 1972; Robert Gildea, *Marianne in Chains*, London 1993.
4. Thomas, *French Empire*, ch. 1.
5. Thomas, *French Empire*, 41–44; for the army's capacity, cf Albert Merglen, 'La France pouvait continuer la guerre en Afrique Francaise du Nord en 1940', *Revue d'Histoire Diplomatique*, 106, 1992, 99–119.

6. TNA CAB 65/8 W.M. 238/40; Dunmore, *Visions*, 230–231; David Day, *The Great Betrayal, Britain, Australia and the Onset of the Pacific War, 1939–1942*, New York 1989, 91.
7. Dunmore, *Visions*, 230–231; M. Simington, 'Australia in the New Caledonia coup d'état of 1940', *Australian Outlook*, 1976, 91; Kim Mulholland, 'The Trials of the Free French in New Caledonia, 1940–1942', *French Historical Studies* 14, 1986. (Thomas, *French Empire*, does not deal with the French Pacific.)
8. Dallek, *Franklin D. Roosevelt*, 235–256.
9. Thomas, *French Empire*, 52–53.
10. Thomas, *French Empire*, 45–49.
11. Thomas, *French Empire*, 56–60.
12. Marder, *Operation 'Menace'*, 6–9.

Chapter 5
1. The best treatment of this episode is Marder, *Operation 'Menace'*; see also John A. Wilson, *Echec à Dakar*, Paris 1967, and Jacques Mordal, *La Bataille de Dakar*, Paris 1956; Sir Edward Spears, *Two Men who saved France*, London 1966, has a firsthand account. Detailed references will not be given in this chapter, since they would be merely repetitious.
2. Llywelyn Woodward, *British Foreign Policy in the Second World War*, vol. 1 London 1970; Thomas, *Britain and Vichy*.
3. *Somerville Papers*, no. 58.
4. Marder, *Operation 'Menace'*, 88–89; Rohwer, *Chronology*, 40.

Chapter 6
1. *Somerville Papers*, nos 65, 66; Rohwer, *Chronology*, 42.
2. *Somerville Papers*, nos 68, 76.
3. Woodward, *British Foreign Policy*, vol. 1, 409–413; Melton, *Darlan*, 90.
4. Woodward, *British Foreign Policy*, vol. 1, 412.
5. Marder, *Operation 'Menace'*, ch. 9.
6. Marder, *Operation 'Menace'*, 161, note 9.
7. Thomas, *French Empire*, 88.
8. *Somerville Papers*, nos 72, 76, 93.
9. Thomas, *Britain and Vichy*, 66–67.
10. Rohwer, *Chronology*, 48.
11. Werth, *De Gaulle*, 120–122; Marder, *Operation 'Menace'*, 149–157; Rohwer, *Chronology*, 48; Thomas, *French Empire*, 75–76.
12. Thomas, *French Empire*, 87–91; Woodward, *British Foreign Policy*, vol. 1, 421–43; Thomas, *Britain and Vichy*, 69–71.
13. Melton, *Darlan*, 84–85; Roskill, *War at Sea*, vol. 1, 255, 292

14. Thomas, *Britain and Vichy*, 94–104.
15. *Somerville Papers*, no. 122.
16. *Somerville Papers*, no. 122.
17. *Somerville Papers*, no. 133.
18. *Somerville Papers*, nos 133, 134.
19. *Somerville Papers*, no. 135.
20. *Somerville Papers*, no. 149.
21. *Somerville Papers*, no. 134.
22. Rohwer, *Chronology*, 56.
23. Rohwer, *Chronology*, 52.
24. Rohwer, *Chronology*, 57.
25. Thomas, *Britain and Vichy*, 74–87.
26. See the scope of his authority as defined by the German Ministry of Foreign Affairs, quoted in Langsam, *Historic Documents*, 47–48.
27. Thomas, *French Empire*, 92–93.

Chapter 7
1. See Artemis Cooper, *Cairo in the War, 1939–1945*, London 1989.
2. Elizabeth Monroe, *Britain's Moment in the Middle East, 1914–1956*, London 1963.
3. Stephen Longrigg, *Syria and Lebanon under the French Mandate*, Oxford 1958; Michael Provence, *The Great Syrian Revolt and the Rise of Arab Nationalism*, Texas 2005.
4. Thomas, *French Empire*, 100–102; Warner, *Iraq and Syria*, 11–20, 31–35.
5. Aviel Roshwald, *Estranged Bedfellows, Britain and France in the Middle East during the Second World War*, Oxford 1980, 25–26.
6. Albert Hourani, *Syria and Lebanon, a Political History*, Oxford 1946, 238.
7. Thomas, *French Empire*, 102–103.
8. Roshwald, *Estranged Bedfellows*, 31–35.
9. Roshwald, *Estranged Bedfellows*, 43–44.
10. Warner, *Iraq and Syria*, 33.
11. Warner, *Iraq and Syria*, 85–87.
12. The accessible accounts of these events are Warner, *Iraq and Syria*, Buckley, *Five Ventures*, Robert Lyman, *First Victory, Britain's Forgotten Struggle in the Middle East, 1941*, London 2006, Smith, *England's Last War*, and Anthony Mockler, *Our Enemies the French*, London 1976. All these contain references to the relevant Official Histories and other sources.
13. Thomas, *French Empire*, 93; Melton, *Darlan*.
14. Warner, *Iraq and Syria*, 122–123.

15. Warner, *Iraq and Syria*, 123–127.
16. Thomas, *French Empire*, 92–93; Paxton, *Vichy France*, 117–121.
17. Lyman, First *Victory*, 169–170; Smith, *England's Last War*, 181–182.
18. Warner, *Iraq and Syria*, 127–130; Jaina L. Cox, 'The Background to the Syrian Campaign, May–June 1941: a Study in Franco-German Relations', *History* 72, 1987.
19. Warner, *Iraq and Syria*, 131; Lyman, *First Victory*, 171–172.
20. Smith, *England's Last War*, 191–192; Lyman, *First Victory*, 168–169; N. E. Bou-Nacklie, 'The 1941 Invasion of Syria and Lebanon: the Role of the Local Paramilitary', *Middle Eastern Studies* 30, 1994.
21. A. B. Gaunson, 'Churchill, de Gaulle, Spears and the Levant Affair 1941', *Historical Journal* 27, 1984.
22. Bou-Nacklie, 'The 1941 Invasion'.
23. Warner, *Iraq and Syria*, 139–141; Thomas, *French Empire*, 106.
24. Gaunson, 'Churchill, de Gaulle'; Martin L. Mickelson, 'Another Fashoda: the Anglo-French Conflict over the Levant, May–September 1941', *Revue Francaise d'Outre-mer* 63, 1976.

Chapter 8
1. Buckley, *Five Ventures*, 53.
2. Thomas, *French Empire*, 104.
3. Buckley, *Five Ventures*, 49.
4. The main official source is TNA WO 106/3076; air operations are in AIR 2/7067; and naval operations in Cunningham Papers and ADM 199/415 and 679. The war is generally well described in secondary works: Warner, *Iraq and Syria*, Buckley, *Five Ventures* are the best accounts; see also Smith, *England's Last War*, Mockler, *Our Enemies*, Lyman, *First Victory*. Detailed citations will not be given for the rest of this chapter, except for the naval operations, which are generally neglected.
5. *Cunningham Papers*, no. 244; Rohwer, *Chronology*, 78.
6. *Cunningham Papers*, no. 244.
7. *Cunningham Papers*, no. 244; Rohwer, *Chronology*, 78.
8. Thomas, *French Empire*, 107–124; A. B. Gaunson, *The Anglo-French Clash in Lebanon and Syria, 1940–1945*, London 1987; Roshwald, *Estranged Bedfellows*; Gloria A. Maguire, *Anglo-American Relations with the Free French*, London 1995, ch. 3.

Chapter 9
1. Ludovic Kennedy, *Pursuit, the Sinking of the Bismarck*, London 1947; David J. Bercuson and Holger H. Herwig, *The Destruction of the Bismarck*, Woodstock NY 2003; a good summary is in Richard Hough,

The Longest Battle, the War at Sea, 1939–45, London 1966, and Roskill, *War at Sea*, vol. 1.

2. *Somerville Papers*, nos 163, 164.
3. *Somerville Papers*, no. 163.
4. *Somerville Papers*, nos 239, 244.
5. Rohwer, *Chronology*, 79, 84, 88; Stuart Gill, *Blood in the Sea, HMS Dunedin and the Enigma Code*, London 2003.
6. Thomas, *French Empire*, 199–200.
7. Rohwer, *Chronology*, 110; Thomas, *French Empire*, 92.
8. Rohwer, *Chronology*, 112.
9. Thomas, *French Empire*, 195–199.
10. Dunmore, *Visions*, 231–232.
11. Thomas, *French Empire*, 131–132.
12. Langer, *Our Vichy Gamble*; Maguire, *Anglo-American Relations*, ch.1.
13. Thomas, *Britain and Vichy*, 112–114; Maguire, *Anglo-American Relations*.
14. Thomas, *French Empire*, 132 and note 11, p. 154.
15. This crisis over the islands has been well studied: Thomas, *French Empire*, 137–139, Thomas, *Britain and Vichy*, 124–126, and Maguire, *Anglo-American Relations*, 27–29 provide summaries; for more detail see Douglas G. Anglin, *The St Pierre and Miquelon Affair of 1941*, Toronto 1966, William A. Christiane, *Divided Island, Faction and Unity of Saint Pierre*, Cambridge MA 1969, Paul M. Coutoure, 'The Vichy-Free French Propaganda War in Quebec, 1940 to 1942', *Canadian Historical Association Historical Papers*, 1978, J. F. Hilliker, 'The Canadian Government and the Free French, Perceptions and Restrains, 1940–44', *International History Review* 2, 1980, Martin Thomas, 'Deferring to Vichy in the Western Hemisphere: the St Pierre and Miquelon Affair of 1941', *International History Review* 19, 1997.
16. John Terraine, *The Right of the Line*, London 1985, 492; Alistair Horne, *Seven Ages of Paris*, New York 2002, 368 misdates the attack and claims much higher casualties.
17. Christopher Buckley, *Norway, the Commandos, Dieppe*, London 1952, 195–225; C. E. Lucas Philips, *The Greatest Raid of All*, London 1958.
18. Robert Gildea, *Marianne in Chains, In Search of the German Occupation of France, 1940–45*, London 2002, 263–264.
19. Langer, *Our Vichy Gamble*.
20. Buckley, *Norway*, 229–269; Ken Ford, *Dieppe 1942*, Oxford 2003; John P. Campbell, *Dieppe Revisited, a Documentary Investigation*, London 1993,
21. Terraine, *Right of the Line*, 496–497.

Chapter 10
1. The official British account of events in Madagascar is William Platt, *Operations of East Africa Command, 1940–1943*, Nairobi 1943, and *British Military Administration in Africa, 1941–1947*, London 1948. Near contemporary accounts are Kenneth Dower, *Into Madagascar*, London 1943, and *The King's African Rifles in Madagascar*, Nairobi 1943, and Eric Rosenthal, *Japan's Bid for Africa: including the Story of the Madagascar Campaign*, Johannesburg 1944. Later accounts are Thomas, *French Empire*, 139–154; Smith, *England's Last War*, 281–356; Buckley, *Five Ventures*, 165–208, and Philip M. Allen, *Madagascar, Conflicts of Authority in the Great Island*, Oxford 1995.
2. Thomas, *French Empire*, 141.
3. Martin Gilbert, *The Road to Victory*, London 1986, 77.
4. H. P. Willmott, *Empires in the Balance, Japanese and Allied Strategies to April 1942*, London 1942.
5. *Somerville Papers*, nos 227–243.

Chapter 11
1. See the sources listed for the previous chapter.
2. Paxton, *Vichy France*, 313, note 42; Thomas, *French Empire*, 145.
3. Rohwer, *Chronology*, 169–170.
4. Thomas, *French Empire*, 144–146.
5. Thomas, *French Empire*, 152.

Chapter 12
1. Richard W. Steele, *The First Offensive, 1942*, London 1973.
2. Dallek, *Franklin D. Roosevelt*, 245–353.
3. Carlo d'Este, *Eisenhower, Allied Supreme Commander*, London 2003, ch. 29.
4. Denis Smyth, 'Screening Torch: Allied Counter-Intelligence and the Spanish Threat to the Secrecy of the Allied Invasion of French North Africa in November 1942', *Intelligence and National Security* 4, 1989.
5. Thomas, *French Empire*, 159–169; Murphy, *Diplomat*, 107–123; Thomas, *Britain and Vichy*, 145–150.
6. Smith, *England's Last War*, 361–362, 366.
7. D'Este, *Eisenhower*, 347; Smith, *England's Last War*, 367.
8. D'Este, *Eisenhower*, 344–347; Murphy, *Diplomat*, 107–123.
9. Melton, *Darlan*; Arthur Layton Funk, *The Politics of Torch*, Lawrence, KN 1974, and 'Negotiating the "Deal with Darlan"', *Journal of Contemporary History* 8, 1973; Langer, *Our Vichy Gamble*, 305–330; David Walker, 'OSS and Operation Torch', *Journal of Contemporary History* 22, 1987.

10. Rohwer, *Chronology*, 210.
11. Smyth, 'Screening Torch'; G. Playfair, *The Second World War: The Mediterranean and the Middle East*, vol. 4, London, 1976, 134–136.
12. Ben MacIntyre, *Operation Mincemeat*, London 2010.
13. Playfair, *Second World War*, vol. 4, 142–150; Alan Moorehead, *African Trilogy*, vol. 3, London 1944; *Cunningham Papers*, vol. 2, nos 28–38; Rick Atkinson, *The Army at Dawn, the War in North Africa, 1942–1943*, London 2003; Corelli Barnett, *Engage the Enemy more Closely*, London 1991, 561–568; Smith, *England's Last War*, 363–410.
14. Carlo D'Este, *Patton, A Genius for War*, New York 1995, 433–441.
15. Rohwer, *Chronology*, 209–210.
16. Charles Mast, *Histoire d'une rebellion, Alger, 8 Novembre 1942*, Paris 1969; Murphy, *Diplomat*, 162–167.
17. Melton, *Darlan*; Funk, 'Negotiating'; Anthony Verrier, *Assassination in Algiers, Churchill, Roosevelt, de Gaulle and the Murder of Admiral Darlan*, London 1990, 225–252; Thomas, *Britain and Vichy*, 151–167.
18. Playfair, *Second World War*, vol. 4, 170–173.
19. *Cunningham Papers*, vol. 2, 39–57.
20. Verrier, *Assassination*, 225–252.

Chapter 13
1. Anthony Clayton, 'A Question of Honour? Scuttling Vichy's Fleet', *History Today* 42, 1992; Simon Ball, *The Bitter Sea, the Struggle for Mastery in the Mediterranean, 1935–1949*, London 2009, 171–172.
2. Basil Liddell Hart, *History of the Second World War*, London 1970, 343–344.
3. The events at Toulon are detailed in L. Noguères, *La Suicide de la flotte Francaise à Toulon*, Paris 1961, Paul Auphan and Jacques Mordal, *The French Navy in World War II*, Westport, CN 1959, and Philippe Masson, *La Marine Francaise et la Guerre 1939–1945*, Paris 1991.

Bibliography

Ageron, Charles Robert, *Les Chemins de la decolonization française de 1936–1956*, Paris 1986.

Alexander, M. S., 'The Fall of France 1940', *Journal of Strategic Studies* 13, 1990.

Allen, Philip M., *Madagascar, Conflicts of Authority in the Great Island*, Oxford 1995.

Anglin, Douglas G., *The St Pierre and Miquelon Affair of 1941*, Toronto 1966.

Auphan, Paul, and Jaques Mordal, *The French Navy in World War II*, Westport CT, 1959.

Azema, Jean-Pierre, *From Munich to the liberation, 1938–1944*, Cambridge 1984.

Ball, Simon, *The Bitter Sea, The Struggle for Mastery in the Mediterranean, 1935–1949*, London 2009.

Barnett, Corelli, *Engage the Enemy More Closely*, London 1991.

Baudouin, Paul, *The Private Diaries of Paul Baudouin*, London 1948

Bell, P. M. H., 'Prologue à Mers el-Kebir', *Revue Historique de la Guerre Mondiale*, 9 1959.

Bell, Philip, *A Certain eventuality. Britain and the fall of France*, Farnborough 1974.

Bell, Philip, *France and Britain in 1940–1994. The Long Separation*, London 1997.

British military administration in Africa, 1941–1947, London 1948.

Bou-Nacklie, N. E., 'The 1941 Invasion of Syria and Lebanon: the Role of the Local Paramilitary', *Middle Eastern Studies* 30, 1994

Bryant, Arthur, *The Turn of the Tide, 1939–1943*, London 1957.

Buckley, Christopher, *Five Ventures*, London 1954.

Charles-Roux, François, *Cinq Mois Tragiques aux affaires étrangeres*, Paris 1949.

Christiane, William A., *Divided Island, Faction and Unity of Saint Pierre*, Cambridge Mass., 1969.

Churchill, Winston S., *Their Finest Hour*, London 1949.

Churchill, Winston S., *The Grand Alliance*, London 1950.

Coutoure, Paul M., 'The Vichy-Free French Propaganda War in Québec, 1940 to 1942', *Canadian Historical Association Historical Papers*, 1978.

Cox, Jaina L., 'The Background to the Syrian Campaign, May–June 1941: a Study in Franco-German Wartime Relations', *History* 72, 1987.

The Cunningham Papers, 2 vols, ed. Michael Simpson, Navy Records Society 1999.

Dallek, Robert, *Franklin Roosevelt and American Foreign Policy, 1932–1945*, Oxford 1979.

De Gaulle, Charles, *War Memoirs*, London 1955–1960.

D'Este, Carlo, *Eisenhower, Allied Supreme Commander*, London 2003.

Dinan, Desmond, *The Politics of Persuasion. British Policy and French African neutrality 1940–42*, Lanham, Md, 1988.

Dower, Kenneth, *Into Madagascar*, London 1943.

Dower, Kenneth, *The King's African Rifles in Madagascar*, Nairobi 1943.

Dunmore, John, *Visions and Realities, France in the Pacific 1695–1995*, Waikanae, NZ, 1997.

Foot, M. R. D., *SOE, the Special Operations Executive, 1940–1946*, London 1984.

Funk, Arthur Layton, *The Politics of Torch*, Lawrence 1974.

Funk, Arthur Layton, 'Negotiating the "deal with Darlan"', *Journal of Contemporary History* 8, 1973.

Gates, Eleanor M., *End of the Affair, The Collapse of the Anglo-French Alliance 1939–40*, London 1981.

Gaunson, A. B., *The Anglo-French clash in Lebanon and Syria, 1940–1945*, London 1987.

Gaunson A. B., 'Churchill, De Gaulle, Spears and the Levant affair 1941', *Historical Journal* 27, 1984.

Gilbert, Martin, *Finest Hour, Winston S. Churchill, 1939–1941*, London 1983.

Gilbert, Martin, *Road to Victory, Winston S. Churchill, 1941–1945*, London 1986.

Gildea, Robert, *Marianne in Chains*, London 1993.

Glubb, John Bagot, *War in the Desert*, London 1950.

Godfroy, Rene, *L'aventure de la Force X à Alexandrie 1940–1943*, Paris 1953.

Hilliker J. F., 'The Canadian Government and the Free French: Perceptions and Restraints 1940–44', *International History Review* 2 1980.

Hinsley, F. H. *British Intelligence in the Second World War*, 5 vols, London 1979–1984.

Hough, Richard, *The Longest Battle, The War at Sea, 1939–1945*, London 1986.

Howard, Michael, *The Mediterranean Strategy in the Second World War*, London 1993.

Jackson, Ashley, *The British Empire and the Second World War*, London 2006.

James, William, *The Portsmouth Letters*, London 1945.

Kersaudy, François, *Churchill and de Gaulle*, London 1981.

Killngray, David, and Richard Rathbone (eds), *Africa and the Second World War*, London 1986.

Kolinsky, Michael, *Britain's war in the Middle East: Strategy and Diplomacy, 1939–42*, Basingstoke 1999.

Krautkramer, Elmar, *Vichy – Alger 1940–1942*, Paris 1992.

Larkin, Maurice, *France since the Popular Front, 1936–1996*, Oxford 1997.

Langer, William L., *Our Vichy Gamble*, New York 1947.

Liddell Hart, B. H., Hi*story of the Second World War*, London 1970.

Longrigg, Stephen, *Syria and Lebanon under the French Mandate*, Oxford 1958.

Lukacs, John, *The Last European War, September 93–December 1941*, London 1976 [1977].

Lukacs, John, *Five Days in London, May 1940*, New Haven RI 2001.

Lyman, Robert, *First Victory, Britain's Forgotten Struggle in the Middle East 1941*, London 2006.

Maguire, Gloria A., *Anglo-American Relations with the Free French*, London 1995.

Marder, Arthur J., *From the Dardanelles to Oran*, London 1974.

Marder, Arthur, *Operation 'Menace', the Dakar Expedition and the Dudley North Affair*, Oxford 1976.

Masson, Philippe, *La Marine Française et la Guerre 1939–1945*, Paris 1991.

Mast, Charles, *Histoire d'une rebellion, Alger, 8 Novembre 1942*, Paris 1969.

Melka R. L., 'Darlan between Britain and Germany, 1940–1941', *Journal of Contemporary History* 8 1973.

Melton, George E., *Darlan, Admiral and Statesman of France 1881–1942*, Westport, Conn., 1998.

Mickelson, Martín L., 'Another Fashoda: the Anglo-Free French Conflict over the Levant, May–September 1941', *Revue Française d'Outre-mer* 63, 1976.

Mockler, Anthony, *Haile Sellassie's War*, London 19.

Mockler, Anthony, *Our Enemies the French*, London 1976.

Munholland, Kim, 'The Trials of the Free French in New Caledonia, 1940–1942', *French Historical Studies* 14, 1986.

Murphy, Robert, *Diplomat among Warriors*, New York 1964.

N'Dumbre, K. A., *Hitler voulait l'Afrique*, Paris 1980.

Noguères, L., *La Suicide de la Flotte Française à Toulon*, Paris 1961.

Ollander, Jerome, *Brazzaville, Capital de la France Libre*, Brazzaville 1980.

Paxton, Robert O., *Parades and Politics at Vichy*, Princeton NJ 1966.

Paxton, Robert O., *Vichy France, old guard and new order, 1940–44*, London 1972.

Philips, C. E. Lucas, *The Greatest Raid of All*, London 1958.

Platt, William, *Operations of East Africa Command, 1940–43*, Nairobi 1943.

Playfair, I. S. O. *et al.*, *The Mediterranean and the Middle East*, 6 vols, London 1954–1988.

Puaux, Gabriel, *Deux années au Levant, Souvenirs de Syrie et du Liban*, Paris 1952.

Queuille, P, 'La politique d'Hitler à l'egard de Vichy', *Revue d'histoire diplomatique* 97, 1983.

Robert, Georges, *La France aux Antilles 1939 at 1943*, Paris 1950.

Rohwer, Jurgen, *Chronology of the War at Sea 1939–1945*, rev. ed., London 2005, 28–31.

Rosenthal, Eric, *Japan's bid for Africa: including the Story of the Madagascar Campaign*, Johannesburg 1944.

Roshwald, Aviel, *Estranged Bedfellows, Britain and France in the Middle East during the Second World War*, Oxford 1980.

Roskill, Stephen, *The War at Sea*, 3 vols London 1956–1960.

Roskill, Stephen, *Churchill and the Admirals*, London 1977.

Sainsbury, Keith, *Roosevelt and Churchill at War*, London 1994.

Smith, Colin, *England's Last War with France, Fighting Vichy 1940–1942*, London 2009.

Smyth, Denis, 'Screening Torch: Allied Counter-Intelligence and the Spanish Threat to the Secrecy of the Allied Invasion of French North Africa in November 1942', *Intelligence and National Security* 4, 1989.

The Somerville Papers, ed. Michael Simpson, Navy Records Society 1995.

Spears, Sir Edward, *Two men who Saved France, Pétain and de Gaulle*, London 1966.

Spears, Sir Edward, *Fulfillment of a Mission. The Spears mission in Syria and Lebanon, 1941–1944*, London 1977.

Stafford, David, *Britain and European Resistance, 1940–1945*, London 1983.

Steele, Richard W., *The First Offensive 1942, Roosevelt, Marshall and the Making of American Strategy*, Bloomington, Ind, 1973.

Terraine, John, *The Right of the Line*, London 1985.

Thomas, Martin, 'Imperial backwater or strategic outpost? The British takeover of Vichy Madagascar in 1942', *Historical Journal* 39, 1996.

Thomas, Martin, 'Deferring to Vichy in the Western Hemisphere: the St Pierre and Miquelon Affair of 1941', *International History Review* 19, 1997.

Thomas, Martin, *The French Empire at War, 1940–45*, Manchester 1998.

Thomas, R. T., *Britain and Vichy, the dilemma of Anglo-French relations, 1940–42*, London 1979.

Warner, Geoffrey, *Iraq and Syria 1941*, London 1974.

Werth, Alexander, *De Gaulle*, Harmondsworth, 1965.

Willmott, H. P., *Empires in the Balance: Japanese and Allied Strategies to April 1942*, London 1982.

Woodward, Llywelyn, *British Foreign Policy in the Second World War*, 3 vols 1970–1974.

Index